Cinemas of Therapeutic Activism

Cinemas of Therapeutic Activism

Depression and the Politics of Existence

Adam Szymanski

Routledge
Taylor & Francis Group
LONDON AND NEW YORK

This book draws on research funded by the Social Sciences and Humanities Research Council of Canada and the Fonds de recherche du Quebec – Societe et culture.

The research leading to these results has received funding from the European Union's Horizon 2020 research and innovation programme under the Marie Skłodowska-Curie grant agreement No 754340.

First published in 2020 by Amsterdam University Press Ltd.

Published 2025 by Routledge
4 Park Square, Milton Park, Abingdon, Oxon OX14 4RN
605 Third Avenue, New York, NY 10158

Routledge is an imprint of the Taylor & Francis Group, an informa business

ISBN: 9789463723121 (hbk)
ISBN: 9781041176985 (pbk)
ISBN: 9781003692560 (ebk)
NUR 670

Cover illustration: *Nachmittag* (*Afternoon*), Angela Schanelec, 2007

Cover design: Coördesign, Leiden

DOI 10.5117/9789463723121

For Product Safety Concerns and Information please contact our EU representative:
GPSR@taylorandfrancis.com
Taylor & Francis Verlag GmbH, Kaufingerstraße 24, 80331 München, Germany

Table of Contents

Acknowledgements 9

Perceiving the Pandemic 11

1 The Psychosocial Image 37

2 The Neuroplastic Paradox 59

3 Belief and the Common World of Experience 83

4 Ecosophy and Peace 111

5 Healing and Decolonization 129

For Therapeutic Activisms 153

Bibliography 157

Filmography 171

About the Author 173

Index 175

List of Illustrations

Image 1	*Il deserto rosso* (*The Red Desert*), Michelangelo Antonioni, 1964	50
Image 2	*Il deserto rosso* (*The Red Desert*), Michelangelo Antonioni, 1964	50
Image 3	*Il deserto rosso* (*The Red Desert*), Michelangelo Antonioni, 1964	50
Image 4	*Nachmittag* (*Afternoon*), Angela Schanelec, 2007	76
Image 5	*Nachmittag* (*Afternoon*), Angela Schanelec, 2007	77
Image 6	*Night Moves*, Kelly Reichardt, 2013	101
Image 7	*Lung Bunmi Raluek Chat* (*Uncle Boonmee Who Can Recall His Past Lives*), Apichatpong Weerasethakul, 2010	124
Image 8	*Lung Bunmi Raluek Chat* (*Uncle Boonmee Who Can Recall His Past Lives*), Apichatpong Weerasethakul, 2010	125
Image 9	*Busong* (*Palawan Fate*), Kanakan Balintagos, 2011	145
Image 10	*Busong* (*Palawan Fate*), Kanakan Balintagos, 2011	146

Acknowledgements

Erin Manning and Thomas Lamarre, thank you infinitely. I never cease to find inspiration in your sincerity of thought and purpose.

Perceiving the Pandemic

Keywords: Depression, Melancholy, Foucault, Anti-Psychiatry, Global Art Cinema

The Pandemic

A depression pandemic is sweeping the globe and its end appears nowhere in sight. Study after study confirms skyrocketing diagnostic rates: now about ten times more prevalent than it was only a few decades ago, depression has become the world's leading cause of disability. Approximately 350 million people live with a depressive disorder and over 800,000 people commit suicide every year.[1] This startling statistical trend has politicians and public health officials scrambling to mitigate a crisis that deepens with every moment by increasing the resources allotted to public mental health services.[2] However well-intentioned these institutional efforts may be, their attempts to quell the depression outbreak have proven largely inept because they are grounded on the credulous presupposition, which has also now become a hallmark of liberal democratic ideology, that increased access to mental health services will actually translate into improved mental health.

Studies on dominant treatment methods are showing their benefits to be as modest as ever, and broad-based initiatives to administer "evidence based treatments" to the public have yielded underwhelming clinical results.[3] To

1 For more statistics on depression see the World Health Organization's factsheet (2016a).

2 Politicians are increasingly making mental health a policy priority. Take for example the UK secretary of health Jeremy Hunt's recent admission that mental health services are the NHS's greatest area of weakness, and his subsequent announcement of £1.4 billion for children and young people's mental health care (Campbell 2016: n.p.). In Canada, mental health funding has become a hot-button issue in failing budgetary negotiations between the federal government and the provinces, due largely to Federal Health Minister Jane Philpott's insistence "that billions in new federal money be devoted specifically to mental health care" (Curry 2016: n.p.).

3 A recent meta-analysis published in the American Psychological Association's *Psychology Bulletin* shows that Cognitive Behaviour Therapy is proving less and less effective as a treatment for depression (Johnsen and Friborg 2015). In the UK, more than a million people have received

Szymanski, A., *Cinemas of Therapeutic Activism: Depression and the Politics of Existence.* Taylor & Francis Group, 2020
DOI: 10.5117/9789463723121_INTRO

make matters worse, no curative breakthrough lies on the horizon since the basic research on depression has long resigned itself to the search for topical solutions. Martin Seligman, a depression researcher and former president of the American Psychological Association, has outed the "dirty little secret" that biological psychiatry and clinical psychology have totally abandoned the search for a cure. "The road has come to a dead end at symptom relief," he writes. "Every single drug on the shelf of the psychopharmacopeia is cosmetic. There are no curative drugs and no drug is in development that I know of that aims at cure" (46). Even after having abandoned the loftier goal of cure to settle for mere symptom suppression, clinicians are witnessing relapse after relapse. Access to first-rate treatment has done little to change the unwavering fact that once someone has been diagnosed with severe depression, it is typical for them to battle with a high risk of relapse for their entire life.[4]

The crisis has gotten so out of control that even the world's financial elite have started to worry about the economic consequences. "This is not just a public health issue—it's a development issue," says Jim Yong Kim, a former President of the World Bank. "We need to act now because the lost productivity is something the global economy simply cannot afford" (World Health Organization 2016b). In support of the World Health Organization's

free CBT as part of a public health inititative that economist Richard Layard launched with the help of Oxford psychologist David Clark (Burkeman 2016; Department of Health 2012). Despite these massive governmental efforts, rates of mental illnesses such as depression are still higher than ever in the UK (Campbell 2016).

There is also a mounting body of literature that questions the effectiveness of psychotropic drugs prescribed in treating depression and points to the economic incetives in place for maintaining their primary role in treatment programs. One of the best summaries of this literature comes from Marcia Angell, the former editor of the *New England Journal of Medicine*. In "The Epidemic of Mental Illness: Why?," a lengthy 2011 review of three authoritative books, she makes echo the criticisms found in Irving Kirsch's *The Emperor's New Drugs: Exploding the Antidepressant Myth*; Robert Whitaker's *Anatomy of an Epidemic: Magic Bullets, Psychiatric Drugs, and the Astonishing Rise of Mental Illness in America*; and Daniel Carlat's *Unhinged: The Trouble With Psychiatry—A Doctor's Revelations About a Profession in Crisis*). She describes the books as "powerful indictments of the way psychiatry is now practiced" and she recounts in some detail how they "document the 'frenzy' of diagnosis, the overuse of drugs with sometimes devastating side effects, and widespread conflicts of interest" (Angell 2011b: n.p.).

The criticisms that Angell shares is corroborated by trends in the medical literature. For a recent patient-level meta-analysis that has raised doubts about the effectiveness of SSRIs for "milder forms" of depression, see Fournier et al. 2012.

4 Depression recurrence statistics show "50 percent of those who recover from a first episode of depression having one or more additional episodes in their lifetime, and approximately 80 percent of those with a history of two episodes having another recurrence" (Burcasa and Iacono 2007: 960)

For depression recurrence statistics, see Burcasa and Iacono's "Risk for Recurrence in Depression."

call for increased government investment into mental health services, Jong Kim underscores the economic advantages of treating depression and anxiety disorders, citing a "fourfold return." Without delving into how destructive this free marketeering of life really is, his statement harbours a telling contradiction that begs to be teased out. By framing the mental health epidemic as a development issue, Jong Kim unconsciously infuses the discourse on depression with a political-economic dimension that psychiatry is wont to conceal, and points to one of the reasons why psychiatry's dominant methods have proven so unsuccessful at alleviating the crisis, to the degree that they could even be considered an aggravating factor. For if psychiatry was really concerned with intensifying health, and not just suppressing the symptoms of mental illness, then it would be obliged to put neoliberal hegemony (and its deleterious effects on the bulk of the world population) into question, and develop a critical auto-reflexivity about its own relationship to power. Instead, psychiatry not only leaves the status quo uncontested, but is instrumental in its reification. The financial elite represented by Yong Kim just "couldn't afford" to have it any other way.

Psychiatry's naturalization of asymmetrical power dynamics is as notable today as it was when Foucault gave his lectures on psychiatric power at the Collège de France in 1973-1974. Foucault refers to a number of historical examples whereby psy-professionals are brought into schools, the army, or the prison in order to reinforce the order of the institution, and these lead him to conceive of psychiatric power as an "intensification of reality" that "is found wherever it is necessary to make reality function as power" (Foucault 2006: 189). One of Foucault's many insights is that there is a fundamental complicity between the discipline of psychiatry and society's dominant institutions, however unconducive to mental health or overall well-being that they may be. The intensification of reality that Foucault describes, whereby psychiatry reifies the power dynamics of society at large, is enacted through psychiatry's diagnostic practice of identifying an individual subject with a mental illness. In the diagnostic scene, an "individual" is clearly demarcated from "society," and as a result of this distinction, society is normalized (no matter how cruel or unjust it may be), and the individual is pathologized (no matter how understandable their suffering may be given the circumstances).[5]

5 For more on moving past the binary between "culture" and the "individual," a true "chicken and the egg problem," see Brian Massumi's chapter "The Political Economy of Belonging and the Economy of Relation" in *Parables for the Virtual*. Massumi explains, "it is an absurdity to speak of them as if they were discrete entities that enter into extrinsic relation to one another, let alone to wonder which term takes precedence over the other in determining stasis and change. [...] In

Psychiatric power renders depression a personal problem that someone "has," and must assume responsibility for managing, thereby intensifying and subtly absolving the neoliberal reality through the act of medical diagnosis.

Psychiatry's awesome power to produce subjectivity is wielded through a perceptual apparatus that Foucault calls the "clinical gaze"—"a way of seeing, saying, and doing in relation to illness, the body, [and] life itself" (Rose and Abi-Rached 79).[6] Based on the research of their "Brain, Self and Society" project, Nikolas Rose and Joelle M. Abi-Rached have identified three dimensions to the clinical gaze: the spatio-temporal, the technological and the institutional (Rose and Abi-Rached 79-80), each of which are operative in the medical perception of depression. In the diagnostic scene, the clinical gaze transforms the patient into a spatio-temporal matrix that allows the doctor to perceive clinically significant patterns and influences (the persistence of symptoms over a set period of time, family history, environmental factors, etc.); diagnostic technologies such as standardized questionnaires and brain scans can be used to glean the targeted symptoms; and mental health institutions and networks of social legitimization (the hospital, the media, the university) provide resources and infrastructure to make the gaze's conclusions operative on a mass scale.

Institutions of medical perception have certainly developed to embrace new (mostly neurological) theories and technologies over the last two centuries, but they have retained the core function that Foucault ascribes to the clinic: that is, they extract the person who is ill from the illness. "In the rational space of disease," Foucault writes,

> doctors and patients do not occupy a place of right; they are tolerated as disturbances that can hardly be avoided: the paradoxical role of medicine consists, above all, in neutralizing them, in maintaining the maximum difference between them, so that, in the void that appears between them, the ideal configuration of the disease becomes a concrete, free form, totalized at last in a motionless, simultaneous picture, lacking both density and secrecy, where recognition of itself opens onto the order of essences. [...] If one wishes to know the illness from which he is suffering, one must subtract the individual, with his particular qualities (Foucault 2003: 9, 14 translation modified).

other words they might be seen as differential emergences from a shard realm of relationality that is one with becoming—and belonging" (71).

6 In *The Birth of the Clinic*, the term "medical gaze" (*regard médical*) is sometimes translated by A.M. Sheridan as "medical perception," as an acquiescence to the unprepared reader (2003: vii).

The clinical gaze neutralizes the patient, whose presence could only introduce possible distortions or variations, and unnecessarily complicate a neatly classifiable and ideal disease with essential qualities.

By constructing an autonomous disease as object of its perception, the clinical gaze subtracts the individual. Yet rather than amount to its overcoming, the individual's subtraction marks its very production.[7] This may seem counterintuitive, but medical perception's subtraction of the individual is at the same time a privileging of the individual—a privileging of what to subtract. The individual's subtraction is made to stand in for the erasure of everything else that disappears in the diagnostic scene, like the plethora of affective ties and libidinally significant relationships which are systematically obscured by the clinical gaze. In search for an autonomous disease, medical perception occludes all that the depressed person brings into the diagnostic encounter, effectively denying their complicated presence—the multiplicity of relations that encompass the individual and are irreducible to it—in the name of scientific objectivity. These relations are swept outside of the clinic's walls and labelled "society." What remains is a standardized shell, a clinical individual, whose role is to play host to an alien disease living inside of it. By bringing disease under the regime of medical perception, the diagnostic scene ritually performs this separation of individual from society, exemplifying Foucault's assessment that "medical authority functions as power well before it functions as knowledge" (2006: 3).

A more contingent theory of subjectivity is warranted if the experience of being profoundly unwell is to be reinfused with an existential and political dimension that allows for escape from the essentialist confines of the "individual," "society" and "depression" triad that psychiatric power reifies so efficiently. A theory of subjectivity-in-the-making is exactly what militant psychoanalyst Félix Guattari proposes through his theory of "assemblages" which he develops in collaboration with Gilles Deleuze. Assemblages are "set up at the intersection of meaning, material and social facts, and, above all, of their transformation" (Guattari 2009d: 209) and they comprise "actions and passions, an intermingling of bodies reacting to one another" as well as "acts and statements" and "incorporeal transformations" (Deleuze and Guattari 1987: 88). The metastable manner of the assemblage, or the way that it tentatively stages the mobile relations between its component parts, articulates a dramatically expanded sense of the term "subjectivity." In "Subjectivities, For Better or for Worse," an essay that Guattari wrote near the

7 Foucault clearly writes: "It seems to me that insofar as power is a procedure of individualization, the individual is only the effect of power" (2006: 15).

end of his life, he builds on the idea of subjectivity as a dynamic assemblage[8] and proposes a provisional definition of subjectivity as "the set of conditions that make it possible for individual and/or collective factors to emerge as a sui-referential existential territory, adjacent or in a determining position to an alterity that is itself subjective" (1996b: 196). Guattari's insistence on the relational and mobile disposition of events of subjectivity production makes evident the inherent limitations of the clinical gaze and suggests the need for an enlarged field of perception that can operate beyond the limits of the individual to sense the manifold forces that condition singular iterations of depression. Guattari makes clear that his theory of subjectivity is not a theory of the individual: "The self-conscious subject should be considered a particular 'option,' a sort of normal madness. It is illusory to believe there exists only *one* subject—an autonomous subject, centered on one individual" (2009: 262). The analyses of subjectivity which fill the following pages of this study build on Guattari's ideas by deploying allied thinkers such as William James, Gilles Deleuze, A.N. Whitehead and Gilbert Simondon whose theories of subjectivity also complicate the bipartite division between the individual and society on which medical perception's authority rests.

The importance of Guattari's assemblage theory of subjectivity for an analysis of depression cannot be overestimated, especially given the context in which it was developed. Guattari wrote prolifically while living and working as a psychoanalyst at La Borde, an alternative psychiatric institution for psychotics that was started by Jean Oury in 1951. The collective psychotherapeutic practices of La Borde greatly influenced his theoretical writings, and their full significance is revealed only when read in light of the therapeutic impulse guiding his life's work. I return to Guattari's work

8 A word of caution is warranted here. Like many of Deleuze and Guattari's concepts, the concept of assemblage proves quite malleable across their two bodies of work. In their rereading of structuralist linguistics in *A Thousand Plateaus*, the most systematic development of the concept distinguishes between "machinic assemblages" and "collective assemblages of enunciation" which together comprise the two poles of the "abstract machine's" horizontal axis. The machinic assemblages are segments of content and the collective assemblages of enunciation are segments of expression. These poles of the abstract machine's horizontal axis are paired with a vertical axis that stretches from deterritorialization to reterritorialization (Deleuze and Guattari 1987: 88). In various other texts, particularly those authored solely by Guattari, the distinction between machinic assemblages and collective assemblages of enunciation starts to collapse. For example, Guattari's later essays cited in this study, such as *Schizoanalytic Cartographies* and "Subjectivities, for Better and for Worse" make next to no mention of "machinic assemblages" and are wholly preoccupied with the pragmatics of collective assemblages of enunciation. One reason for this slight but significant terminological shift could be that by the late 1980s and early 1990s, Guattari had already justified the expressivity of content and no longer felt the need to dialogue with the postulates of Saussurean linguistics in the same way.

throughout this book precisely because of how his theories of subjectivity production are intimately linked to therapeutic practice.

Never one to accept biological reductionism, Guattari always insisted that nonnormative psychic states which qualify for cateogorization as mental illness must first and foremost be conceived of as an existential problem of subjectivity production. The schizoanalytic praxis he developed at La Borde works on precisely this premise. At once analytic and creative, schizoanalysis discovers unconscious blockages and breaks through them by diagramming lines of flight towards novel assemblages of subjectivity whose existential territories could prove creative of therapeutic value for all involved. Premised on the assemblage theory of subjectivity quoted from above, schizoanalysis reinfuses the problem of depression with the existential and political dimension that is stripped away by psychiatric power and its perceptual apparatus. Once depression is regarded as an impasse in the machinic production of assemblages of subjectivity, it regains the existential and political dimensions that psychiatric power obscures through its naturalization of the biological disease model. Through adopting an assemblage approach to subjectivity, it is no longer possible to demarcate where individual, society, or disease begins and ends.

By isolating a disease as if it were autonomous and producing an individual subject through perceptual subtraction, the clinical gaze parses out the bulk of the "machinic assemblage" that informs how (a patient's) life can be lived. Psychiatry's production of the individualized subject, cut off from its conjoined assemblages, makes for what Deleuze calls a "clinical state" of subjectivity that "does not open out onto anything" (Deleuze 1998: lv). Strangely enough, given the therapeutic mandate of medicine, the inherent sclerosis of the clinical state stemming from its ritualized reification of individual and society lends itself to a sense of isolation and existential sterility. Guattari was known to suffer from recurring bouts of depression throughout his life[9] and in *Chaosmosis*, a book dedicated to the analysis of the production of subjectivity, he allies the sensation of feeling like a discrete individual—the sort of individual that the clinical gaze produces—to the experience of depression. He writes: "The phenomenological apprehension of being existing as inert facticity only occurs in the case of limit experiences such as existential nausea or melancholic depression" (109). Psychiatric

9 The François Dosse biography, *Gilles Deleuze and Félix Guattari: Intersecting Lives*, recounts Guattari's recurring struggles with depression. A collection of Guattari's essays from the 1980s even bears the title *The Winter Years* (*Les années d'hiver*) in reference to the severe depression he experienced towards the end of his life (Dosse 16-17; 425-427).

power's production of the clinical individual through its imposition of the disease model thus makes for a highly alienating scenario, whereby an essential disease reifies a depressive sense of self, all remarkably in the name of mental health.

Schizoanalysis searches for techniques to overcome the depressive sense of self that arises in moments of being made to feel like an isolated individual, or "being existing as inert facticity," cut off from the movements of the world's assemblages and their resingularizing potential. By remapping the subjective cartography, schizoanalysis introduces an aesthetic, or "critical," element into the clinical domain of mental health. In Deleuze's remarkable "critical and clinical" project, which articulates a limit point shared between art and medicine, he develops the concept of critique in a new direction as "the literary technique and style of the writer" (Smith li). The guiding thesis of his project is that artists, using aesthetic technique and style, can imaginatively perceive new constellations of subjectivity, that when transposed to the clinic, could become verifiable medical classifications. The classic examples he gives are the literary figures Marquis de Sade and Leopold von Sacher-Masoch,

> whose names were used as labels in the nineteenth century to denote two basic 'perversions' in clinical psychiatry. [...] This encounter between literature and medicine was made possible, Deleuze argues, by the peculiar nature of the symptomatological method. Medicine is made up of at least three different activities: symptomatology, or the study of signs; etiology, or the search for causes; and therapy, or the development and application of a treatment. While etiology and therapeutics are integral parts of medicine, symptomatology appeals to a kind of limit-point, premedical or submedical, that belongs as much to art as to medicine. [...] Deleuze strongly suggests that artists and authors can go further in symptomatology than doctors and clinicians, precisely "because the work of art gives them new means [...] " (Smith xvi-xvii)

If artists can go further than clinicians, perceiving symptoms of emergent subjectivities, and not only of a disease whose symptoms are already known and medically classified, then they are in the perfect position to complicate essentialist narratives about depression that are derived from the intrinsically limited scope of the clinical gaze and subsequently recounted by the medical-industrial complex's media appendages.[10] The shared emphasis on

10 For a Canadian example of a highly concerted corporate media effort to reify psychiatric power's understanding of mental illness, see the Bell "Let's Talk" campaign.

perceiving assemblages of subjectivity is the point where Deleuze's "critical and clinical" project and Guattari's lifelong commitment to elaborating schizoanalytic praxis dovetails. In both cases, the revolutionary function of art, and even pure science, is its ability to make critical discoveries that fall outside of the clinic's established classifications.

The cinema is no exception to the rule, and is equally well equipped with the critical capacity to symptomatologically perceive emergent assemblages of subjectivity. Periodically throughout his life, Guattari turned to the cinema as a way to better understand the workings of desire "*before* the separation between the familiarized self and the social field" takes place (Guattari 2009a: 245). In creating images that index processes of subjectivity production, and not merely the reified, individual subjects produced by the clinical gaze, the cinema trades critical perception for clinical perception to enact a radical symptomatology of a world ravaged by a depression pandemic. The stark differences between these two modes of perception are reflected in their respective symptomatologies. Psychiatry's diagnostic handbook, the *Diagnostic and Statistical Manual of Mental Disorders*, fifth edition lists nine symptoms of "major depressive disorder," each of which are found in the patterns of the depressed patient's feelings, thoughts and behaviours (feelings of worthlessness, thoughts of death, psychomotor disturbances, etc.).[11] If Deleuze and Guattari's machinic theory of subjectivity is taken seriously, and subjectivity is seen as a dynamic event irreducible to the individual, then the sort of symptoms that are listed in the *DSM* and perceived (as signs) by the clinical gaze can be considered as complete or exhaustive only under highly reductive conditions.

The cinema's symptomatology is entirely different. Its critical mode of perception opens onto the site of subjectivity production, where it discovers event-based symptoms of depression. Through a close analysis of key filmic examples, this book foregrounds four of such symptoms: the depotentialization of neuroplasticity, alienation from a common world of experience, the foreclosure of an encounter with alterity, and the erosion of Indigenous values by capitalist modes of valuation.[12] By shifting focus from the standardized clinical subject (psychiatry's privileged symptomatological

11 For the official list of symptoms corresponding to depressive disorders, see pages 155-189 of the *DSM-5*.

12 These symptoms are by no means exhaustive. Art cinema's melancholy aesthetics is much more extensive than the case studies that comprise the following pages, and I claim no interest in reconsolidating a definitive list of symptoms. The inherent ambiguity of the term "melancholy" offers the advantage of sidestepping the clinical drive towards establishing sharply defined disorders.

site), onto the plane of immanence where subjectivity is produced, the films discussed in this project implicitly challenge the disease model of depression and its dependence on an individual subject who must house the disease, and be made responsible for managing it. Once the symptoms of depression can no longer be found in or on an individual but in the world and its relations, then what the symptoms begin to index is not necessarily a disease—natural, ideal, essential—but a highly contingent manner of subjectivity production, and its conditioning by power. The following study is allied to the cinema's critical symptomatology and the far-reaching consequences this perceptual shift.

True to the critical force of art, contemporary cinema's symptomatology markedly differs from what medical institutions consensually recognize depression to be. So much so, that the perceptual shift from the clinical to the critical welcomes a terminological shift. The term "depression" is loaded with clinical baggage that doesn't make itself very amenable to studies of cinema, even when filmmakers make their art in response to the waves of acute emotional pain cascading across the globe. The term "depression," denotes a clearly definable clinical entity corresponding to an exhaustive list of symptoms, whose meaning couldn't be more precise. The concept of melancholy, on the other hand, retains an ambiguity that honours the cinema's perception of subjectivity production, and the re-existentialization and repoliticization of depression that follows from these critical acts of perception. One reason for melancholy's ambiguity has to do with the sheer historical longevity of the concept. Long before the notion of clinical depression came into common usage after the publication of the *DSM-I* in 1952, artists, poets, philosophers and physicians made recourse to melancholy to describe a number of historically contingent ways of feeling, with epoch after epoch adding to the concept's polysemy.[13] Already by the early seventeenth century, could Robert Burton pen the following line: "The Tower of Babel never yielded such confusion of tongues as this Chaos of Melancholy doth variety of symptoms" (Burton 108). Whether an imbalance of black bile in Aristotle's great statesman[14], the sin of acedia afflicting St. Theresa of Avila's melancholy nuns[15], or the sense of dejection that fills the flâneur in Charles Baudelaire's macabre symbolist poetry[16], melancholy mutates throughout

13 Raymond Klibansky, Erwin Panofsky and Fritz Saxl's *Saturn and Melancholy: Studies in the History of Natural Philosophy, Religion and Art* is the touchstone text on melancholy's various historical iterations.

14 See Aristotle's "Brilliance and Melancholy" in Radden's *The Nature of Melancholy.*

15 See Theresa of Avila's "Melancholy Nuns' in Radden's *The Nature of Melancholy.*

16 See Baudelaire's "Autumn Song" and "Spleen" in Radden's *The Nature of Melancholy.*

history, taken up when needed to describe the painful tedium, despair and despondency that has wrought so many lives, in so many different ways.

The visual arts' longstanding fascination with melancholy is one of the main reasons for its fruitful ambiguity. The exhibit *Melancholy: Genius and Madness in the Occident*, which was presented at the Galeries nationales du Grand Palais in Paris (October 2005-January 2006) and the Neue Nationalgalerie in Berlin (February-May 2006), presents this historical relationship in great depth. Documented in an oversized book of the same name edited by Jean Clair, it meticulously shows how melancholy has inspired artistic creations as stylistically and historically diverse as antiquity's votive stencils (*Melancholy Athena*), paintings of medieval religious experiences (Hieronymus Bosch's *St. John the Baptist in the Wilderness*, Albrecht Dürer's famous renaissance engravings (*Melancholia I*), and the modern paintings of Edvard Munch (*Melancholy III*), to name just a few.

Due in large part to this aesthetic tradition carrying melancholy down through the ages, discovering its qualities in ever-novel assemblages, melancholy has a noteworthy reputation of being applied, as Jennifer Radden explains, "not only to persons but landscapes and events" (30). It is precisely this depersonalized, event-based conception of melancholy coursing through art history that is activated in this study of contemporary art cinema's melancholy aesthetics. It bears repeating: whereas depression is mired in the confines of the clinical state productive of an essential disease and reified individual, melancholy lends itself to the critical functions of art and schizoanalysis, which open onto the collective, evental conditions of subjectivity production.

The terminological shift from depression to melancholy enables a re-politicized and re-existentialized manner of perceiving the mental health crisis in the realm of the aesthetic, and it is also for this reason that I opt for the term melancholy instead of its companion "melancholia." History has witnessed much slippage between these two terms to the extent that they are virtually indistinguishable, but if one slight difference can been maintained, it parallels the one teased out above between melancholy and depression: that melancholia is a distinctly psychoanalytic clinical entity, whereas melancholy describes a generalized affective tonality coursing through art history that mutually includes a variety of conjoined emotional states such as suicidial despair, unwavering psychic distress, exhaustion, loneliness, isolation, resignation and lapsed faith.

There is no loss in the assemblage. Practically all literature on melancholia from the 20th century onwards refers back to Freud's 1917 Ur-text "Mourning and Melancholia." The basic premise of his text is that melancholia is the result of the failure to mourn a lost love object. Instead of detaching from the object through a process of reality-testing and replacing it with a new one in cases of successful mourning, melancholia takes hold when the libido "regresses into the ego" (Freud 1957: 257) and internalizes its ambivalence towards the lost object, resulting in symptoms such as "painful dejection, cessation of interest in the outside world, loss of the capacity to love, inhibition of all activity, and a lowering of the self-regarding feelings to a degree that finds utterance in self-reproaches and self-revilings, and culminates in a delusional expectation of punishment" (Freud 1957: 243). These psychoanalytic symptoms of melancholia appear in slightly modified form in the *DSM-V*'s list of criteria for clinical depression, and acknowledge the sort of emotions that the melancholy aesthetics of art history put on display. This book moves from "depression" and "melancholia," which carry precise but weighty clinical defintions, to the more nebulous "melancholy" and its aesthetic heritage. Through latching onto the leeway afforded by a term like "melancholy" it becomes possible to trade off a clinical ethos for a critical one, and to reorient the site of symptomatology from the clinical individual to the eventful assemblage.[17]

A crucial effect of this perceptual displacement is that by shifting the symptomatological site towards the event of subjectivity production, the cinema's melancholy aesthetics potentialize an analogous reappraisal of depression's corresponding etiologies and therapies. The book's second half seizes this newfound opportunity to examine how experimental processes of subjective recomposition can double as acts of therapy and activism.[18] By exploring the coordinates of melancholic assemblages of subjectivity, and experimenting with their recomposition, the filmmakers featured in this study challenge the uncompromising ossification of what depression has

17 The ossification of the term "melancholia" is attributable to the fact that his "Mourning and Melancholia" essay has been so heavily influential in 20th Century thought, effectively eclipsing all previous iterations of melancholy and melancholia and cementing the latter term as the one of serious study. In all fairness to Freud, he himself was sure to acknowledge the hypothetical nature of his theory, and "from the outset drops all claims to general validity for our conclusions" (Freud 1957: 237).

18 My use of the term therapy here, and throughout this study, should not be confused with the personalist connotations that the term comes loaded with, and that *Anti-Oedipus* rails against. Dana L. Cloud describes the connotations as follows: "the discursive pattern of translating social and political problems into the language of individual responsibility and healing is a rhetoric because of its powerful persuasive force" and its rhetoric a form of "therapy" because "of its focus on the personal life of the individual as a locus of both problem and responsibility for change" (xiv).

been made to mean, and even more importantly, how it may be diagnosed and treated, and by whom.

Thus it could be said that the filmmakers who populate the following pages are nothing less than therapeutic activists.[19] They effectively corroborate Philippe Pignarre's contestation that the depression pandemic is a pandemic in the medicalization of existential problems (104), by taking the speculative risk of viewing it through the critical lens offered by the cinema. In adopting such an ethos they politicize the problem of existence in ways that enable therapeutically acting in line with collective well-being, without waiting for the sanction of medical authorities.

In the throes of a pandemic exacerbated by neoliberal power's devaluing of life itself, a devaluing reified by psychiatry's clinical apparatus, such lay acts of relational healing through the recomposition of subjectivity would amount to nothing less than an urgently needed praxis of both therapy and activism—or what we could call therapeutic activism: a way of acting on Foucault's reminder in the closing lines of *Discipline and Punish*, that in the apparatuses of normalization that are intended "to provide relief, to cure, to help," one should hear "the rumbling of battle" (Foucault 308).

The Films

The following investigation into the production of melancholic subjectivity and the conditions for its therapeutic reassemblage is enacted through encounters with five different films: *The Red Desert* (Michelangelo Antonioni, 1964), *Afternoon* (Angela Schanelec, 2007), *Night Moves* (Kelly Reichardt, 2013) *Uncle Boonmee Who Can Recall His Past Lives* (Apichatpong Weerasethakul, 2010), and *Palawan Fate* (Kanakan Balintagos, 2011). *The Red Desert* announced the arrival of the "cinema of poetry" by blending the aesthetic strategies of neorealism and expressionism to create a "free indirect" image that confounds the distinction between objective and

19 The term "therapeutic activism" is inspired by Franco 'Bifo' Berardi and Josep Rafanell i Orra. Channeling the ethos coursing through Guattari's life work, Bifo writes, "Political action must happen according to modalities analogous to therapeutic intervention" (2009: 140). Rafannell i Orra reinforces this idea by exposing how psychotherapeutic services of all kinds have become an uncritical appendage of the neoliberal economy, indissociable from new technologies of control, which he calls, "therapeutic capitalism" (Rafanell i Orra 268). He goes on to make a claim very similar to Bifo, and equally indebted to Guattari, when he writes: "Healing, before wanting to ask, 'How can I heal?' presupposes a prior question: 'What world must be actualized?'" (2011: 284.)

subjective perspectives, and between the psyche and the socius (the social body). The film's aesthetic accomplishment in turn created the artistic conditons for the latter four films to explore the "psychosocial" dynamics of the depression pandemic.

Each of these four contemporary films begs to be read in light of a broader film movement with visibility in the global cinemascape: The Berlin School, American Neo-Neorealism, New Thai Cinema and Fourth Cinema. Over the course of the book, I situate the case studies within the political and artistic context of these film movements, since it helps to show how these films' concern for the precarity of well-being under global capital is part of a broader artistic awareness of the issue. In making this gesture, I do not mean to claim that these film movements are to be read primarly and solely as responses to the depression pandemic, since that narrow of interpretation would limit many other productive ways of reading these films and the film cultures in which they take part. However, I do contend that the political and existential contours of the contemporary depression pandemic can be found in many of the new millenium's most artistically signficiant film movements.

I have decided to limit the scope of this book to these five case studies. A more all-encompassing presentation of melancholy aesthetics in contemporary cinema would likely touch on related film movements, such as the Iranian New Cinema (Jafar Panahi, Abbas Kiarostami), the Taiwanese Second New Wave (Tsai-Ming Liang), recent Québecois cinema (Rodrigue Jean, Ivan Grbovic), the Danish Dogme movement (Lars von Trier, Thomas Vinterberg), and a slate of other active auteurs including Lav Diaz (*Melancholia*, 2008), Pedro Costa (*In Vanda's Room*, 2000), Joachim Trier (*Oslo, Ausust 31st*, 2011), Steve McQueen (*Shame*, 2011), Carlos Reygadas (*Silent Light*, 2007) and Béla Tarr (*The Turin Horse*, 2011). I do not intend for the five films that I have chosen as my case studies to be taken as representatives of this greater set of films, and they would undoubtedly fail to uphold the weight assigned to them should they be tasked with representing what these other films have to say about life in the depression pandemic. Rather, they have been chosen for their ability to function as limit-cases of how the cinema can render melancholy experience aesthetic and offer an alternative to the reigning psychiatric models which dictate the sense of depression and define the range of legitimate therapeutic responses to it.

At first glance, the five films that I have chosen as my case studies may seem to have little in common other than their melancholic tonality. *The Red Desert* predates the other four films by over thirty-five years; each film comes from a different country (Italy, Germany, USA, Thailand, and the Philippines); and each features dialogue in their respective languages

(Italian, German, English, Thai, and Palawano). Moreover, they each relay quite different narrative intrigues: psychosis in an industrial zone; a breakup in a bourgeois cottage; the direct action of a group of ecological activists; an ailing man's recollection of his past lives; and a couple's search for a shaman who can heal the wounds of colonialism. Politically and culturally speaking, they contrast as well, with each film making meaning in relation to a unique site of power relations: 1960s Italy's "economic miracle"; post-unification Germany; the climate of economic collapse in post-2008 America; Thailand's anti-communist history; and the neocolonization of the island of Palawan by multinational resource extraction companies.

Given the high degree of variance between the films focused on in this study, it begs the question as to how such thematically, geographically, linguistically and culturally distinct films could possibly be grouped together. All of this book's case studies could be categorized under the rubric of two separate, but sometimes overlapping, fields of study: global art cinema and minor cinema. In what follows, I will lay out how the category of global art cinema informs my choice of case studies, by articulating how otherwise disparate filmmakers share in a common artistic heritage and enter into dialogue with one another on the global festival circuit. Afterwards, I will supplement the global art cinema framework with the theory of minor cinema to explain how these films also engage in a political aesthetics of anti-psychiatry that puts into question the clinical construct of depression and its inherent individualism, in opening onto an event-based understanding of melancholy experience.

In their edited anthology entitled *Global Art Cinema*, Rosalind Galt and Karl Schoonover privilege the global nature of contemporary art cinema and include essays that emphasize the commonalities between East Asian, Latin American, American, African and European art cinemas. "'Global,'" they argue is not merely one of art cinema's themes "but an inherent element, alongside and interpenetrating 'art' and 'cinema'" (20). The editors offer four criteria of art cinema,[20] but for the purposes of this study, which ranges in purview from West to East to Global South, from First World to Fourth, the aspect of art cinema that warrants deepest emphasis is none other than its globality. Published in 2010, the *Global Art Cinema* anthology amounts to what its authors themselves admit is a polemic (20). The reason why adding

20 The four criteria that Galt and Schoonover identify can be summarized as follows: an "impure spectator at the level of textual address and in the history of its audiences", "ambivalence with regards to location," an "ambivalent relationship to stardom and authorship," and lastly, a "troubling of genre" (6-8).

the qualifier "global" amounts to a polemic about art cinema at this historical moment is because, as Galt and Schoonover point out, "in traditional film historiography, art cinema has been a way to organize national cinema in canons of 'great directors,'" which amounts to a "critical tendency [that] conflates art cinema with national cinema" (7). What the collection's editors argue instead is that "art cinema always carries a comparitivist impulse and transnational tenor" (7).

Influential film theorist Dudley Andrew adds weight to this global conception of the art film in his preface to the edition. He says straightforwardly that art cinema "is by definition pan-national, following the urge of every ambitious film to take off from its point of release, so as to encounter other viewers and other movies, elsewhere and later" (vi). For Andrew, the "international address" of a film is what warrants its consideration as art cinema, in contradistinction to national cinemas, which address local populations (and are often unintelligible or indecipherable outside of that linguistic-cultural context). He gives the example of Philippine cinema, where

> out of a hundred films made each year this past decade, only fifteen or so can be identified as part of the Philippine art cinema, specifically those that have been selected to screen abroad. [...] So there would seem to be two distinct Philippine cinemas, one based on cultural belonging, bound to the Tagalog language, and the other taken up by a polyglot international audience who can access the films at festivals or download them on their computers (vii).

What Andrew's conception of art cinema offers is a way to emphasize how films not only enter into relation with one another on global circuits of exhibition that cross national borders, but are constructed with this deterritorialized encounter in mind.

The international address of a work of Philippine art cinema, like *Palawan Fate*, which can also be categorized as a Fourth Cinema title (these are not mutually exclusive categories), does not subtract from its imbrication in local political issues. Though sometimes, as Dudley Andrew points out, this relationship between internationally recognized auteurs and their home countries is undeniably strained.[21] Apichatpong Weerasethakul's relationship to Thailand perfectly encapsulates this tension. He ultimately decided not to show his most recent film *Cemetery of Splendour* in his homeland mainly

21 Andrew gives the example of Taiwanese auteur Edward Yang who refused to let *Yi-Yi* be screened in the country where it was shot (Andrew: x).

"because he fears it would run foul of the ruling military junta" if he did not edit the film in accordance with Thailand's strict censorship laws. "I feel there is more violence in our country than in others that are in similar situations and I am sad to see that I don't have any power or rights to speak, because I know if I speak, harm will come." (Child: n.p.) In defiance of the grave risks, art cinema's global address is more than an institution, aesthetic practice, or genre[22], but a downright political necessity. Apichatpong may freely live in Thailand, but his films, banished from Thai movie theatres, are made with the knowledge that they will become nomadic exiles.

The other auteurs who I focus on don't suffer from the same sort of censorship legislation, but they do share Apichatpong's unease towards their respective nations and national cinemas. For example, Antonioni's oeuvre—and especially *The Red Desert*—is a meditation on the feeling of alienation that can arise in one's own country, particularly when dealing with a modern factory setting made of chemical smoke, industrially coloured steel, and empty streets. In the context of the Berlin School films, even when they are shot in Germany, featuring local settings and subject matter, one would be hard pressed to try and squeeze these filmmakers into a national cinema discourse due to how drastically they differ in style, theme, and tone from their nationalist counterparts.[23] Ulrich Köhler, one of Angela Schanelec's Berlin School contemporaries, even goes so far as to deliberately rail against the mainstream German cinema and its sanitized liberal politics. For her part, Kelly Reichardt demonstrates a repeatedly ambivalent relationship to her home nation. Her films sympathize with marginalized and downtrodden characters all the while quietly indicting the American political system for exacerbating their misery. As one of the most relevant American independent filmmakers, she could have easily transitioned into a career in Hollywood. At least until now, Reichardt has opted to find alternative financing for her films in an effort to preserve her creative autonomy, effectively cementing her as an outsider in her own domestic market. Lastly, Kanakan Balintagos, who would undoubtedly

22 The defining frameworks for understanding art cinema has traditionally been split into two camps: one which conceives of art cinema as institution, the other as an aesthetic practice or genre. Steve Neale advocates the former approach in his widely read *Screen* article, "Art Cinema as Institution." The latter approach is derived from David Bordwell's equally well-recognized essay, "The Art Cinema as a Mode of Film Practice."

23 A defining characteristic of Schanelec's oeuvre is its wandering protagonists who drift beyond zones of local belonging. For example, *Marseille* (2004) follows a woman who travels between Berlin and the city in southern France, and in her more recent *Orly* (2010) is shot in the Orly airport as an homage to Jacques Tati's interstitial epic *Playtime* (1967).

qualify as one of the "ten to fifteen art cinema auteurs" from the Philippines that Dudley Andrew references, reaches out to a broad cross-section of publics to express diverse facets of his hybrid existence. As an Indigenous man from the Global South, inspired as much by his ancestral myths as European and modern Philippine art cinemas, his films appeal to festival publics as diverse as Cannes, ImagiNative (Toronto), Cinemalaya (Manila), and Frameline (San Francisco). Though widely celebrated on the indie film circuit in his home country, Balintagos is still somewhat of an anomaly in Philippine film culture since he tells the types of stories that rarely make their way onto domestic screens. He is a true "wanderer between worlds," as ethnologist of Filipino psychology, Katrin de Guia has so eloquently said, in reference as much to the national and cultural borders he straddles as to his shamanic capabilities (139).

These filmmakers' international mode of address has brought them into a global exchange, through which they have all been marked by aesthetic and thematic contagion. Rajendra Roy articulates this phenomenon in his introduction to the Museum of Modern Art's coffee table book on the Berlin School, when he points out how one of the movement's filmmakers, Christoph Hochhäusler "situates the Berlin School on a global terrain, noting that filmmakers such as Abbas Kiarostami, Apichatpong Weerasethakul, and Howard Hawks have been at least as influential as [German filmmakers] Fritz Lang, Rainer Werner Fassbender or Werner Herzog" (11). The reference to Apichatpong should not go unnoticed. In the very same book, Hochhäusler's telling essay "On Whose Shoulders: The Question of Aesthetic Indebtedness," imparts the secret that Berlin School directors "are in agreement over the influence of Apichatpong" and additionally suggests that Kelly Reichardt should be regarded as a contemporary of the Berlin School (Hochhäusler 24). A couple of other clever cinephilic links between Apichatpong and the Berlin School are hard to ignore. In 2011, Ulrich Köhler directed a film called *Sleeping Sickness*, and only three years later, Apichatpong, whose oeuvre has long displayed a fascination with all things oneiric, decided to make *Cemetery of Splendor*, a film about the epidemic spread of a mysterious sleeping sickness where hallucinations become indistinguishable from reality. Another uncoincidental connection between these parties crops up in a *Cinema Scope* piece on Angela Schanelec and her film (aptly titled *The Dreamlike Path*) (2016). Its author makes the keen observation that both Schanelec and Apichatpong's earlier efforts *Marseille* (2004) and *Tropical Malady* (2004) are structured as diptychs, and happened to premiere at Cannes the very same year (Williams 13). Consciously and unconsciously, it is safe to say that there is a stylistic and thematic contagion between art cinema directors, as this brief example between Apichatpong and the Berlin School indicates, regardless of the gaps between their respective national cultures.

Perhaps this mutual indebtedness should not come as much of a surprise, since many art film auteurs, particularly the ones who comprise this study, are the inheritors of a specific current of art cinema called the cinema of poetry that has a history of casting psychologically unstable protagonists and using a free indirect aesthetic to interrogate their psyche's relational underpinnings. Each of the films discussed in the following pages reactivate this tradition inaugurated in the 1960s to express a common concern for well-being in the midst of a depression pandemic which is as global as art cinema itself.

The theory of minor cinema is useful for articulating the anti-psychiatric politics behind this perceptual shift from the individual to the event, and it provides the means for thinking these films together based on shared affinity, sensibility and concern rather than shared identity, which is the more common way of organizing studies of film. Minor cinema is now a film studies concept with widely acknowledged currency in the discipline, but its roots date back to Deleuze and Guattari's 1975 book *Kafka: Toward a Minor Literature*. In their collaborative study of Kafka, Deleuze and Guattari deploy the concept of minor literature to explain the political aesthetics of Kafka's work in a manner that challenges the two types of readings that had dominated interpretations of his work up until that point in time: natural (psychoanalytic) and supernatural (theological) interpretations. According to Réda Bensmaïa, "one misses the mark in Kafka either by putting him in the nursery—by oedipalizing and relating him to mother-father narratives—or by trying to limit him to theological-metaphysical speculation to the detriment of all the political, ethical, and ideological dimensions that run through his work and give it a special status in the history of literature" (Bensmaïa ix). Deleuze and Guattari's theory of minor literature consists of three fundamental criteria. The first is "a high coefficient of deterritorialization" characteristic of a minority's use of a major language, as is the case of Kafka's Prague German (1986:16). "The second characteristic of minor literatures," Deleuze and Guattari write, "is that everything in them is political. In major literatures, in contrast, the individual concern (familial, marital, and so on) joins with no other less individual concerns, the social milieu serving as a mere environment or background. [...] Minor literature is completely different, its cramped space forces each individual intrigue to connect immediately to politics" (1986: 17). Deleuze and Guattari then go on to write, "The third characteristic of minor literature is that everything takes on a collective value [...] There isn't a subject, *there are only collective assemblages of enunciation* [...] " (1986: 18, italics in original). The three characteristics of minor literature that Deleuze and Guattari find in Kafka's work lead them to the conclusion that "the minor no longer designates specific literatures but the revolutionary conditions for every literature within the heart of what is called great (or established) literature" (1986: 18).

Their conclusion is an important one, and it should be taken as a reminder that even though this book uses the concept of minor cinema to expound the anti-psychiatric politics of select art films which serve as limit-cases, by no means should that be misconstrued to suggest that all of art cinema is somehow a minor cinema. To translate Deleuze and Guattari's maxim from literature into the realm of cinema, we can say that the minor no longer designates specific cinemas, but the revolutionary conditions for every cinema, within the heart of what is called great (or established) cinema. The films that comprise this project's case studies are minor limit-cases of global art cinema, and the majoritarian structure that they inflect from within is not a specific language or cinematic genre, much less the art cinema's institutions, but psychiatry's mode of clinically perceiving—and producing—mental illnesses such as depression. The reason why it can be said that these films undo psychiatric perception from within, much in the same way that Deleuze and Guattari speak of minor literatures as acting on the revolutionary conditions within established literatures, is that the object of psychiatry's clinical gaze—the (mentally ill) individual—also happens to be the subject of neoliberal political life par excellence. To shake psychiatry's clinical gaze from within doesn't require making a film inside of a doctor's office or hospital (though it could), since the individual, and the individualism, that the gaze naturalizes and reifies can be found across diverse fields of subjectivity production adjacent to various social spaces and instutions. Only in the most acute cases is psychiatry now practiced in an asylum or hospital context; the vast majority of psychiatric subjects, especially those who are diagnosed with depression, carry their diagnoses and treatments—points of subjection—around with them in the quotidian. Psychiatry is an institution of the everyday and the everywhere. Unsettling the effects of its ways of seeing on the production of subjectivity requires intervening into the quotidian spaces of its operations—(battle)fields of subjectivity production where minor cinemas of melancholy aesthetics and therapeutic activism stake a claim.

The three charcateristics of minor literature that Deleuze and Guattari advance in *Kafka* articulate with remarkable clarity what happens when psychiatry's clinical gaze is traded for cinema's critical perception. Firstly, the territory on which the clinical construct of depression is built comes undone, and is extended to new, destratified linkages. In these cases, the cinematic image is invested with a high coefficient of deterritorialization because it opens onto an event of subjectivity production that precedes and exceeds the bounded individual on all sides and in all tenses. It becomes impossible to speak of this or that person's depression, as if they were the proprietiers of an internalized disease, since the entire image, and the event of subjectivity production that it perceives, is inundated with a melancholic affective tonality. The "territory" of the depressed individual is deterritorialized onto a relational field of melancholy. Secondly, in minor cinemas of melancholy and therapy, the depression which is routinely (mis)taken for an individual concern in psychiatry is made to connect immediately to politics. Private emotions are exploded in favour of a generalized affective tonality that is coterminous with the spaces that give rise to them. The "immediacy" of this connection between the private affair and politics follows from the deterritorialization of the clinical individual upon which this bipartitie division is constructed. In minor cinemas, there is no mediator between the personal and the political, as if each could claim an autonomous reality of its own—there is only the political immediacy of events of subjectivity production. Thirdly, depression's becoming-melancholy through this process of deterrritorialization takes on a collective value as the subject of depression is replaced by a melancholic collective assemblage of subjectivity. In these limit-cases of minor cinema, what psychiatry frames as a disease belonging to a clinical individual, becomes an immediately political impasse in the composition of collective existence. Taken together, we can see why the three chacteristics of Deleuze and Guattari's minor literature are so useful for elucidating my case studies' perceptual shift from a clinical to a critical view of the depression pandemic: they articulate the political and existential stakes that are gained in melancholy's line of flight from the confines of clinical depression.

These minor films of melancholy and therapy may not share an identity, but they do share an affinity. Not content to have psychiatric power dictate the meaning of the widespread existential malaise that saturates their film worlds, the makers of minor cinemas that fill the pages of this book shift perception away from the clinical individual to re-existentialize and repoliticize the pandemic by harnessing the critical force of art. Together, these filmmakers can be considered therapeutic activists, or practicing schizoanalysts, who in fathoming the world in which they are mired, open perception onto existential horizons of subjectivity production far beyond the clinic's sightlines, thus finally making it possible to act, to therapeutic effect, in the midst of a pandemic that has for too long been left to the professionals—professionals who are still all too competent (Deleuze and Guattari 1983: 380).

Bibliography

American Psychiatric Association. *Diagnostic and Statistical Manual of Mental Disorders. Fifth Edition. DSM-5*. Washington, DC and London, England: American Psychiatric Association, 2013.

Andrew, Dudley. "Foreward." *Global Art Cinema: New Theories and Histories*. Eds. Rosalind Galt and Karl Schoonover. Oxford and New York: Oxford University Press, 2010. v-xi.

Angell, Marcia. "The Epidemic of Mental Illness: Why?" *The New York Review*. 23 June 2011a. Online. www.nybooks.com/articles/2011/06/23/epimeic-mental-illness-why/?pagination=false

Angell, Marcia. "The Illusions of Psychiatry." *The New York Review*. 14 July 2011b. Online. http://www.nybooks.com/articles/2011/07/14/illusions-of-psychiatry/

Bensmaïa, Réda. "Foreward: The Kafka Effect." *Kafka: Toward a Minor Literature*. Trans. Terry Cochran. Minneapolis: University of Minnesota Press, 1986.

Berardi, Franco 'Bifo'. *The Soul at Work: From Alienation to Autonomy*. Trans. Francesca Cadel and Guiseppina Mecchia. Los Angeles: Semiotext(e), 2009.

Bordwell, David. "The Art Cinema as Mode of Film Practice." *Film Theory and Criticism: Introductory Readings. Sixth Edition*. Eds. Leo Braudy and Marshall Cohen. New York and Oxford: Oxford University Press, 2004: 774-782.

Burcasa, Stephanie L. and William G. Iacono. "Risk for Recurrene in Depression." *Clinical Psychology Review* 27.8 (December 2007): 959-985.

Burkeman, Oliver. "Therapy Wars: The Revenge of Freud." *The Guardian*. 7 January 2016. Online. https://www.theguardian.com/science/2016/jan/07/therapy-wars-revenge-of-freud-cognitive-behavioural-therapy

Burton, Robert. *The Essential Anatomy of Melancholy*. Mineola, New York: Dover Publications, 2002.

Campbell, Denis. "NHS Mental Health Services Failing Young People, Say Psychiatrists." *The Guardian*. 26 December 2016. Online. https://www.theguardian.com/society/2016/dec/26/nhs-mental-health-services-failing-young-people-say-psychiatrists

Carlat, Daniel. *Unhinged: The Trouble with Psychiatry. A Doctor's Revelations About a Profession in Crisis*. New York: Free Press, 2010.

Child, Ben. "Apichatpong Weerasethakul: I Won't Censor My Work for Thailand." *The Guardian*. Online. Accessed Oct 19, 2016. https://www.theguardian.com/film/205/2015/oct/16/apichatpong-weerasethakul-cemetery-of-splendour-cannes

Clair, Jean. *Mélancolie: génie et folie en Occident*. Paris, Gallimard, 2005.

Cloud, Dana L. *Control and Consolation in American Culture and Politics: Rhetoric of Therapy*. Thousand Oaks: Sage Publications, 1998.

Curry, Bill. "Philpott warns premiers she won't budge on effort to expand mental-health funding." *The Globe and Mail.* 20 December 2016. Online. https://beta.theglobeandmail.com/news/politics/philpott-warns-premiers-she-womt-budge-on-effort-to-expand-mental-health-funding/article33397386/

De Guia, Katrin. *Kapwa: The Self in the Other. Worldviews and Lifestyles of Filipino Culture-Bearers.* Quezon City: Anvil Publishing, 2005.

Deleuze, Gilles. *Essays Critical and Clinical.* Trans. Daniel W. Smith and Michael A. Greco. London and New York, 1998.

Deleuze, Gilles and Félix Guattari. *A Thousand Plateaus: Capitalism and Schizophrenia.* Trans. Brian Massumi. Minneapolis: University of Minnesota Press, 1987.

Deleuze, Gilles and Félix Guattari. *Anti-Oedipus: Capitalism and Schizophrenia.* Trans. Robert Hurley, Mark Seem, and Helen R. Lane. Minneapolis: University of Minnesota Press, 1983.

Deleuze, Gilles and Félix Guattari. *Kafka: Toward a Minor Literature.* Trans. Dana Polan. Minneapolis and London: University of Minnesota Press, 1986.

Department of Health. *IAPT three-year report: The first million patients.* Department of Health. November, 2012.

Dosse, François. *Gilles Deleuze and Félix Guattari: Intersecting Lives.* Trans. Deborah Glassman. New York: Columbia University Press, 2010.

Foucault, Michel. *Discipline and Punish: The Birth of the Prison.* Trans. Alan Sheridan. New York: Vintage Books, 1995.

Foucault, Michel. *Psychiatric Power: Lectures at the Collège de France 1973-1974.* Eds. Jacques Lagrange, François Ewald, Alessandro Fontana and Arnold I. Davidson. Trans. Graham Burchell. Basingstoke and New York: Palgrave Macmillan, 2006.

Foucault, Michel. *The Birth of the Clinic: An Archeology of Medical Perception.* Trans. A.M. Sheridan. London and New York: Routledge, 2003.

Fournier, Jay C., Robert J. DeRubeis, Steven D. Hollon et al. "Antidepressant Drug Effects and Depression Severity: A Patient-Level Meta-analysis. *JAMA* 303.1 (2010): 47-53.

Freud, Sigmund. "Mourning and Melancholia." *The Standard Edition of the Complete Psychological Works of Sigmund Freud, Volume XIV (1914-1916): On the History of the Psycho-Analytic Movement, Papers on Metapsychology and Other Works.* London: The Hogarth Press and The Institute of Psycho-Analysis, 1957. 237-258

Galt, Rosalind and Karl Schoonover. *Global Art Cinema: New Theories and Histories.* Oxford and New York: Oxford University Press, 2010.

Guattari, Félix. *Chaosmosis: An Ethico-Aesthetic Paradigm.* Trans. Paul Bains and Julian Pefanis. Bloomington and Indianapolis: Indiana University Press, 1995.

Guattari, Félix. *Chaosophy: Texts and Interviews 1972-1977.* Ed. Sylvère Lotringer. Trans. David L. Sweet, Jarred Becker, and Taylor Adkins. Los Angeles, CA: Semiotext(e), 2009.

Guattari, Félix. *Les années d'hiver: 1980-1985*. Paris: Les Prairies Ordinaires, 2009c.

Guattari, Félix. *Schizoanalytic Cartographies*. London and New York: Bloomsbury Academic, 2013.

Guattari, Félix. "Subjectivities, For Better or for Worse." *The Guattari Reader*. Ed. Gary Genosko. Cambridge and Oxford: Blackwell Publishers, 1996b. 193-203.

Guattari, Félix. "The Schizoanalyses." *Soft Subversions: Texts and Interviews 1977-1985*. Ed. Sylvère Lotringer. Trans. Chet Wiener and Emily Wittman. Los Angeles, Semiotext(e), 2009d. 204-225.

Hochäusler, Christoph. "On Whose Shoulders: The Question of Aesthetic Indebtedness." *The Berlin School: Films from the Berliner Schule*. New York: The Museum of Modern Art, 2013. 20-29.

Johnsen, Tom J. and Oddgeir Friborg. "The Effects of Cognitive Behavioural Therapy as an Anti-Depressive Treatment is Failing: A Meta-Analysis." *Psychological Bulletin* 141.4 (July 2015): 747-768.

Kirsch, Irving. *The Emperor's New Drugs: Exploding the Antidepressant Myth*. New York: Basic Books, 2010.

Klibansky, Raymond, Erwin Panofsky and Fritz Saxl. *Saturn and Melancholy: Studies in the History of Natural Philosophy, Religion and Art*. London: Nelson, 1964.

Massumi, Brian. *Parables for the Virtual: Movement, Affect, Sensation*. Durham and London: Duke University Press, 2002.

Neale, Steve. "Art Cinema as Institution." *Screen* 22.1 (1981): 11-40.

Pignarre, Philippe. *Comment la depression est devenue une épidémie*. Paris: Éditions la découverte, 2012.

Radden, Jennifer. *The Nature of Melancholy: From Aristotle to Kristeva*. New York: Oxford University Press, 2000.

Rafanell i Orra, Josep. *En finir avec le capitalism thérapeutique: soin, politique, communauté*. Paris: Éditions la Découverte, 2011.

Rose, Nikolas and Joelle M. Abi-Rached. *Neuro: The New Brain Sciences and the Management of the Mind*. Princeton and Oxford: Princeton University Press, 2013.

Roy, Rajendra. "Introduction." *The Berlin School: Films from the Berliner Schule*. New York: The Museum of Modern Art, 2013. 10-13.

Seligman, Martin. *Flourish: A Visionary New Understanding of Happiness and Well-Being*. New York: Free Press, 2011.

Smith, Daniel W. "Introduction: 'A Life of Pure Immanence': Deleuze's 'Critique et Clinique' Project." *Essays Critical and Clinical*. Trans. Daniel W. Smith and Michael A. Greco. London and New York, 1998. xi-liii.

Whitaker, Robert. *Anatomy of an Epidemic: Magic Bullets, Psychiatric Drugs, and the Astonishing Rise of Mental Illness in America*. New York: Crown Publishers, 2010.

Williams, Blake. "Saying Something: The Films of Angela Schanelec." *Cinema Scope* 68 (Fall 2016): 12-15

World Health Organization. "Depression: Fact Sheet." *World Health Organization*. April 2016a. Online. www.who.int/mediacentre/factsheets/fs369/en

World Health Organization. "Investing in Treatment for Depression and Anxiety Leads to Fourfold Return. Depression and Anxiety Disorders Cost the Global Economy US$1 Trillion Each Year; Countries and Development Partners to Discuss Way Forward During World Bank-WHO Events." Online. 13 April 2016b. http://www.who.int/mediacentre/news/releases/2016/depression-anxiety-treatment/en/

1 The Psychosocial Image

Abstract

Chapter One charts a stylistic history of the cinema which shows how the 1965 arrival of Michaelangelo Antonioni's film *The Red Desert* and Pier Paolo Pasolini's concept of the cinema of poetry led to the emergence of a new kind of image: the psychosocial image. This psychosocial image overcomes a distinction that had previously been maintained between the psyche and the socius. In the expressionist and neorealist currents of the cinema, either the psyche was made to represent the socius, or vice versa. The specifically psychosocial quality of the cinema of poetry and its free indirect mode of perception opens the possibility for crafting images of psychological nonnormativity.

Keywords: Cinema of poetry, Pier Paolo Pasolini, free indirect discourse, Michelangelo Antonioni

Faith in the Image, Faith in Reality

The history of film style is structured by a division between two types of images, each with a unique relationship to the reality that they have commonly been understood to represent. André Bazin's canonical essay "The Evolution of Film Language" established this critical distinction between two "stylistic families with fundamentally different conceptions of cinematic expression": "filmmakers who put their faith in the image and those who put their faith in reality" (Bazin 2009: 88). Whereas the silent-era "realists" (epitomized by the work of Stroheim, Flaherty, Murnau and Dreyer) exercised their faith in reality through an "objective" style that sought to reproduce the spatial coordinates and temporal duration of profilmic reality as accurately as possible, the "imagists" (German Expressionists and Soviet Montagists) did violence to the "plastic" surface (lighting, décor, composition, acting) or altered the inherent duration of filmed events through recourse to montage-style editing, to articulate "subjective" states of mind. The

Szymanski, A., *Cinemas of Therapeutic Activism: Depression and the Politics of Existence.* Taylor & Francis Group, 2020
DOI: 10.5117/9789463723121_CH01

imagists dominated the cinema from 1915-1930, but by the late 1930s they were unseated by Italian neorealism and the "spatial realism" of American auteurs Orson Welles and William Wyler. Bazin famously praised the realist overcoming of the imagists as a dialectical step forward in the history of film style towards ever-greater realism.

Yet the clear-cut division between the realists and the imagists starts to muddy when faced with the following question: How can faith be put in the psychic—and not just social—dimension of reality? If Bazin had lived past his untimely death in 1958, he would have witnessed the emergence of the "cinema of poetry," a seismic shift in the history of film style whose creative potential is yet to be exhausted. Significantly, it also happens to offer a resolution to this schism between the realists and the imagists founded on a metaphysical distinction between social and psychic realities. The cinema of poetry was christened by none other than Pier Paolo Pasolini, filmmaker and colossal figure of Italian literature, according to whom this ground-breaking tendency in art cinema is most fully incarnated by Michelangelo Antonioni's *The Red Desert*. The 1964 film is remarkable because it puts its faith in the psychic life of its protagonist's neurosis; an artistic commitment that necessitated a stylistic break from Italian neorealism's "objective" orientation. While still very much caring for the reality that Bazin and the neorealists held dear, the 1960s cinema of poetry began to re-incorporate some of the imagists' plastic distortions to express the intricacies of character psychology. Faced with the artistic task of expressing the psychic pain throbbing underneath the surface of the objective, realist image, the cinema of poetry found it necessary to do some violence to the plastics of the image and detour through non-realism in order to be true to the psychic dimension of reality; effectively overcoming the definitive distinction that Bazin had drawn between the directors who put their faith in the image and those who put their faith in reality.

Dating back to its origins, cinema has regularly articulated character psychology.[1] What the cinema of poetry invented was an aesthetic that could express mental interiority and social exteriority with equal fidelity and undivided faith. The technique deployed by the cinema of poetry to hold these two opposing poles of the cinematographic image in experiential

1 Early film theorists such as Béla Balázs and Hugo Munsterberg were enamoured with the psychological dimension of cinema, and even considered psychological expressivity to be one of the cinema's defining features, distinguishing it from otherwise comparable art forms such as theatre. For an example of this perspective, see Balázs' *Theory of the Film* as well as Munsterberg's *The Film: A Psychological Study*.

tension with one another is what Pasolini calls the "free indirect point of view shot" (Pasolini 176). Neither a classical point of view shot (the cinematic equivalent of literature's "direct discourse") nor a non-point of view, objective shot (the equivalent of literature's "indirect discourse"), the free indirect introduces a real ambiguity as to whether or not an image is seen "through the eyes" of a particular character. This ambiguity is creative of a situation where many of the binaries that structure both Bazin's classification of the history of film style[2] as well as the etiology of depression start to collapse into one another. Subjective and objective, interior and exterior, psychic and social: the image of psychosocial reality that comes to perceptibility in the cinema of poetry grasps these categorical distinctions that structure the "faith in reality/faith in the image" schism, and reassembles them into relational poles co-inhabiting the very same image.

The Subjective and Objective Poles of the Cinematographic Image

To better situate how the cinema of poetry resolves this tension coursing through the history of film style, I will trace the two separate lineages of directors who put their faith in the image and those who put their faith in reality, and show how each cultivated either a subjective or an objective aesthetic orientation. These two tendencies within the history of film style can be neatly mapped onto Bazin's distinction between those directors who put their faith in the image and those who put their faith in reality. But as I will show here, expressionism's subjective/psychological focus, or faith in the image, and neorealism's objective/social inclination, or faith in reality, never precluded a concern with the other camp's emphasis on either psychic or social reality. Italian neorealism, the cinema which epitomizes a faith in reality, tends towards the objective pole of the image. However, neorealism's objective orientation and aesthetic commitment to a faithful representation of social exteriority never implied an abandonment of psychological inquiry. The humanist spirit of neorealism encapsulated by films such as

2 Bazin's history of film style has found a renewed importance for contemporary authors who have attempted to broach the "crisis of indexicality" that has accompanied the shift from analog to digital filmmaking. Important accounts of this include authors such as Dudley Andrew (*What Cinema Is!*), D.N. Rodowick (*The Virtual Life of Film*) and André Gaudreault (*The End of Cinema? A Medium in Crisis in the Digital Age*). David Bordwell's *On the History of Film Style* is also heavily influenced by Bazin's distinction between the imagists and the formalists, and the book investigates cinematic techniques such as montage and découpage, which for Bordwell's reading of Bazin, structures the division between these two tendencies of the cinema.

Germany Year Zero (Roberto Rossellini, 1948), *The Bicycle Thief* (Vittorio De Sica, 1948) and *The Earth Trembles* (Luchino Visconti, 1948) led to a sincere concern for the experience of living in post-war poverty. *Germany Year Zero* famously ends with the suicide of a young boy who jumps off the scaffold of a bombed-out building. He couldn't bear the trauma of war and the moral guilt of having euthanized his ailing father with poison. In *The Bicycle Thief*, an otherwise honest man is reduced to petty bike thievery in an effort to gain employment, and is brutally shamed in front of his son when caught committing the crime. *The Earth Trembles* focuses on young Sicilian fishermen who face a glum future after their revolt against exploitative fish merchants is suppressed. Gripped by the despair-inducing reality of war, neorealism has narrated the psychological despair of poverty since its very beginnings.

This narration of a wretched socio-political reality and its detrimental psychological effects was enabled by aesthetic innovation. As Deleuze writes in the very first lines of *Cinema 2: The Time-Image*, "Against those who defined Italian neorealism by its social content, Bazin put forward the fundamental requirement of formal aesthetic criteria. [...] The real was no longer represented but 'aimed at'" (Deleuze 1). For both Deleuze and Bazin, neorealism consists of an aesthetic breakthrough that enabled the expression of the Italian post-war experience—an experience that would have been impossible to express through past aesthetic strategies. The feeling of poverty couldn't just be plugged into the stylistic coordinates of the white telephone drama that previously dominated Italian screens during the fascist era. Rather, it took on-location shooting combined with long shot and long take cinematography for the neorealists to express the plight of the people with genuine sincerity, to "aim at" expressing their reality, including its psychological dimension.

Poverty can be filmed with little manipulation of the plastics of the film image and even less recourse to montage. War-torn cities show up well in long shot, the arduous search for a stolen bicycle lends itself well to long take, and everyday objects like potatoes and fishing nets that are charged with narrative significance naturally emerge from the environment in which they are filmed. Bazin praised the neorealists for respecting the spatio-temporal coordinates of the scene: the situatedness of objects and people in space, and their unfolding in duration. Mobile, long-take cinematography allowed the neorealists to craft a newfound respect for the reality they aimed at and a renewed fidelity to the social actuality in which they intervened. Through fidelity to the social actuality—its materiality, spatiality, and temporality—the neorealists found a way of articulating faith, not just in social reality, but even in the psychological reality of post-war alienation.

For Bazin, the faith that the neorealists put in reality was a humanist and spiritual accomplishment that distinguished them from the expressionists who made the error of putting their faith in the image. According to Bazin's definition of "faith in the image,"

> "image" implies broadly speaking, everything that the depiction of a thing on the screen can add to the thing itself. This contribution is complex but it can basically be reduced to two kinds: the plasticity of the image and the resources of editing. By plasticity, [Bazin means] the style of the make-up and décor and even, to a certain extent, of the acting; in addition of course to the lighting and framing, the basis of composition." (Bazin 2009: 88)

The expressionist aesthetic of distortion-through-addition included the use of extreme contrast lighting, man-made sets, exaggerated makeup and costume, and heavily stylized acting. Though operating from a very different set of aesthetic values—from a faith in the image—the expressionists shared with the neorealists a concern for the psychological effects of war. German expressionist films made during the inter-war period such as *The Cabinet of Dr. Caligari* (Robert Weine, 1920), *Pandora's Box* (G.W. Pabst, 1929) and *The Testament of Dr. Mabuse* (Fritz Lang, 1933) all sought the aesthetic resources to articulate their fears over the rise of fascism.

Caligari famously concludes in the asylum of an evil psychiatrist with totalitarian impulses; *The Testament of Dr. Mabuse* contains scenes of mind control wherein human cognitive faculties are overtaken by the animal magnetism of a villainous hypnotist, and *Pandora's Box* blends sexual desire with murderous impulses in an exploration of Berlin's criminal underworld. The German cineastes expressed an unparalleled mass anxiety about the rise of Nazism and return to war that was to come after the fall of the Weimar republic. To avoid betraying their subject matter, the expressionists could not help but put their faith in a dark, obtuse and violent image—the only kind that could anticipate their nation's historical development. By exploring the interwar unconscious, the expressionists found a way to elucidate the coming socio-political actuality of World War II.

Siegfried Kracauer's seminal study on Weimar cinema *From Caligari to Hitler: A Psychological History of the German Film* argues that cinema is the most useful art for revealing the depths of the collective unconscious: "What films reflect are not so much explicit credos as psychological dispositions—those deep layers of collective mentality which extend more or less below the dimension of consciousness" (Kracauer 6). According to Kracauer, for this psychic dimension to be expressed in the cinematographic image, hidden mental processes need to be rendered aesthetic through a process of exteriorization. He writes:

> Inner life manifests itself in various elements and conglomerations of external life, especially in those almost imperceptible surface data which form an essential part of the screening treatment. In recording the visible world—whether current reality or an imaginary universe—films therefore provide clues to hidden mental processes. (Kracauer 7)

By exteriorizing and uncovering "inner" mental processes, the expressionists sought a sociological truth: the impending rise of fascism, which could only be possible in a world of irrational men, prone to herd mentality and willing to sacrifice their freedom, or even their lives, for their collective affirmation in totalitarian values.

Even though German expressionism and Italian neorealism constitute opposite sides of the realism-formalism divide laid out by Bazin, they unexpectedly mirror each other's preoccupations. German expressionism rendered aesthetic the psychic roots of pre-war social actuality, whereas the neorealist image showed the social conditions responsible for post-war psychological misery. Both expressionism and neorealism are "partial" cinemas, for both gain access to one half of the psyche-social binary, but only by consigning the other half to metaphoric abstraction.[3] In its search for the psychic conditions that made the rise of fascism possible, expressionism had to invent an entire set of signifying codes for psychological malaise—and it was wildly successful in doing so. As a result, expressionism invented a psyche that became quasi-fantastical and broke from social reality through an image that flaunted plastic excesses. In its most stylized moments, expressionism invents an abnormal psyche as an allegory for pre-fascist society, but never films the social reality with any fidelity to its spatio-temporal coordinates.

A similar impasse lies at the heart of neorealism, and is only resolved by the cinema of poetry's arrival ten years after its end. In a humanist spirit, neorealism sought to express psychological truths about the traumatic

3 It should go without saying that by using the word "partial" here to refer to how German expressionism and Italian neorealism each directly access only one half of the psycho-social binary, I by no means intend to impart a slighted value judgment. Both cinemas artistically flourished within the means and concerns particular to it, and fulfilled its historical role in Bazin's dialectic of film language. They are "partial" only in the sense that they have committed their aesthetic fidelity to one half of the psyche-social binary.

effects of war through a sociologically and politically committed cinema. Looking at the rubble and decay of bombed-out post-war Europe, neorealist films evoked a certain feeling of what it must be like to inhabit such a bleak landscape. The neorealist image starts from the exterior social world, and uses its shape to deduce a corresponding psychological state. Most orthodox readings of Italian neorealism dismiss the psychological current running throughout the neorealist canon as merely incidental and opts to emphasize its sociological and objective tendencies of its aesthetic. Robert Kolker's *The Altering Eye* best encapsulates this view: "An essential component of the neorealist endeavour was its concern, really for the first time, to deal objectively with the working class. That it could not avoid sentimentalizing its subject is ultimately unimportant. [...] They replaced psychological inquiry with depictions of external struggle with the social environment, the government, the economic and political state of postwar Italy" (Kolker 272). Kolker effectively depreciates the psychological pole of the neorealist image as incidental sentimentalism.

Conversely, I suggest that neorealism's psychological layer is in fact a fundamental component of the image whose brooding presence generated the stylistic conditions for the cinema of poetry's later emergence.[4] Neorealism has always carried a concern for the psychology of poverty and war. In mirror movement to the operations of expressionism, neorealism detours through the social to arrive at the psychological. Without directly filming the psyche, the psychological pole of the image is made felt abstractly through its implication in the filmed social actuality. The psychological pole gained increasing prominence as the neorealist movement developed historically, interpenetrating with its sociological pole to such a degree that the objective-subjective binary eventually collapsed, giving rise to a new type of cinema: the cinema of poetry. What follows is an account of this stylistic tension in Italian neorealism leading up to the cinema of poetry's historical emergence, as illustrated through some of the most movement's most significant films.

Perhaps the only neorealist film to really attempt at crafting an entirely sociologically objective aesthetic is Luchino Visconti's *The Earth Trembles*. In Bazin's analysis of the film he describes it as "a film almost entirely composed of long-takes where the concern with embracing the *totality of the event* is expressed by deep focus shots and endless pans" (Bazin 2009: 103).

4 In his essay, "Pasolini's Exquisite Flowers: The 'Cinema of Poetry' as a Theory of Art Cinema," John David Rhodes also makes the argument that the cinema of poetry grows out of "the experiments of [Italian] neorealism.".

Non-diegetic, voice-of-God narration punctuates the film and authoritatively explicates the injustice that saturates the downtrodden livelihood of a Sicilian fishing community. Though the film's images could certainly speak for themselves and make this very point, Visconti opts for the closure of any possible misinterpretation by having the facts of life dictated aloud. *The Earth Trembles* strives to capture the totality of the event as objectively as cinematically possible.

Perhaps it was this canonical reading of *The Earth Trembles*, or assumptions about the aims of Italian neorealism that has led to the wide disregard of this film movement's psychological undercurrent which Bazin endeared with great nuance. Influential filmmaker and *Cahiers du cinéma* critic Eric Rohmer even went so far as to erroneously claim that "the whole body of Bazin's work is based on one central idea, an affirmation of the objectivity of the cinema" (Bazin 2011: 5). While Bazin is indeed quick to notice that many shots in neorealist films sought a degree of sociological objectivity, his writings on film realism intrinsically recognized the latent psychological pole harboured in the neorealist image. A prime example of this overlooked facet of Bazin's work is his relishing of what he calls the "objective psychology" at work in *Germany Year Zero* (Bazin 2009: 206), a film that expresses a psychological dimension through close attention to the social actuality. Prominent historian of Italian film Peter Bondanella echoes Bazin when he finds the "moral emptiness" of its child protagonist (Edmund) reflected in the "external means" of the film (Bondanella 81). The film evokes his psychic states without delving "into" his troubled mind or modulating the plastics of the image in the manner of the expressionists (with unnatural lighting, makeup, props, etc.). For its director Roberto Rossellini, such modulations would constitute a superfluous aesthetic excess since the filmed social actuality (in neorealist style) is devastating enough for its psychological effects, especially on such a young and impressionable lead character, to be conjured up. There are even moments when Edmund's psychology is reflected in the urban landscape, in the most objective of long shots.

Unlike Visconti's *The Earth Trembles*, *Germany Year Zero* does make considerable use of close-up and point-of-view shots that serve to link the bombed-out urban landscapes to Edmund's psychic state. For example, a point of view shot of the bottle of poison that Edmund uses to kill his father raises the object into an ethical dilemma that bears on character psychology and the overall meaning of the film. Though the film never goes "inside the mind," in the style of many expressionist films, its latent concern for character psychology hints at the direction of Italian cinema's eventual development.

Vittorio De Sica's late neorealist work *Umberto D* (1952) and Roberto Rosselini's post-neorealist *Voyage to Italy* (1954) begin to trade off the movement's earlier proclivity towards sociological objectivity in favour of aesthetic techniques that could more directly articulate the psychological dimension of the post-war subject's modern alienation—an alienation that could be derived from poverty as much as from bourgeois existential malaise. *Umberto D* is often cited as the last neorealist film.[5] It retains a de-narrativized emphasis on the quotidian as relayed through the canonized long shot/long take cinematography, yet fully delves into the psychology of poverty, old age and single motherhood. The film focuses on the lives of two principle characters who share in the weariness of economic precarity: Umberto D (Carlo Battisti) and Maria (Maria Pia Casilio), his landlady's maid. Umberto is an elderly man who has lost his pension to post-war inflation and he lives at constant risk of being thrown out of the room he has occupied for years. Maria is in an even tougher position, since she is unmarried and newly pregnant, unsure of the prospective father's identity. A now-famous kitchen scene conjures up the psychological impact of their dire situations.

The scene is detailed in Bazin's essay "Umberto D: A Great Work," and Deleuze reinforces its importance in the opening pages of his book on the time-image, where he describes it as follows:

> The young maid going into the kitchen in the morning, making a series of mechanical, weary gestures, cleaning a bit, driving the ants away with a water fountain, picking up the coffee grinder, stretching out her foot to close the door with her toe. And her eyes meet her pregnant woman's belly, and it's as though all the misery in the world were going to be born. (Deleuze 2007: 2)

This scene holds the objective and subjective poles of the cinematic image in tension with one another by intercutting long take cinematography of the maid's wavering movements with close-up shots of Umberto's face that punctuate this quotidian scene with his surprise and dread. The scene could qualify as objective due to its cinematography and mise-en-scène, yet as both Deleuze and Bazin point out, the scene is expressive of the

5 For an example of this standard film-historical demarcation, see David A. Cook's *A History of Narrative Film*, page 363. Kristin Thompson and David Bordwell are more flexible in marking the end of Italian neorealism, but also admit, "By the early 1950s, the Neorealist impulse had spent its force" (333). See page 331 of their *Film History: An Introduction. Third Edition* for a timeline of the movement that ends with *Voyage to Italy*.

characters' thoughts, feelings, and dashed hopes. This late neorealist film manages to express a troubled psychic interiority just as effectively as a purely expressionist mise-en-scène, but without doing the violence to the plastics of the image that expressionism so routinely carried out. Instead, the camera dwells in the room with the characters, absorbing their pain and sympathizing with them through its extended presence. The long take—a technique allied to the objective pole of the image—begins to turn in on itself, to make felt the scene's subjective tenor, in yet another variant of the "objective psychology" paradigm that flashed up at key moments in the neorealist canon that I discussed above, such as *Germany Year Zero*.

Released only two years after *Umberto D*, *Voyage to Italy* straddles a very thin dividing-line between late neorealism and the cinema of poetry in its full embrace of the psychological pole of the image. It departs from the standard neorealist theme of poverty to narrate the marital listlessness and bickering of an English couple that travels to Italy to sell a luxurious estate they have inherited. Throughout the course of the film their marriage continues to break down, to the point where Alex (George Sanders) and Katherine Joyce (Ingrid Bergman) decide to spend time apart. Left alone by her husband, Katherine goes sightseeing around Naples, and the city begins to reflect her mental and moral distress by procuring an endless stream of morbid images. The catacombs that she visits are lined with skulls, the streets filled with funeral processions, and when she is summoned to the scene of an archaeological discovery, she witnesses the excavation of a couple who were buried alive during the volcanic eruption at Pompeii. As Bazin evocatively writes: "It is Naples 'filtered' through the consciousness of the heroine. If the landscape is bare and confined, it is because the consciousness of an ordinary bourgeoise itself suffers from great spiritual poverty. Nevertheless, the Naples of the film is not false. It is rather a mental landscape at once as objective as a straight photograph and as subjective as pure personal consciousness" (Bazin 2011: 169).[6] Entire scenes craft Katherine's psyche out of the landscape in which she is found,[7] so that in arguably the last

6 In his "Mental Landscapes" essay in *Cinema Journal*, Justin Horton makes recourse to *Voyage to Italy* to argue convincingly that Bazin was much more nuanced than the "naive realist" that critics writing in the political modernist tradition accused him of being, precisely because his theory of realism took account of both the subjective and objective poles of the image and anticipated Pasolini's discovery of the free indirect subjective in 1965.

7 Commenting on these "surprising" architectural landscapes and "direct aesthetic" expressive of this psychological dimension, Jacques Rivette boldly hailed *Voyage to Italy* as an example of "modern cinema" (Rivette 1985: 192, 198). Some Italian critics, like Guido Aristarco, saw this "modern" development as a regression, a slippery slope away from the supposed purity of

neorealist film, Rossellini takes realist aesthetics to their limit, and uses all of its formal resources to express the psychic life of its characters.

At this limit of expression, *Voyage to Italy* begins to destabilize the subjective and objective poles of the image, but not in so far as to break with the spatial and temporal coordinates of reality, as the expressionists had done in the pre-war era. Katherine is a troubled character, she is suffering and she is existentially exhausted. As morbid as Katherine's visions are, however, they are visions, and not hallucinations. They never break off from the world that she holds in common with all of the people around her. The other characters in the film observe the skulls, skeletons and funeral processions, and bear equal witness to these omens of death and signifiers of psychic trouble—these people just so happen to be more well-adjusted and less impressionable. Katherine's neurosis is just that, a personal neurosis, and it never contests the foundations of the world in which she suffers. The mental landscape renders her psychology palpable through symbolism and metaphor, whereby an inferential leap from the plastic surface of the social exterior is required to subsequently deduce her mental interiority.

The "mental landscape," as Bazin calls it, is the result of an artistic compromise that Rossellini was forced to make when confronted with the dilemma of whether to express full fidelity to the singular truth of Katherine's psychic pain—and the many ways it overspills the logic and scope of symbolism (skulls, catacombs, etc.)—or to the social reality before the camera. In an oblique manner, Bazin alluded to this privileging of the social over the psychic in his "Defense of Rossellini" essay, where he observes how "[Rossellini's] characters are more apt to be affected by the settings through which they move than the settings are liable to be affected by their movement" (Bazin 2011: 170). By maintaining the rigidity of the plastic surface, and exhibiting the utmost fidelity to spatio-temporal contours of social actuality, the materiality of the world cramps and closes in on the psyche, but the psyche never liberates itself and re-makes the world. Allowing it to do so would have broken from neorealism's "faith in reality"—which has proven itself to be a faith in *social reality*[8]—and had

neorealism's earlier years. Yet in his essay "Defence of Rossellini," Bazin countered this criticism by advancing an understanding of neorealism as "an ideal" that is only "approached more or less" (Bazin 2011: 170). For Bazin, there is no neorealist purity to be lost, only a creative striving for fidelity to the events it depicts.

8 Neorealism's faith in a particularly social reality explains why the controversial miracle sequence at the end of *Voyage to Italy* is, as Bazin points out, a very particular type of miracle, that Rosselini claims is nothing but "noise and crowd movements that people are in the habit of calling a miracle" (Bazin 2011: 170). Rossellini approaches even the most supernatural scene

character psyches affect the plastics of the image. If this were to be the case, Rossellini would have found a way of sincerely filming the "totality of the event," inclusive of both its psychological and sociological poles. He would have made the assertion, through aesthetic experimentation, that psychic fluxes, once thought to be the domain of an interiorized psychology, shape the social milieu in which they exist. But this development in the history of film style would have to wait for the maturity of another Italian cineaste, Michelangelo Antonioni, whose cinema of poetry discovered a reality that is immediately psychosocial.

The Cinema of Poetry

Pier Paolo Pasolini christened the cinema of poetry at a conference roundtable held at the 1965 Pesaro Film Festival, after seeing films by modernist auteurs such as Jean-Luc Godard, Bernardo Bertolucci, and most importantly, Michelangelo Antonioni. What prompted Pasolini to hail the arrival of the cinema of poetry and pen an influential essay expounding its virtues and limitations is these auteurs' reimaginaing of character subjectivity. Each of them, Pasolini argues, develops a free indirect relationship between themselves and their protagonists. As a result of this new type of image, the longstanding distinction between subjective and objective images that was maintained in German expressionism and Italian neorealism was proven inadequate. In the lexicon of film form, subjective shots capture a character's point of view, as if through his or her eyes, and objective shots are non-point of view shots that emanate from the eyes of the filmmaker who looks at the characters positioned infront of the camera lens. In a free indirect schema, the filmmaker and their protagonist share a pair of eyes, and a way of looking at the world, so that it is no longer possible to clearly distinguish between subjective and objective images. Free indirect images are both objective and subjective, all at once. Of additional significance is that these films regularly feature mentally disturbed protagonists whose psychic nonnormativity aids the free indirect schema in troubling the binary between objective and subjective perspectives.

Antonioni's *The Red Desert* best articulates this shift from neorealism to the cinema of poetry and watching it side by side with *Voyage to*

just as he does any other: by respecting the spatio-temporal coordinates of social reality and the integrity of its plastic surface (which in this case happens to be crowd movements).

Italy illuminates how differently these two film movements conceive of psychic torment. In *Voyage to Italy*, Katherine's psyche was troubled by the world, but never in turn troubles the world, precisely because neorealism preserved the ontological distinction between the objective and the subjective, and remained faithful to the objectivity of the exterior, social world until is final days. As much as Rossellini cares about the psychological conditions of his characters and goes to great lengths to infer what they are thinking and feeling, his deep faith in social reality during this neorealist period ultimately grants primacy to the objective pole of the image. It is in this way that neorealism implicitly localized the psyche, and its troubles, as residing inside the individual subject and as only being representable through the mediation of symbolism. The cinema of poetry offers a radically different account of the psyche's locale and relationship to the social. By harnessing the power of the free indirect, it destabilizes the distinction between objective and subjective poles of the image, making it impossible to tell where objectivity and subjectivity begin and end. Without this clear demarcation, mental distress breaks out of the space it was once-assigned. No longer contained by the personal domain of subjective interiority, "mental illness" becomes a psychosocial phenomenon.

A close look at some specific images from *The Red Desert* will help to show how the cinema of poetry uses the free indirect to craft psychosocial images of psychic non-normativity. The film focuses on Guiliana (Monica Vitti) and the anguish she endures when adapting to her newly industrialized surroundings of "economic miracle" Italy. Antonioni's camera uses specific cinematographic techniques that lend the psyche a renewed significance by systematically eroding the border between objective and subjective perspectives. For example, in one of the film's most important moments, Guiliana and her companion Corrado (Richard Harris) notice a floating piece of newspaper. This sequence opens with what seems like a shared point of view shot, but before long, the two characters remarkably walk into the shot. What begins as a subjective shot ends as an objective shot.

But this reversibility to the image indicates that it is of another variant entirely. In other important moments that build on this approach, Antonioni uses an extreme shallow focus shot from behind Guiliana's head that expresses her confusion; unnatural colour schemes that reveal her unease with the industrial invasion of her psychic life; and the sound of a boat horn whose origin is unknown. The cinema of poetry throws neorealist reality and the cinema's longstanding distinction between the objective and subjective poles of the image into relief: Does the boat horn actually sound,

Image 1 *Il deserto rosso (The Red Desert)*, Michelangelo Antonioni, 1964

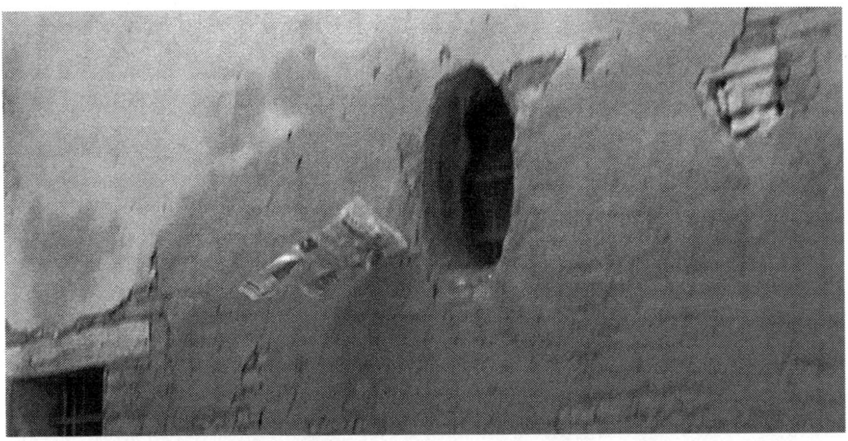

Image 2 *Il deserto rosso (The Red Desert)*, Michelangelo Antonioni, 1964

Image 3 *Il deserto rosso (The Red Desert)*, Michelangelo Antonioni, 1964

or is it just "in her head"? Is the factory smoke actually bright yellow, or does it just appear that way to Guiliana? Is that piece of floating newspaper really there, or is she imagining things that don't really exist? Where the border is to be drawn between her perceptions and the "real world" is totally unknown, because the free indirect image creates an assemblage that mutually includes both the social and the psyche to arrive at an image that is immediately psychosocial and throw divisions between interior and exterior into relief.

The free indirect's capacity to create a psychosocial image is first insinuated by Pasolini, but is only really conceived in Deleuze's later rereading of Pasolini where he de-personalizes the free indirect schema. In his cinema of poetry essay, Pasolini expounds the free indirect schema through the relationship between Michelangelo Antonioni and his protagonist Guiliana:

> Antonioni looks at the world by immersing himself in his neurotic protagonist, re-animating the facts through her eyes (she, not by accident, clearly needs professional care, having already tried to commit suicide). By means of this stylistic device, Antonioni has freed his most deeply felt moment: he has finally been able to represent the world seen through his eyes, because he has substituted in toto for the worldview of a neurotic his own delirious view of aesthetics, a wholesale substitution which is justified by the possible analogy of the two views. (Pasolini 179)

Pasolini's formulation of the free indirect privileges the auteur-protagonist relationship and how their perspectives dovetail though a free indirect system of enunciation. The strong emphasis he places on the auteur as a pivotal figure who establishes the free indirect schema can likely be attributed to the historical conditions of its conception. Pasolini was working and writing in the heyday of auteurism. As a well-known cultural figure, much like Antonioni, his films were largely disseminated and marketed within an auteurist paradigm. Furthermore, film criticism of the 1960s was heavily influenced by the auteurist approach of *Cahiers du cinema*, and Andrew Sarris (who spoke on a panel with Pasolini at the 1966 New York Film Festival) published his "Notes on Auteur Theory" essay just a couple of years prior to the publication of Pasolini's on the cinema of poetry.

Pasolini's ground-breaking writing on the cinema of poetry creates the conditions for a theory of the psychosocial image, yet the passage cited above poses a couple of hurdles to contend with, stemming from the gendered connotations of his unabashed auteurism. If taken at face value, it implies that neurotic experiences are little more than a substitute for the vision of a great (male) auteur who needs to cast a fragile muse to achieve his delirious vision of aesthetics. Experience in itself is turned into an alibi for a greater vision. In the free indirect schema as Pasolini advances it here, the limit separating the subjective and objective poles of the image is dissolved, yet identities (between filmmaker and protagonist), and the hierarchy of values they imply, remain intact.

It is Deleuze who is the first to excavate the impersonal and machinic qualities of the free indirect assemblage. According to his rereading of Pasolini in *Cinema 1*, in the free indirect style, "objective and subjective images lose their distinction, but also their identification, in favour of a new circuit where they are wholly replaced, or contaminate each other, or are decomposed and recomposed" (Deleuze 148-149). In this passage and the pages surrounding it, Deleuze moves away from the auteurist and gendered connotations of Pasolini's configuration cited above by insisting that the free indirect initiates a "loss of identification." Rather than an interpersonal relationship between an auteur and his muse, the free indirect is here conceived of as "assemblage of enunciation, carrying out two inseparable acts of subjectivation simultaneously, one of which constitutes a character in the first person, but the other of which is present at his birth and brings him on to the scene"[9] (Deleuze 73). According to this reading, no longer do two subjects (the character and the auteur) bring the free indirect into being. Instead, the free indirect itself brings them into being, and modifies them in the process, by creating the conditions for a group subject in free indirect relation with its component parts. In the cinema of poetry, both subject and object, auteur and protagonist, participate in the life of the free indirect schema's operations by moving across and between the psychic and social poles of the cinematographic image.

Faced with a free indirect system that dissolves the borders of objectivity and subjectivity, "one might say, then, that free indirect discourse allows a subtler means by which to grant the interior the right to comingle with the exterior" (Horton 34). At least that is the conclusion that Justin Horton arrives at in his recent article on mental landscapes in *Cinema Journal*. And his conclusion is certainly correct, since the free indirect style overcomes the mutual exclusivity of interior (psyche) and exterior (social) by equally

9 It is noteworthy that Deleuze's rereading of Pasolini's essay on the cinema of poetry detaches the free indirect schema from the model of auteurist agency, especially since one of the common critiques of Deleuze's cinema books their adherence to the *Cahiers du cinema* canon of great auteurs. While his books do certainly deploy the auteurist canon to construct a taxonomy of cinematic signs, he privileges above all else the impersonal and machinic quality of the cinematic image-as-event and the quantum of experience that it expresses.

and simultaneously privileging these two poles of the image that have long found themselves opposed in the history of film style. Yet in their comingling, the analogical relationship that "interior" and "exterior" maintain with the psyche and the social ceases to be tenable, and instead gives way to an entirely new reality very different from the one in which the neorealists put their faith; a reality that can only be described as immediately psychosocial.

The cinema of poetry can then be seen as advancing its own variant of realism, true to the psychosocial reality of what Simondon calls the "transindividual." The transindividual is a preindividual force immanent to events of subjectivity production, or "individuation" to use Simondon's language.[10] It "appears not as that which unifies individual and society, but as a relation interior to the individual (defining its psyche) and a relation exterior to the individual defining the collective: The transindividual unity of two relations is thus a relation of relations" (Combes 26). This transindividual relation of relations between the interior and exterior is precisely where Simondon situates psychology, and he even goes to the length of stating that "transindividual reality *is* psychological reality" (Simondon 2005: 281). For Simondon, psychology is intrinsically psychosocial, and belongs to the event in which the individual takes part rather than to the individual herself. "The psychological world," Simondon reminds us, "should be called the transindividual world because it does not have an independent existence" (Simondon 2005: 279). By perceiving the transindividual through its free indirect aesthetic, the cinema of poetry doesn't just make "psychic interiority" and "social exteriority" comingle with one another, it produces a qualitatively distinct third term which is more than the sum of its parts: a psychosociality throbbing at their relational limit.

The gulf separating *Voyage to Italy* and *The Red Desert* attests to this key difference between an image that safeguards the mutual exclusivity of interior and exterior, and a truly free indirect perception of transindividual psychology's psychosociality. As previously mentioned, in *Voyage to Italy*, narratively significant symbols, objects, and people are made to stand in for the lead character's interior psychic trouble. Only via these representations does the image access her psyche, which is personalized, localized and interiorized. Conversely, in *The Red Desert*, Guiliana's psychology contaminates

10 Simondon's concept of the transindividual is not to be confused with the more widespread notion of "intersubjectivity" or interactivity between individuals. He clearly distinguishes the concept of the transindividual from what he calls the "interindividual." Whereas the interindividual "goes from individual to individual" but "does not penetrate individuals," the transindividual "characterizes the real relation between all interiority and exteriority with regards to the individual" (Simondon 2005: 191, 157).

and stains every frame of the film. The psychic trouble which she undoubtedly endures modulates the plastics of the image, effectuating what Pasolini calls a "delirious aesthetic"—even in non-point of view shots—rendering it futile to try and anticipate where her subjective hallucinations end and where a stable, objective, social reality with common perceptual coordinates begins. This film, like so many examples from the cinema of poetry canon, is highly effective at articulating character psychology without resorting to symbol or metaphor, because it free indirectly perceives psychology's transindividual scope, effectively confounding the longstanding impulse to aesthetically privilege interior or exterior at the expense of the other.

The transindividuality undergirding *The Red Desert*'s world affects each of its characters, and effectuates a depersonalization and delocalization of psychology. The delirious hallucinations can't simply be attributed to Guiliana or to Antonioni, they belong to the collective psychological atmosphere. For example, when Corrado is away from Giuliana and "her" neurosis, giving a speech to a group of workers who are considering moving to Patagonia, the camera begins to drift, capturing abstract shapes and intensities of colour in varying degrees of focus. Guiliana's deliruium has followed him and actively conditions his experience as well.

In another scene, these two characters enter the home of a worker who Corrado is trying to recruit for overseas work, the adulterous tension building between them erupts in such a way that all of the other guests begin to feel their desire. The couples splay out in a room adorned with deep red walls and find themselves interpellated into Guiliana's hallucinatory psychology. In a quasi-fantastical moment, she makes a quail egg transpire out of thin air, to the amazement of her friends, who nevertheless corroborate her vision without hesitation. One person's psyche cannot be parsed out from another's, nor can the delirious be parsed from the normative: they are all mutually included in, and produced by, the inherent relationality of the transindividual.

The cinema of poetry's free indirect images of transindividual psychology depicts various facets of psychic life that Deleuze and Guattari delineate in *Anti-Oedipus: Capitalism and Schizophrenia*, a project which, perhaps not coincidentally, was written in the years following the 1965 Festival of Pesaro. In the opening lines of *Anti-Oedipus*, Deleuze and Guattari embrace the id's reserve of instinctual energy, and free it from its position within the Freudian topography as the domain of that which is negated and repressed by the ego's mode of organization (Laplanche and Pontalis: 199, 474). In Deleuze and Guattari's eventful and productive unconscious, "the self and the non-self, outside and inside, no longer have any meaning whatsoever" (Deleuze and Guattari: 2). Deleuze and Guattari elaborate:

> There is no particular form of existence that can be labeled 'psychic reality.' [...] There is no such thing as the social production of reality on the one hand, and a desiring-production that is mere fantasy on the other. [...] The truth of the matter is that social production is purely and simply desiring-production itself under determinate conditions. [...] There is only desire and the social, and nothing else. (Deleuze and Guattari: 27, 28, 29).

There is only desire and the social, and nothing else, except for the immediate relation of their mutual co-production—the point at which psychology, or the transindividual, resides.

"Faith in reality" thus takes on an entirely different sense after the cinema of poetry's emergence. Having discovered psychology to be indistinguishable from the transindividual, to be a "realist" in the Bazinian sense, entails a faith in reality's psychosociality. The following chapters are filled with examples of contemporary filmmaking[11] that build on the cinema of poetry's legacy by embodying aesthetic strategies expressive of such faith. Each of these films gives life to the reality of the transindividual by constructing psychosocial images that overcome expressionism's use of the psyche to metaphorize the social and neorealism's use of the social to symbolize the psyche. What the contemporary art films that feature in the following chapters inherit from the cinema of poetry is its penchant for psychosocial images, where, just as in *The Red Desert*, neither psyche nor socius represents the other, but are co-constituted as "empirically inseparable"[12] by the reality of a transindividual relation immanently productive and mutually inclusive of

11 Film studies scholars John Orr and John David Rhodes have argued that contemporary art cinema is the inheritor of the cinema of poetry. In his foreword to *Contemporary Cinema* (Edinburgh: Edinburgh University Press, 1998, pp. ix), Orr singles out the cinema of poetry as "a dominant and guiding feature in the development of the cinema over the last thirty years [1960s-1990s]" and for his part, in "Pasolini's Exquisite Flowers," Rhodes asserts that Pasolini's cinema of poetry essay provides the theoretical basis for a discrete mode of political filmmaking called "art cinema" (which differs from Bordwell's depoliticized formulation of the term). See pages 151, 154 and 158-159 in Bordwell's *On the History of Film Style*.

12 A transindividual conception of psychology conceives of the psyche and the social much in the same way that Brian Massumi describes individuals and societies as "not only empirically inseparable," but "strictly simultaneous and consubstantial" (Massumi 2002: 71). As simultaneous and consubstantial, neither precedes nor produces the other, because they are not discreet entities. Instead, they "can be seen as products, effects, coderivatives of an immanent relation that would be change in itself. In other words, they might be seen as differential emergences from a shared realm of relationality that is one with becoming—and belonging" (Massumi 2002: 71). Psychology, in the Simondonian sense, is this immanent relation ("exterior to its terms"); "change in itself," whose relational movements produce singular psychosocial compositions where "individual" and "society" can only be spoken of as abstractions out from the psychosocial event.

them both. Having analyzed how the major schism governing the history of film style is reconciled by the development of the cinema of poetry and its remarkable ability to free indirectly perceive the creatively co-compositional relations between the social and the psychic, the objective and the subjective, the exterior and the interior, it is finally possible to corroborate Maurizio Lazzarato's provocative statement that "Pasolini overcomes the distinction between the image and what it represents" (Lazzarato: 126). For no longer must the psyche be made to represent the social or vice versa; Pasolini's cinema of poetry puts its faith the transindividual primacy of psychosocial reality, which immediately saturates the free indirect image.

Bibliography

Andrew, Dudley. *What Cinema Is!* Chichester, West Sussex: Wiley-Blackwell, 2010.

Balázs, Béla. *Theory of the Film: Character and Growth*. Trans. Edith Bone. New York, Dover Publications, 1970.

Bazin, André. *Bazin and Italian Neorealism*. Ed. Bert Cardullo. New York: Continuum, 2011.

Bazin, André. *What is Cinema?* Trans. Timothy Barnard. Montreal: Caboose, 2009.

Bondanella, Peter. *A History of Italian Cinema*. New York and London: Continuum, 2009.

Bordwell, David and Kristin Thompson. *Film History: An Introduction*. New York: McGraw-Hill, 2010.

Bordwell, David. *On the History of Film Style*. Cambridge, MA: Harvard University Press, 1997.

Combes, Muriel. *Gilbert Simondon and the Philosophy of the Transindividual*. Trans. Thomas LaMarre. Cambridge and London: The MIT Press, 2013.

Cook, David A. *A History of Narrative Film*. Fourth Edition. New York and London: W.W. Norton & Company, 2004.

Deleuze, Gilles. *Cinema 1: The Movement-Image*. Trans. Hugh Tomlinson and Barbara Habberjam. Minneapolis: University of Minnesota Press, 2006.

Deleuze, Gilles. *Cinema 2: The Time-Image*. Trans. Hugh Tomlinson and Robert Galeta. Minneapolis: University of Minnesota Press, 2007.

Gaudreault, André and Philippe Morion. *The End of Cinema? A Medium in Crisis in the Digital Age*. New York: Columbia University Press, 2015.

Horton, Justin. "Mental Landscapes: Bazin, Deleuze, and Neorealism (Then and Now)." *Cinema Journal* 52.2 (Winter 2013): 23-45.

Kolker, Robert. *The Altering Eye: Contemporary International Cinema*. Oxford: Oxford University Press, 1983.

Kracauer, Sigfried. *From Caligari to Hitler: A Psychological History of the German Film*. Princeton: Princeton University Press, 1947.

Laplanche, Jean and J.-B. Pontalis. *The Language of Psychoanalysis*. Trans. Donald Nicholson-Smith. London: Karnac Books, 1988.

Lazzarato, Maurizio. *Signs and Machines: Capitalism and the Production of Subjectivity*. Trans. David Joshua Jordan. Los Angeles: Semiotext(e), 2014.

Munsterberg, Hugo. *The Film: A Psychological Study*. Trans Richard Griffith. Mineola, New York: Dover Publications, 1970.

Orr, John. *Contemporary Cinema*. Edinburgh: Edinburgh University Press, 1998.

Pasolini, Pier Paolo. "The 'Cinema of Poetry'". *Heretical Empiricism*. Trans. Ben Lawton and Louise K. Barnett. Washington, DC: New Academia Publishing, 2005. 167-186.

Rhodes. John David. "Pasolini's Exquisite Flowers: The 'Cinema of Poetry' as a Theory of Art Cinema." *Global Art Cinema: New Theories and Histories*. Eds. Rosalind Galt and Karl Schoonover. Oxford and New York: Oxford University Press, 2010. 142-163.

Rivette, Jacques. "Letter on Rossellini". *Cahiers du Cinéma: The 1950s: Neo-Realism, Hollywood, New Wave*. Ed. Jim Hillier. Cambridge, Massachusetts: Harvard University Press, 1985: 192-204.

Rodowick, D. N. *The Virtual Life of Film*. Cambridge, Massachusetts and London, England: Harvard University Press, 2007.

Simondon, Gilbert. *L'individuation à la lumière des notions de forme et d'information*. Grenoble: Éditions Jérôme Millon, 2005.

Simondon, Gilbert. *L'individuation psychique et collective à la notion lumière des notions de Forme, Information, Potentiel et Métastabilité*. Paris: Éditions Aubier, 1989.

2 The Neuroplastic Paradox

Abstract
Chapter Two turns to a discussion of the Berlin School, one of cinema of poetry's contemporary inheritors. It provides a close analysis of Angela Schanelec's film *Afternoon* (2007) and proposes the first of four event-based symptoms of melancholy: the depotentialization of neuroplasticity. To explain the political significance of this symptom and the reason why the cinema is particularly apt to perceive it, Chapter Two delves into the neuroscience of mental illness and invokes Deleuze's writing on the neurology of the cinematic image. One of the terms that appears recurringly throughout this chapter is "plastics." It is used in dual reference to "neuroplasticity," or the malleability of the brain, and to Bazin's "plastics of the image."

Keywords: Angela Schanelec, Berlin School, neuroplasticity

The Berlin School: A Melancholic Film Movement

Throughout its twenty-year history, the film movement known as the "Berlin School" has proven itself to be one of the most important inheritors of the cinema of poetry.[1] Film critics began using the term "Berlin School"[2] in

1 In his essay on the Berlin School, film critic Dennis Lim cites Antonioni as an influential predecessor of this "cinema of drift and alienation" (89).
2 Film critic Merten Worthmann is credited as being the first to use the term "Berlin School," though not without some confusion. In their article on the history of the Berlin School first published in Austrian film magazine *kolok.film* and later translated in *Senses of Cinema*, Michael Baute, Ekkehard Knrer, Volker Pantenburg, Stefan Pethke and Simon Rothler originally identified Rainer Gansera as coining the term in his article on Angela Schanelec, Thomas Arslan and Christian Petzold, "Glücks-Pickpocket" ("Pickpocket of Happiness") published in *Süddeutsche Zeitung* on 3 November 2001. After the publication they "received an email from the film critic Rüdiger Suchsland in which he pointed out that the term 'Berlin School' had already been used prior to this date, namely by Merten Worthmann in *Die Zeit*. In an article entitled 'Mit Vorsicht genießen' ('To be taken with a pinch of salt') on Angela

Szymanski, A., *Cinemas of Therapeutic Activism: Depression and the Politics of Existence.* Taylor & Francis Group, 2020
DOI: 10.5117/9789463723121_CH02

acknowledgement of the similarities between filmmakers Angela Schanelec, Thomas Arslan and Christian Petzold, all graduates of the Deutsche Film- und Fernsehakademie Berlin (The German Film and Television Academy, or simply the DFFB). The term has since been applied to an expanding group of filmmakers around Germany with different educational backgrounds, including Ulrich Köhler, Christoph Hochhäusler, Maren Ade, Henner Wickler and others.[3] Interestingly enough, a preoccupation with melancholy may in fact be the Berlin School's defining characteristic, particularly when faced with the difficulty of grouping the movement's films together through more established categories of criticism. Without unity of place or programme, the Berlin School is a fairly dispersed network of filmmakers who only occasionally collaborate with one another and have no overarching film manifesto.[4] The absence of a clear political programme, coupled with the movement's sustained refusal to narrate topical macropolitical issues in contemporary Germany has provoked accusations of political apathy amongst mainstream film critics and cultural commentators who are left frustrated and bewildered by the films' brooding melancholy. In contradiction to these sorts of reactions, what I would like to suggest here is that the Berlin School's melancholy aesthetics are its political gesture, because these aesthetics investigate how feeling unwell is a psychosocial problem conditioned by the imperatives of neoliberal power.

Building on Antonioni's pioneering work in the field, a number of the movement's key auteurs consistently harness free indirect perception to create film worlds that are psychosocially saturated with melancholic transindividual psychology. A few examples should suffice to paint the picture of how the Berlin School's political aesthetics, which are tied to this stylistic development, are easily misconstrued. In the introduction to his book-length study of the Berlin School, Marco Abel explains that a "common criticism of Berlin School films is that they supposedly lack

Schanelec's *Mein langsames Leben* (*Passing Summer*), Worthmann writes: ' [...] watching the films of the 'Berlin School', one notices a very similar treatment of time and space' " (Baute et al.: n.p.).

3 For a more exhaustive list of the Berlin School filmmakers, particularly one that is sensitive to the chronology of how its two different waves have emerged, see Marco Abel's canon-forming text *The Counter-Cinema of the Berlin School*.

4 The Berlin School's absence of a manifesto seems all the more glaring when the movement is considered in light of its direct historical antecedent, the New German Cinema and its Oberhausen manifesto. These two movements constitute German Cinema's two "new waves" but are not to be confused with one another despite their sometimes being referred to with the same terminology. In French film criticism, it is common to see the Berlin School referred to as *la nouvelle vague allemande*.

interest in the political and instead present us with, in the words of film critic Christina Nord a 'bourgeois poetics of middle class navel gazing'" (Abel 2013: 12). Director and journalist Oskar Roehler echoes this criticism when he characterizes the Berlin School as bitter and severe, lacking intelligible narratives. "Nothing actually happens in these films," Roehler laments. "They are always slow, always depressing, nothing is ever really said in them—and that is what is called 'the Berlin School'" (Clarke 2012: 135). Another filmmaker, Dietrich Brüggemann critiques the Berlin School auteurs, who in his opinion "'have digested all of film history, who think up one pretentious title after another, but who are not capable of generating one single authentic feeling [...] '" (Baer 2013: 80). The Berlin School's films are imbued with feeling, it just so happens that melancholy doesn't offer the sort of pleasures that Brüggemann hopes to find in his national cinema.

These reactions are reflective of how starkly the Berlin School's political aesthetics differ from the state-sanctioned German national cinema that has won Oscar nominations and topped syndicated critics' "best of" lists since the turn of the millennium. Whereas Berlin School films employ "minimalist aesthetics and long takes, with melancholic slow narratives set in modern-day Germany," (Vinogradova 2010: 158) box-office successes usually narrate an internationally recognizable chapter in German history with drama and passion. Some of the most familiar films of this variety include *Downfall* (Oliver Hirschbiegel, 2004), *The Lives of Others* (Florian Henckel von Donnersmarck, 2006) and *Goodbye Lenin!* (Wolfgang Becker, 2003). They combine standardized narrative techniques with a sanitized liberal politics to advance plots about the downfall of Hitler, state surveillance in East Germany, and the fall of the Berlin wall.

In his provocative essay "Why I Don't Make Political Films," Berlin School director Ulrich Köhler identifies these "topical, message-driven films, that package political enlightenment in stories" as driving the "aesthetic program of social-democratized cultural politics" (2009: 11). He takes this tendency within German filmmaking to task by underscoring how self-congratulatory and ultimately nationalistic it really is.

> The governmental funding agency likes films that 'wrap up' political education in narratives—citizens should not strain themselves too hard," he writes. "Producers know that they get money thrown at them as soon as they make projects against racism, Nazism, oppression of minorities or poverty in distant lands: political education and culture stewing the same pot (Köhler 2009: 11).

Köhler's essay, not to mention his entire body of film work, rails against the institutional and economic imperative to cloak didactic messages in neatly wrapped narratives that are ready to be consumed by spectators who want to feel good about themselves without ever having to put the dominant economic or political order into question. As he points out, it's easy to cultivate a sense of righteousness in contemporary spectators by endlessly exploiting history to show the barbarism of Nazi Germany or the Stasi's violation of personal privacy in the GDR.

Unlike these examples of supercilious filmmaking that celebrate the "post-ideological" lacuna of the present by contrasting it to the totalitarian past, Angela Schanelec's political aesthetics enact a symptomatology of the contemporary moment's melancholic impasse.[5] Ulrich Köhler may argue that he does not make political films, in the sense of narrating political themes, but his films, like Schanelec's, are radically political in that they offer a subversive symptomatology of the current depression pandemic that free indirectly perceives neoliberal power's conditioning of the production of subjectivity in line with the tenets of individualism, which effectuates a depotentialization in the neuroplasticity of the event of subjectivity production. Taking her film *Afternoon* as a case study, this chapter articulates how Schanelec assumes the role of artist-physician to perceive a novel symptom of melancholy: the depotentialization of the event's (neuro)plastic potential for qualitative subjective change.

The Brain is the Screen

As discussed at length in the previous chapter, the cinema of poetry's use of the free indirect overcomes the tenuous distinction between subjective

5 The Berlin School is made up of truly contemporary filmmakers, not only in the sense that it is a fairly recent film movement (originating in the mid-1990s), but more significantly because all of their films take place in the moment of their production. The Berlin School is typically characterized by a stark focus on the daily lives of historically insignificant people. This began to change in 2012, when two of the movement's foremost auteurs (Christian Petzold and Thomas Arslan) released historical dramas *Barbara* (2012), *Gold* (2013) and *Phoenix* (2014). Petzold and Arslan are two of the movement's founding figures, but I think their turn to the historical drama constitutes a break from the original ethos of the Berlin School, and should thus be considered as the start of a new phase whose developmental arc is still not entirely intelligible. Ulrich Köhler has also recently modified his aesthetic strategies, evidenced by *Sleeping Sickness* (2013) which ends on a magical realist note. As a way to make the point that some of the movement's directors have began searching for new forms and strategies, Berlin School auteur Christoph Hochhäusler has declared, "school's out" (Hochhäusler 28).

psychic states and objective social facts, in the creation of a psychosocial image that immediately perceives psychology's transindividuality without recourse to metaphor or symbolism. Schanelec's *Afternoon* bears some remarkable similarities to Antonioni's *The Red Desert*, the cinema of poetry's Ur-text, most importantly in its psychosocial conception of psychological suffering. By conceiving of psychology in such a light, political power enters into the picture quite suddenly, since the site of power's operations is none other than the relational field of transindividuality where collective psychology, or subjectivity, is produced. The film under discussion, like many others in the Berlin School, is attentive to the political dimension of psychology's relational co-composition, and in its own way, poses a variance on the question that prompted Judith Butler to write her book on melancholia, namely: "What is the psychic form that power takes?" (Butler 1997: 2).

Butler's eventual engagement with that question leads to a psychoanalytic theory of subjectivity production that lends a crucial role to melancholy. For Butler, "Melancholy is precisely what interiorizes the psyche" (170). She goes on to write:

> [M]elancholia involves the production of an internal world as well as a topographical set of fictions that structures the psyche. If the melancholic turn is the mechanism by which the distinction between internal and external worlds is instituted, then melancholia initiates a variable boundary between the psychic and the social, a boundary [...] that distributes and regulates the psychic sphere in relation to the prevailing norms of social regulation. (Butler 1997: 171)

Butler's theory of melancholia takes its cues from Freud's *The Ego and the Id*, where he insists on the division between external and internal worlds, the former a real world and the latter a psychic one, to explain the conflicts that the ego must endure between its ideals and the impositions of its environment.[6] At first glance, Butler's Freudian investment in a distinction between internal and external worlds seems inherently incompatible with a psychosocial understanding of melancholy, since it separates out a zone of discrete mental interiority. Yet her formulation contains the indispensible intuition that one of the most prevalent symptoms of melancholy is the sensation that a boundary between psyche and socius does indeed exist.

6 Freud writes: "Conflicts between the ego and the ideal [...] ultimately reflect the contrast between what is real and what is psychical, between external and internal world" (Freud 2001: 36).

Caught in melancholy's treacherous hold, it is habitual to feel disconnected and alienated from the world, and as if one's life may not even be worth living. In moments like these, moments which can go on for months, years, and entire lifetimes in the most chronic of cases, the sense of an insurmountable boundary creates an isolated sense of self, and produces the felt fiction of an interiorized melancholic psyche, drowning in a pain that nobody else can see, feel or understand. Here, in the midst of melancholic experience, psychology's psychosocial relationality is betrayed by the feeling of being psychically isolated by an insurmountable and interiorizing boundary.

Turning to Deleuze's much-cited aphorism, "the brain is the screen" (Deleuze 2000: 366) offers a way to work productively with the contradiction between Butler and Simondon's divergent conceptualizations of the psyche and its relation to the social. To restate: for Butler, following Freud, the psyche is a discrete topography divided from the social by a boundary, whereas for Simondon the psyche and the social are conjoined by a relation of relations. Deleuze situates his concept of the brain at this relational limit straddling the psyche and the social, and the qualities he ascribes to it help to see how "relation" and "boundary" need not be wholly incompatible terms.

Deleuze's conception of the brain may seem a bit counter-intuitive at first; it is not the common-sense notion of the brain inside of the human head, which is couched in material reductionism,[7] but the brain as a depersonalized screen, immanent to the relational movement of the psychosocial event. Using language that strikingly anticipates Butler's terminology in *The Psychic Life of Power*, Deleuze writes: "the brain is *precisely this boundary* of a continuous two-way movement between an Inside and Outside, this membrane between them" (Deleuze 1995: 176, my emphasis). Depending on this two-way movement, the brain is entirely contingent and indeterminate, a brain for the making and in the making. As Deleuze goes on to say, "subjectification, events, and brains are more or less the same thing" (Deleuze 1995: 176).

The emphasis here on a two-way movement shaping the brain's composition provides a clue, corroborated by Schanelec's film *Afternoon*, as to what happens when melancholy settles into an event of subjectivity production

7 Materialist reductionism is a cluster of beliefs within neuroscience research that explains all human experience, especially mental illness, in terms of biological processes. Jeffrey Schwartz and Sharon Begley explain this position as follows: "To the mainstream materialist way of thinking, only the physical is real. Anything nonphysical is at best an artifact, at worst an illusion" (Schwartz and Begley 2002: 24). It is easy to see how such a perspective is commensurate with the depoliticization of mental illness since it completely disengages the brain from the psychosocial field of relation and its conditioning by power.

and the feeling of individual isolation begins to take hold. Instead of the relational boundary being actively shaped from both sides, in melancholic circumstances, it is dominated by a sort of "one-way movement," heavy and stifling, that is analogous to the scene of melancholy-formation Butler describes, where the psychic sphere is regulated "in relation to the prevailing norms of social regulation" (Butler 1997: 171). This is not to say that neoliberal power is unilateral or unidirectional in its implementation of social regulation, but rather to say that in cases of melancholy, power erects a malleable boundary immanent to the plastic fluctuations of the brain that creates the felt fiction of living as an autonomous and isolated individual, or "being as inert facticity," to once again evoke Guattari's description of melancholy mentioned in the introduction. This boundary creates an ossified sense of self that obfuscates the stirring of the transindividual and stifles the recomposition of novel assemblages of subjectivity that could have therapeutic as well as political effects. To better understand how neoliberal power (which works with and through psychiatric power) manages to implement such a depotentializing barrier in the relational juncture of brain, a discussion of neuroplasticity's promises and liabilities in the era of the "control society" is warranted.

The Neuroplastic Paradox

Long gone are the days when scientists thought that the brain finished developing during childhood, and that adults were stuck with a "hard wired" brain that could only diminish in capacities due to physical trauma, mental illness or aging. The rationale that the adult brain can heal from even severe impairments is now commonplace, and constitutes the basis for a vast array of therapeutic options, that all seek, through different means, to modify the plastic structure of the brain into some non-pathological form. The scientific term for the malleability of the brain is "neuroplasticity."

Neuroplasticity has become what philosopher of science Catherine Malabou calls "the dominant concept of the neurosciences." "Today," she argues, "it constitutes their common point of interest, their dominant motif, and their privileged operating model, to the extent that it allows them to think about the brain as at once an unprecedented dynamic, structure, and organization" (Malabou 2008: 4). In the words of obsessive compulsive researcher Jeffrey Schwartz, "Neuroplasticity refers to the ability of neurons to forge new connections, to blaze new paths through the cortex, even to assume new roles. In shorthand, neuroplasticity means rewiring the brain"

(Schwartz and Begley 2002: 15). The brain's ability to be rewired, even into adulthood, has promised a new wave of hope for the treatment of mental illnesses (now also frequently referred to as "brain disorders") and a host of other conditions.

But even from a neuroscientific point of view, plasticity cannot be uncritically celebrated in and of itself, for it is as liable to cement patterns of emotional suffering into the brain as it is to prompt therapeutic transformations.[8] This contradiction is partially explained by "the plastic paradox," which Norman Doidge describes through the following predicament: "the same plasticity which allows for the brain to change and heal, even in adulthood, is also the same plasticity that reinforces patterns of behaviour and habits of perception, and consequentially can entrench a number of disorders into the brain" (Doidge 2007: xx).

Today's dominant medical strategies for treating depression are built on, and justified by, the promises of neuroplasticity. The two most practiced treatments for depression in current usage are the prescription of psychotropic medication (antidepressants) and a form of psychotherapy known as Cognitive Behaviour Therapy. The rationale behind prescribing antidepressant medication is that the depressed brain has a chemical imbalance that can be regulated through medication. CBT operates on the principle that depression is characterized by a deficit of accurate thinking and a surplus of "cognitive distortions." The depressed person's thoughts are trapped within the "cognitive triad" (a reinforcing loop of negative thoughts) which makes life situations seem worse than they really are. What undergirds both this former psychiatric practice and latter psychological one (which differ quite remarkably in their approach but are often practiced in unison) is the neuroscientific discovery that the brain can change, either by introducing new chemical compounds or thought patterns. What I argue in the following pages is that the therapeutic efficacy of these institutionally sanctioned

8 Even though neuroscience has nothing to say on the question of how the plasticity of the brain is conditioned by the operations of power in the field of its emergence, philosophers of the brain do not miss out on this crucial point. Drawing on the work of Luc Boltanski and Eve Chiapello in *The New Spirit of Capitalism*, there are moments where the Deriddean philosopher Catherine Malabou echoes, perhaps unconsciously, Deleuze's formulation of the brain as a decentralized eventful screen composed in tandem with the psychosocial flows of desire. Malabou writes: "Neuronal functioning and social functioning interdetermine each other and mutually give each other form (here again the power of plasticity) to the point where it is no longer possible to distinguish between them" (Malabou 2008: 9). As a result, "the functional plasticity of the brain deconstructs its function as the central organ and generates the image of a fluid process, somehow present everywhere and nowhere, which places the outside and the inside in contact [...] " (Malabou 2008: 35).

methods can be easily thwarted by neoliberal power's immanence to brain plasticity. Neuroplasticity may provide a solid scientific basis for insisting on the possibility of at least some form of therapeutic cure, even in the deepest bouts of despair. Yet this optimism fuelled by various neuroscientific research initiatives is tempered by a harrowing contradiction: that the epoch of neuroplasticity is the same epoch that has witnessed the outbreak of a global depression epidemic.

What institutionally sanctioned therapies fail to critically engage with is the political operation of how the brain becomes subject. Perhaps unconsciously, or perhaps out of willful blindness, the dominant medical strategies in place for treating depression uncritically lend themselves to the neoliberal free marketeering of life—the transformation of life into capital. They each assist this transformation by creating brain chemistries or thought patterns that facilitate the maintenance, or even enhancement, of one's "human capital." It is precisely through this becoming subject of the brain to assume its role as capital that the plastic paradox I would like to foreground here (a politicized variant of the one proposed by Norman Doidge) presents itself: that despite its therapeutic promise, there is nothing inherent to neuroplasticity which prevents the production of subjectivity in line with affective suffering. After all, neoliberal power works immanently to the brain, so that (neuro)plastic qualities of movement, modulation, transformation, or restructuring cannot in and of themselves be valourized for their therapeutic value, since there is nothing preventing power from enticing these changes to serve its own interests, to the detriment of psychic and social life. The subsumption of mental health services to the demands of the market (what Josep Rafanelli I Orra calls "therapeutic capitalism") may not sound all that bad. After all, it is still "therapeutic." But when analyzing therapeutic capitalism's subjectifying apparatuses, Christian Marazzi's reminder rings as pertinently as ever: "If we want to produce capital through life, we need to remember how little life is worth in the eyes of power" (150).

As the shift in emphasis from the "psy" to the "neuro" continues to intensify across a broad range of societal discourses and institutions, especially those pertaining to the management of health,[9] the reductionist temptation to desubjectify the depression pandemic presents itself as strongly as ever. Take for example, the words of pioneering researcher in brain plasticity, Michael Mezernich: "Contemporary neuroscience is revealing, for the first time in our history, our true human natures," he says. "Human wisepersons

9 For more on this shift from the "psy" to the "neuro" see Nikolas Rose and Joelle M. Abi-Rached's *Neuro: The New Brain Sciences and the Management of the Mind.*

and societies have had great fun pondering about the mysteries of the origins of the 'self'. [...] We now have first-level scientific answers to these questions. We now understand the basic processes that underlie the genesis of the 'self'" (Merzenich n.p.). If the self can be reduced to primary brain processes, then what distinguishes a life coloured by depression from an exuberant one, a life on the verge of suicide from a life with an appetite for more? According to this material reductionist viewpoint, the difference between these two tendencies of life lies in the brain. And make no mistake, it undoubtedly does, but only if the brain is granted an expanded sense that confounds its orthodox usage in the neurosciences.

As Gilles Deleuze and Félix Guattari's own theoretical turns from the "psy" to the "neuro" in the 1980s and 1990s attest, theories of subjectivity production that seek to break from established analytic topographies are apt to explore a neurological dimension. The real schism between a reductionist scientism and a politicization of subjectivity is that the former thinks the brain in isolation, "outside of organism and milieu" (Rose 2016: n.p.), whereas the latter thinks the brain as milieu, "event," or "screen" (Deleuze 2000: 366; Deleuze 1995: 176). By constructing an isolated brain as the essence of subjectivity (and psychological affliction), neuroscience and the hegemonic therapies couched in it all too frequently treat the "social as a supplement" (Rose 2016: n.p.), effectively effacing the political contingency of the brain's plastic composition.

Deleuze may have advanced a "materialist psychiatry," but his take on the brain couldn't differ more from material reductionist schemas. That's because the materiality of the brain is thoroughly psychosocial, a membrane at the limit of the psyche and the social. Such a conception of the brain may seem a bit counter-intuitive at first; it is not the brain inside of the head, but the brain as the screen, as materially immanent to the plastic movements of the psychosocial event. Deleuze elaborates:

> One might equally well speak of new kinds of event, rather than processes of subjectification: events that can't be explained by the situations that give rise to them, or into which they lead. They appear for a moment, and it's that moment that matters, it's the chance we must seize. Or we can simply talk about the brain. [...] I think subjectification, events, and brains are more or less the same thing. (Deleuze 1995: 176)

Rather than the originator of experience, or the building block of some essential human self, as is posited by the material-reductionist hypothesis, the brain is an eventful milieu of subjectivity production—a milieu that can engender the hardened confines of an unshakeable depression, or even the most unexpected of therapeutic recompositions.

The shift in neoliberal strategies of governance from industrial capitalism's emphasis on discipline towards the deployment of control has seized the potential of brain plasticity. "Control society" is the term that Deleuze uses to describe a new type of power that emerges in the late 20th century, in contradistinction to Europe's "disciplinary" and "sovereign" societies that figure prominently in Michel Foucault's work on discipline and punishment in the 19th and 18th centuries. Strategies of control augment the state-run disciplinary institutions of confinement such as the military barracks, the classroom and the psychiatric ward by governance through more decentralized and corporatized means. New forms of subjectivity have been produced as a consequence of this shift in power. Whereas disciplinarity operates by molding its subjects from the outside (through confinement, repetitive drills and exercises as well as moral strictures), control works more seductively to induce conformity by way of modulation from within the subject who performs its own enterprising sense of self (by incurring debt, seeking motivation and conducting self-audits). Significantly for this study of plasticity and power, Deleuze attunes to how these strategies of power are to be distinguished by their tendency to either mold or modulate. He writes: "Confinements are molds, different moldings, while controls are a modulation like a self-transmuting molding continually changing from one moment to the next, or like a sieve whose mesh varies from one point to another" (1995: 178). Of key importance here is that rather than restricting change by confining and disciplining movements through molds that hold for a set period of time (the school day, the tour of duty, etc.), control societies work immanently to change, by directing, inflecting and modulating it indefinitely—"In control societies you never finish anything" (Deleuze 1995: 178).

The rise of the control society poses a whole new set of questions about political resistance that were absent from the discourse of political modernism. Neoliberalism has, at least in many "advanced capitalist" pockets, ceded to worker demands for more free time and less rigid work structures; demands for gender fluidity and non-normative relationships; and postcolonial demands for minority recognition. But at the same time that many of the 20th century's desires are seeing themselves fulfilled, and stifling old molds have given way to some more flexible identities, schedules and borders, power has not ceded any of its capacity to modulate modes of existence.

This modulatory style of control is emblematic of what Mark Fisher calls "capitalist realism," the idea that it may be easier to imagine the end of the world than the end of capitalism. For Fisher, capitalist realism "entails subordinating oneself to a reality that is infinitely plastic, capable of reconfiguring itself at any moment. [...] We are presented with what Jameson calls 'a purely fungible present in which space and psyches alike can be processed and remade at will'" (2009: 199). In the control society, power entices never-ending adaption to a plastic reality in perpetual change and modulation, regardless of how ecologically unsustainable or unconducive to wellness such economic imperatives have proven to be. Faced with this neoliberal reality, political resistance cannot be content with only working towards the abolishment of confining structures and identities.

Catherine Malabou and Marc Jeannerod address this predicament at the heart of the neuroplastic paradox in the most politicized passages of the book *What Should We Do with Our Brain?* In order to salvage the concept of plasticity, they propose a distinction between the neoliberal economy's demands for infinite flexibility and the potentially therapeutic qualities of neuroplasticity. They warn:

> Let us not forget that plasticity is a mechanism for adapting, while flexibility is a mechanism for submitting. Adapting is not submitting, and, in this sense, plasticity ought not to serve as an alibi for submitting to the new world order being dreamed up by capitalism. [...] What flexibility lacks is the resource of giving form, the power to create, to invent or even to erase an impression, the power to style. Flexibility is plasticity minus its genius. (Jeannerod: xiv; Malabou: 12)

The distinction that Malabou and Jeannerod set up between plasticity and flexibility posits plasticity's creative capacity to challenge the neoliberal demand of interminable flexibility. According to their formulation, plasticity actively shapes the world, whereas flexibility submits to the shape that the world has already taken. For these thinkers, the act of giving form, creating, inventing, erasing and styling constitute the pragmatic and experimental basis for resistance. Conversely, flexibility would entail a subduing of this creative capacity to accept the form of the world as it is (perpetually in its becoming), and submit to its modulatory impositions, rather than contribute to its ongoing formation through acts of creation.

It is hard not to see the appeal of this sort of optimistic assertion that creative actions can defy the control society's demand of endless flexibility. Yet what needs to be emphasized here is that even plasticity's creative capacity cannot escape the "plastic paradox" outlined above; the paradox that plasticity can habitually reinforce psychological suffering as much as its therapeutic overcoming, political oppression as much as emancipation. What scholarship on the various incarnations of the control society points to is that the creative capacity to give form far from guarantees a break from the logic of "the new world order being dreamed up by capitalism." In a control society, modulatory controls work immanently to plastic creation and change, and find ways to strategically revive old disciplinary molds in key instants.

Franco 'Bifo' Berardi elaborates this idea in his extensive writings on the political conditions that enable widespread depression. His approach advances the view that neoliberalism strategically abandons a politics of repression, and instead entices creative expression and novel change. This idea comes from Deleuze, who in bemoaning the excess of communication in late capitalist society, writes, "repressive forces don't stop people from expressing themselves, but rather, force them to express themselves" (Deleuze 1995: 129). Berardi builds on this idea most overtly in his article "Repression, Expression, Depression" where he writes: "The pathologies of our epoch are effectively no longer the neurotic pathologies produced by the repression of the libido, but rather the schizoid pathologies produced by the expressive explosion of 'just do it' " (189). In "Re-Assessing Composition: 40 Years After the Publication of Anti-Oedipus" he reiterates this view: "Psychic suffering does not come so much from repression but mainly from the hyper-expressive compulsion [...]" (Berardi 2012: 114). The overarching concern running throughout Bifo's recent work on the politics of depression is neoliberalism's ability to promote aggressive and exhausting competition by inducing labourious performances for economic gain, or even just for mere survival.

I include these extracts to show how Malabou and Jeannerod's plasticity-flexibility binary that allies plasticity to creativity and flexibility to submission is troubled by the fact that neoliberal economics depend on creativity, expressivity and novelty in order to extract surplus value and reproduce its lecherous rapport between capital and life. This is not to say that all actions are inherently coopted and futile, and that we should follow Bifo in his most depressive moments by withdrawing from the scene of activism, but simply to point out that in the control society, power is savvy enough to encourage the expressive, creative, and modulatory capacities of (neuro) plasticity, but in ways that never risk its dominance.

This insight that neoliberal power works as much through expressivity as through repression was speculatively glimpsed in *Anti-Oedipus*. In Foucault's preface to the English translation, he famously articulates this strange paradox that repressive forces don't stop people from expressing themselves as inherent to the "molecular fascism" that Deleuze and Guattari went to such great lengths in that book to identify and eradicate. Molecular fascism, Foucault writes, is "the fascism in us all, in our heads and in our everyday behaviours, that causes us to love power, to desire the very thing that dominates and exploits us" (Foucault 1983: xiii). The desire for power, or for fascism, is always already productive. Not coincidentally, what one of the subjective formations it is productive of, particarly in a neoliberal, post-totalitarian era, is none other than the individual: "The individual is the product of power" (Foucault 1983: xiv).

One of neoliberal power's most enduring strategies for maintaining its dominance amidst the deterritorializing effects of a plastic reality that incessantly expresses, creates and modulates is to reterritorialize onto the site of the individual. If there is a historical through-line linking the disciplinary society to the control society, which should be taken as evidence that one type of society does not replace the other but that it emerges over and on top of the other, like an archaeological site or palimpsest, it is the enduring and unwavering presence of the individual. This individualized subject is not a natural given, though neoliberal ideology often presents it as such. It is the result of a highly abstract form of subjectivity production that parses the individual from the machinic assemblages in which it is immersed as a component part. Nevertheless, this parsing of the individual from the "dividual" is a fundamental aspect of the capitalist production of subjectivity that Maurizio Lazzarato calls "social subjection." Found in regimes of power based both on disciplinarity and control, the apparatus of social subjection assigns "subjectivity an identity, sex, profession, nationality, and so forth" to produce "an 'individuated subject' whose paradigmatic form in neoliberalism has been that of 'human capital' and the 'entrepreneur of the self' (Lazzarato 2014: 24). Though really inseparable from the creativity and novelty of the dynamic, plastic assemblages in which it takes part, power parses an individual who is made "guilty and responsible for his fate" (Lazzarato 2014: 24). In an ondular reality of endless modulations, characterized as "infinitely plastic," the individual and its lingering mold incessantly returns as a dominant refrain, confirming power's vested interest in an ontology that separates self from world and makes the former unduly responsible for all that happens in the latter.

If the individual is the product of power, and if power subjects the individual in such a way as to encourage its performance as modulatory "human" capital, then there is no reason to believe that the individual's ability to creatively shape the plastics of its world would somehow mark power's undoing. Nor is there reason to believe that therapeutic methods which encourage brain plasticity to move more in sync with the economic demands of life under neoliberalism would somehow lead to wellness or flourishing, even if it may lead to being "symptom-free." Plasticity, as much as flexibility, can constitute a total submission to the status quo, without us even being cognizant of it—hence the plastic paradox. After all, there is nothing unusual about desiring "the very thing that dominates and exploits us," and thus producing its (and by extension, our) very existence.

The Berlin School's Plastics of Depotentialization

In the previous section's analysis, the "plastic paradox" has revealed itself to be paradoxical in two interrelated ways: one therapeutic and one political. Therapeutic, because the same neuroplasticity "which allows for the brain to change and heal [...] can entrench a number of disorders into the brain" (Doidge 2007: xx). And political, because plasticity's capacity for modulation, change and creation—the sorts of transformations that can break from disciplinary forms of repression—have turned into neoliberal imperatives complicit with control societies' apparatuses of power which also work through social subjection, or individualization. Furthermore, we have seen the limits of a reality sometimes described as infinitely plastic: Longstanding molds persist within the plasticity of control societies, with the individual—responsible and guilty—proving to be an important landing site for power's reterrritorializations.

Angela Schanelec, like the other artist-physicians whose films fill the pages of this project, perceive this play of neuroplasticity for what it is: a contingent production of subjectivity conditioned by power. She sees the autonomous individual as a highly abstract entity which is not at all natural, but whose production—whose divorce from the world and its relations—gives rise to melancholy sentiment that is not liable to be easily overcome. Shift as neuroplastics may, neoliberal power has shown itself unwilling to abandon the mold of the individual whose firm contours it labours to maintain, even in the most plastic and dynamic of milieus.

Just like the brain, the cinematic image can also be said to be plastic. As mentioned in the previous chapter, André Bazin used the phrase "plastics of the image" in reference to "the style of the make-up and décor and even, to a certain extent, of the acting; in addition of course to the lighting and framing; *the basis of composition*" (Bazin 2009: 88, my emphasis). In the film analysis that follows, Angela Schanelec activates all of these formal resources, particularly the lighting and framing ("the basis of composition"), to free indirectly perceive a psychosocial symptom of melancholy immanent to the paradox of neuroplasticity. What she perceives is none other than the depotentialization of the event for collective subjective recomposition; depotentialized because the brain, the milieu of transindividual psychology, is laced with modulatory plastic barriers that serve the aims of "social subjection" by creating a really felt fiction of an isolated self cut off from the world.[10]

Afternoon is a very slow film and homage to Anton Chekov's *The Seagull*. Like all Schanelec's directorial efforts, it is almost entirely devoid of dramatic intrigue. Set at the summerhouse of a family of writers, it follows their minute actions throughout the course of a long, scorching hot afternoon. A gloomy young playwright named Konstantin (Jirka Zett) and his girlfriend Agnes (Miriam Horwitz), a university student, discuss their crumbling relationship and decide to break-up. Konstantin's uncle Alex muses about his anti-depressant medication and passes his time playing card games. Irene (played by Schanelec), Konstantin's mother, lugs herself around the house, often speechless, edging toward a total psychological collapse. The nonchalant pace of the film is punctuated by two suicide attempts, one unsuccessful halfway through, and another at the film's conclusion when Konstantin decides to take a few handfuls of sleeping pills in an effort to end his life. The narrative is very simple and quite unremarkable, but it enables an aesthetic exploration of melancholy (neuro)plastics.

One of the film's artistic achievements is the development of a free indirect aesthetic that perceives the event's depotentialization by modulatory boundaries that enforce an isolated sense of self. It is true that practically all of the characters in this film exhibit some localized melancholy traits—on their face, in their body, through their dialogue—and that for this reason, the film can be confidently placed within the trajectory of melancholy iconography that populates the history of Western art.

10 The difference between potential and possibility is an important distinction to make, since foreclosure of potential for subjective recomposition, when the brain begins to feel like the unforgiving boundary of a one-way movement, is what signals that melancholy has settled into the event's plasticity. In a blog post about Whitehead and Kant's influence on Deleuze, Steven Shaviro offers a concise and instructive reading of the possible. He elaborates as follows:
"For Deleuze, the possible is an empty form, defined only by the principle of non-contradiction. To say that something is possible is to say nothing more than that its concept cannot be excluded a priori, on logical grounds alone. This means that possibility is a purely negative category; it lacks any proper being of its own. Mere possibility is not generative or productive; it is not enough to make anything happen" (Shaviro 2007: n.p).
Whereas potential, on the other hand, is a positive and productive quality: it perpetually introduces novelty into the movement of the event, producing real change (Massumi 2011: 1-2).

These emphatic, iconographic moments, however, are immersed in a free indirect schema that perceives how the brain's transindividuality is made to feel like a boundary, cutting the characters off from sharing in a re-existentializing conjunction. In crafting a melancholy aesthetics of evental plastic depotentialization, Schanelec's free indirect vision perceives the emergence of modulatory barriers that relationally move in tandem with the characters, delimiting the quality of their interactions, and making them feel all alone, even when they are in close proximity. The brain-screen's melancholic plasticity is just as stifling and unrelenting for everyone, leading them all to suffer from a sort of existential paralysis that Agnes briefly manages to put into words as she and Konstantin mutually process their seemingly unmotivated breakup: "When I came here I suddenly felt paralyzed."

The lighting and framing of a vast number of shots construct shifting boundaries between the characters, isolating them out from one another and imposing unconscious restrictions on their movement. The best example of this is the recurring shots of the chalet's glass doors separating the inside of the home from the patio overlooking the lake outside.

Seen on their own, the plastic configuration is banal and unthreatening. It may even read as conducive to movement: the open doors and the translucency of the windows connote bidirectionality and threshold crossing. As soon as one of the characters enters the frame, however, the function of the set's architecture shifts dramatically. The free indirect is made operative, as a seemingly objective shot begins to articulate the melancholic sense of self that haunts the character who has entered the frame. The image becomes the brain, coterminous with transindividual psychology's relational movement. Except that here, in a moment of severe melancholic suffering, the movement only seems to tend in one direction: neoliberal power's individualization and responsibilization of depression determine the image's plastics, thwarting the potential for subjective recomposition immanent to the group of people who inhabit the space.

The angle through which the doors are shot tightly frames the characters. For example, in this image the chalet's architecture has instantaneously gone from being an open passageway to a mobile prison—a modulatory mold—cutting the characters off from one another and their surroundings. In these solitary moments, the boundaries immanent to the brain-screen's plasticity insist that these characters live, struggle and suffer alone. It would be impossible to perceive this shift were it not for the free indirect and its ability to express with equal fidelity, in one image, an objectively true fact (the architecture's arrangement) and a subjectively true feeling (the way

Image 4 *Nachmittag (Afternoon)*, Angela Schanelec, 2007

the characters are existentially isolated from one another and the world around them).

One effect of Schanelec's use of the free indirect is a real indeterminacy between where melancholy begins and ends, or between whom it does and does not affect. In *Afternoon*, melancholy saturates the entire brain-screen. Konstanstin's two suicide attempts which punctuate the film appear each time as completely startling since he doesn't appear to be a more likely self-harm candidate than any of the other characters. The suicides could just as easily have been attempted his girlfriend, mother or uncle. Leading into this final suicide scene, Konstantin walks into the kitchen to pour the glass of water that he will use to swallow his sleeping pills, and crosses right past his family members who are casually conversing at the kitchen table. Not one of them cues into his fatal intentions. In a plastically depotentialized world where everyone is mired in their own unrelenting sense of self and power has foreclosed re-existentializing relational movements, Konstanin's suicidal behaviour doesn't even stand out.

The free indirect is also what enables Schanelec to create an image of plastic depotentialization in the film's harrowing conclusion. In the suicide that closes out the film, the shot begins with an empty frame, before Konstantin enters and takes a seat on the edge of his bed, facing a dark grey wall. His back faces the camera in a five-minute-long static shot. This scene depicts what must be for Konstanin a moment of extreme suffering that has pushed him to the brink of self-willed death. Compositionally speaking, it is one of the film's darkest, as the natural light that filters through the rest of the film's daytime scenes has faded. The tight interior framing shows nowhere for his body to move, no possible line of advance, no window to offer

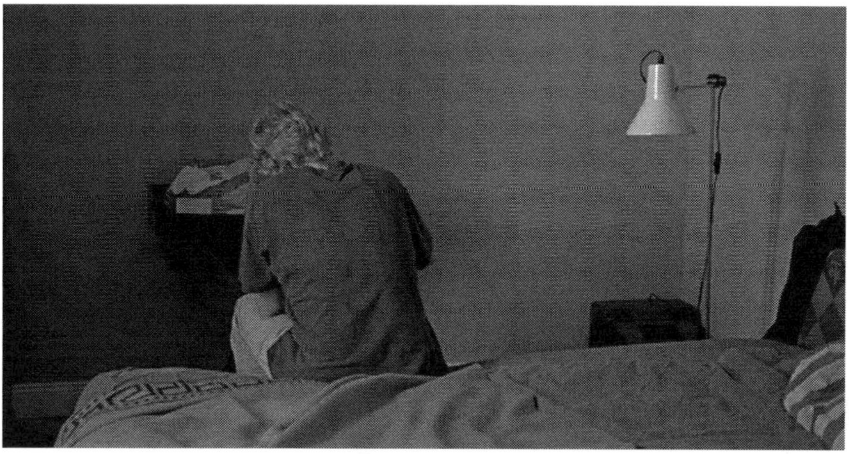

Image 5 *Nachmittag (Afternoon)*, Angela Schanelec, 2007

a fresh view of things, no door to escape through and nobody to reach out to for help. An ordinary bedroom, with plenty of potential to be inhabited in a myriad of ways, when graced with Konstantin's presence, turns into a hellish confine where suicide seems like the only way out. An objective space, turns into a free indirect subjective space, where it is impossible to parse its physical manifestation from the psychic pain that inhabits it. The image of the room is coterminous with a brain on the brink of suicide. The free indirect is operative here in the way that the image never needs to break with the objective reality to construct some fantastical or iconographic image that could do symbolic justice to the psychic gravity of the scene.

A luminous bourgeois chalet, where he could come and go and do as he pleases, in this moment of suicidal despair, modulates and turns into a malleable and dispersed prison of existential paralysis. The walls of the home have turned into barriers preventing Konstantin's world from being otherwise, not because they are fundamentally of such nature, or because he is really physically trapped, but because Schanelec's delirious aesthetic pictures them in such a way so as to articulate how neoliberal power's strategic individualism has made him—one part of a collective assemblage of subjectivity—feel responsible for the entirety of the melancholic pain saturating the event. The modulatory barriers that depotentialize the brain-screen account for why, even when Konstantin swims out to the floating dock to die in the film's very last scene, he doesn't have a change of heart and begin to see the beauty of the world, even though the sun is shining above a pristine lake with plenty of open air, with room to move and presumably, other people to meet. Feeling the barriers that usurp potential immanent to the plastics of his bourgeois Western European world and reinforce the felt fiction of his individuality, Konstantin could sense all too well the usurping of potential for therapeutic subjective recomposition, and embraces his death—the only viable release from an inescapable sense of self.

A similar aesthetic strategy punctuates Angela Schanelec's other films as well as those of her Berlin School contemporaries. What they depict is a free indirect expression of both the subjective and objective in one immediately psychosocial image. Yet again, windows—boundaries between the inside and outside, just like Deleuze's brain-as-screen—play an important role in shaping the image plastics and their potential for shaking the isolation of a depressive sense of self. In Ulrich Köhler's *Windows on Monday*, a bourgeois couple named Nina (Isabelle Menke) and Freider (Hans-Jochen Wagner) are renovating the home that they share with their young daughter Charlotte (Amber Bongard). They both seem completely dissatisfied with their lives and relationship, but are trying to keep busy and make good financial investments by retiling their floor and installing new pine windows. In spite of having these home improvement projects, not to mention a daughter in common with her husband, Nina makes a spur of the moment and seemingly unmotivated decision to abandon her family. One evening, Nina goes to pick Charlotte up from the babysitter while Freider is at home working on the renovations then suddenly decides that she would simply rather not perform the familial duties expected of her. Without saying a word or giving any noticeable prompt, she turns the car around and drives away from the babysitter's home where Charlotte is waiting. When Frieder calls Nina on her cellphone to inquire as to why she still hasn't come back with their daughter, she shrugs off the situation, says that she doesn't know why she has made the decision that she has, but that she is sure that she will not return. This scene of abandonment initiates her wandering attempts at overcoming the melancholy that has instilled itself in the fabric of her conjugal and familial life.

After giving up on her family, Nina goes to visit her brother in the woods where he is living in a cabin with his girlfriend. Across the way from their cabin is a resort hotel that piques her interest and draws her in. Once inside, Nina is presented with a host of seductive opportunities to break out of the monotonous existence that she has tried so hard to escape, but malleable boundaries keep separating Nine out from the scenes of her desire. She peeps in on a jovial tennis match, a pool party, a chic gala from the opposite side of the windows that cut her out of the action. Even after having broken free from the stifling confines of her family home Nina finds herself in what seems like and endless string of situations that continue to provoke melancholic plastic compositions.

Other films in the Berlin School continue to play on the trope of the window as malleable boundary that reinforces a depressive sense of self. Much like in *Windows on Monday*, Christoph Hochhäusler's *This Very Moment* depicts the frustrations of another bourgeois woman stifled by her home renovations. In *Forest for the Trees*, a school teacher's car window marks her suicidal confinement and in *Bungalow* the window of a military bus encases a disenchanted young soldier on the brink of going AWOL. Other Angela Schanelec films such as *Passing Summer, Marseille*, and *Places in Cities* repeatedly play on the window motif in *Afternoon* to render plastic the psychological suffering of young women who face amorous discontent, listlessness and loneliness.

By free indirectly perceiving one of melancholy's symptoms as being the depotentialization of the event for subjective recomposition, Schanelec manages to corroborate Butler's guiding intuition that there is nothing more melancholic than being made to feel like an individual. Ultimately, this Berlin School film shows why transindividual psychology, or the brain, a relation of relations, can in cases of melancholy double as a boundary: because as much as neoliberal power entices the plastic expanse of boundless creativity, it cannot yet do without strategically reinforcing the artificial limits of the self and its ontological distinction from the world of relations in which it is immersed, and assigning it undue responsibility for managing the melancholic sentiments that arise from this alienating divide. In the Berlin School's existential gridlock, like in the control society, plastics shift, shifting possibilities, all while foreclosing potential for collective subjective recompositions with therapeutic effects to be made.

Bibliography

Abel, Marco. *The Counter-Cinema of the Berlin School*. Rochester, New York: Camden House, 2013.

Bazin, André. *What is Cinema?* Trans. Timothy Barnard. Montreal: Caboose, 2009.

Baer, Hester. "Affectless Economies: The Berlin School and Neoliberalism." *Discourse* 35.1 (Winter 2013): 72-100.

Baute, Michael, Ekkehard Knrer, Volker Pantenberg, Stefan Pethke, Simon Rothler. "The Berlin School – A Collage." *Senses of Cinema* 55 (July 2010): n.p. Online. http://sensesofcinema.com/2010/feature-articles/the-berlin-school-%E2%80%93-a-collage-2/

Berardi, Franco 'Bifo'. "Re-Assessing Composition: 40 Years After the Publication of Anti-Oedipus." *Subjectivity* 5.1 (2012): 111-119.

Berardi, Franco 'Bifo'. "Repression, Expression, Depression." *The Guattari-Effect*. Ed. Éric Alliez and Andrew Goffey. London and New York: Continuum, 2011b.

Boltanski, Luc and Even Chiapello. *The New Spirit of Capitalism*. London: Verso, 2005.

Butler, Judith. *The Psychic Life of Power: Theories in Subjection*. Stanford, California: Stanford University Press, 1997.

Clarke, David. "'Capitalism has no more natural enemies': The Berlin School." *A Companion to German Cinema*. Eds. Terri Ginsberg and Andrea Mensch. West Sussex, UK: Wiley-Blackwell. 2012.

Deleuze, Gilles. "Control and Becoming." *Negotiations: 1972-1990*. New York and Chichester, West Sussex: Columbia University Press, 1995. 169-176.

Deleuze, Gilles. "The Brain is the Screen: An Interview with Gilles Deleuze." *The Brain is the Screen: Deleuze and the Philosophy of Cinema*. Ed. Gregory Flaxman. Minneapolis and London: University of Minnesota Press, 2000. 365-373.

Doidge, Norman. *The Brain that Changes Itself: Stories of Personal Triumph from the Frontiers of Brain Science*. London: Penguin, 2007.

Fisher, Mark. *Capitalist Realism: Is There No Alternative?* Winchester, UK and Washington, USA: o Books, 2009.

Foucault, Michel. "Preface." *Anti-Oedipus: Capitalism and Schizophrenia*. Minneapolis: University of Minnesota Press, 1983.

Freud, Sigmund. "The Ego and the Id." *The Standard Edition of the Complete Psychological Works of Sigmund Freud, Volume XIX (1923-1925): The Ego and the Id, and Other Works*. London: Penguin (Vintage Classics), 2001.

Gansera, Rainer. 2001. "Glücks-Pickpocket." Süddeutsche Zeitung November 3. Online. http://archiv.sueddeutsche.apa.at/sueddz/index.php?id=A13298091_OGTPOG

Hochhäusler, Christoph. "On Whose Shoulders: The Question of Aesthetic Indebtedness." *The Berlin School: Films from the Berliner Schule*. New York: The Museum of Modern Art, 2013. 20-29.

Köhler, Ulrich. "Why I don't Make Political Films." *Cinema Scope* 28 (Spring 2009): 10-13.

Lazzarato, Maurizio. *Signs and Machines: Capitalism and the Production of Subjectivity*. Trans. David Joshua Jordan. Los Angeles: Semiotext(e), 2014.

Lim, Dennis. "Moving On: The Next New Wave." *The Berlin School: Films from the Berliner Schule*. New York: The Museum of Modern Art, 2013. 88-97.

Malabou, Catherine. *What Should We Do With Our Brain?* Foreword by Marc Jeannerod. Trans. Sebastian Rand. New York: Fordham University Press, 2008.

Marazzi, Christian. *Capital and Affects: The Politics of the Language Economy*. Trans. Guiseppina Mecchia. Los Angeles and Cambridge, Massachusetts: Semiotext(e), 2011.

Massumi, Brian. *Semblance and Event: Activist Philosophy and the Occurrent Arts.* Cambridge, Massachusetts and London, England: The MIT Press, 2011.

Merzenich, Michael. “The brain plasticity revolution.” *“On the Brain” with Dr. Michael Merzenich.* http://www.onthebrain.com/2009/07/brain-plasticity-revolution

Rose, Nikolas. “Brain, Self and Society.” Andrew F. Holmes Dean of Medecine Distinction Lectures. McGill University. Montreal, Canada. 27 October 2016. Public Lecture.

Rose, Nikolas and Joelle M. Abi-Rached. *Neuro: The New Brain Sciences and the Management of the Mind.* Princeton and Oxford: Princeton University Press, 2013.

Schwartz, Jeffrey and Sharon Begley. *The Mind and the Brain: Neuroplasticity and the Power of Mental Force.* New York: Regan Books, 2002.

Shaviro, Steven. “Kant, Deleuze and the Virtual.” *Pinnochio Theory.* Blog Post. 9 May 2007. http://www.shaviro.com/Blog/?p=577

Vinogradova, Maria. “The Berlin School as a Recent New Wave in German Cinema.” *Acta Univ. Sapientiae, Film and Media Studies* 3 (2010): 157-168.

Worthmann, Merten. “Mit Vorsicht genießen.” *Die Zeit* 27 (September 2001). Online. http://zeit.de

3 Belief and the Common World of Experience

Abstract
Chapter Three analyzes Kelly Reichardt's *Night Moves* and the "American Neo-Neorealsim" film movement. The relational symptom of melancholy which it proposes is the erosion of belief in a common world of experience. By closely investigating the plastic composition of Reichardt's images and how they engender a play of asymmetrical beliefs, this chapter questions the degree of fidelity to which the cinematic image can depict an experience so singular and incommensurate as melancholy, and proposes that the firee indirect style maintains an ontological link between the film image and profilmic experience since it can psychosocially perceive the play of beliefs that give rise to melancholic isolation, even if that isolation can never be known in and of itself.

Keywords: Kelly Reichardt, American independent cinema, pure experience, William James

American "Neo-Neorealism"

At a historical moment that overlaps with the Berlin School's productions, a cluster of American independent filmmakers also decided to invoke the cinema of poetry tradition to aesthetically interrogate the conditions of contemporary melancholy. This loosely connected wave of filmmakers that began to emerge around 2005 has come to be called "American Neo-Neorealism," and it includes the likes of Kelly Reichardt and her contemporaries such as Julia Loktev, Ramin Bahrani, Lance Hammer, Ryan Fleck and Anna Boden. American Neo-Neorealism is comparable to the Berlin School since film after film dwells on protagonists whose affective well-being is found to be at complete odds with the socioeconomic system in which they live. The most aesthetically refined of these filmmakers, such as Kelly Reichardt,

Szymanski, A., *Cinemas of Therapeutic Activism: Depression and the Politics of Existence.* Taylor & Francis Group, 2020
DOI: 10.5117/9789463723121_CH03

augment melancholic themes by crafting psychosocial film worlds out of free indirect perspectives that discover yet another evental symptom of melancholy: singular breaks from the common world of experience. This symptom of melancholy is especially vivid in Kelly Reichardt's *Night Moves*, the film which I focus on in this chapter, as it meticulously renders aesthetic the psychological dimension of a group of ecological activists who come together to explode a hydroelectric dam, but whose collective then fractures once the act is completed, leaving three troubled individuals alienated from the world and the beliefs that they once held in common. By cueing into yet another symptom of melancholy that resides in the event itself, surpassing the individual on all sides, Kelly Reichardt intensifies Angela Schanelec's implicit critique of the psychiatric gaze and its penchant for reducing problems of evental breadth down to the scale of the individual. Attuned to the event of subjectivity production, like Schanelec, Reichardt's work taps into the reasons why a given event can produce the melancholic sensation of feeling like an isolated individual. In Angela Schanelec's film world, this feeling was brought about through modulatory plastic boundaries that foreclosed the potential for a re-existentializing encounter. Here in the parallel world of Kelly Reichardt, a similar operation takes place: power conditions what types of collective beliefs are permissible, so that activist desires for real political change that could recompose a collective subjectivity, end up abstracting individuals out from one another, dooming them to the singular depths of melancholic isolation, to incommensurate existential territories fated to never again intersect.

Before delving into the aesthetic and theoretical details of this melancholic dynamic in the work of Kelly Reichardt, a brief description of American Neo-Neorealism's history and thematic preoccupations will help to contextualize her filmmaking practice. The term was coined by *New York Times* film critic A.O. Scott in his widely read article "Neo-Neo Realism: American Directors Make Clear-Eyed Movies for Hard Times."[1] Therein, Scott aptly points out that films such as *Wendy and Lucy* (Reichardt, 2008), *Sugar* (Fleck and Boden, 2008), *Man Push Cart* (Bahrani, 2005), and *Ballast*

1 The article prompted a minor scuffle with *New Yorker* critic Richard Brody, who took exception to the premise of Scott's article that America has never before had a neorealist film movement. Scott replies to Brody's criticisms in a *New York Times* blog post that reiterates his vision of neorealism and why the American films that Brody cites do not fit the category. The exchange is also notable for how it teases out the often-held assumption, this time advanced by Brody, that neorealism puts "emphasis on outer life at the expense of inner life." See Brody's "About Neo-Neo Realism" and "A.O. Scott Responds to New Yorker Blog on the Value and Definition of Neorealism."

(Hammer, 2008) invoke Italian neorealism's humanist concern with the dignity of the working class and offer a timely critique of the discourse of upward mobility which holds sway over so many of the films' protagonists. Not surprisingly, the struggle to deal with economic precarity is a recurring theme in these films that were released amidst the U.S. Invasion of Iraq and the impending 2008 Wall Street collapse. In *Wendy and Lucy* an unemployed young woman (Michelle Williams) stranded in Portland tries to scrounge up enough gas money to reach Alaska with her dog, where her hopes for a better future rest on a fish-canning job. *Sugar* follows a young Dominican baseball player (Algenis Perez Soto) with his eyes set on cracking the major leagues and its seven-figure salaries, all while washing dishes in a New York City restaurant. Ahmad (Ahmad Razvi), the protagonist of *Man Push Cart*, sells coffee and doughnuts while desperately counting on a wealthy friend to help revive the short-lived music career that once earned him celebrity status in Pakistan. In *Ballast*, Lawrence (Michael J. Smith Sr.) holds out faith that the grocery store he owns can catalyze his broken family's recovery from drug addiction, suicide and hunger. All of these protagonists grasp onto the slim but real hope that one big break could lift them out of their entrenched class position. However, as Scott points out, "in these movies, dreams generally do not come true" (Scott 2009b: MM38). In spite of the protagonists' optimism, the film worlds they inhabit are unforgiving and thoroughly expressive of "capitalist realism"—the pervasive feeling that there is no escape from the dictates of capital (Fisher 2009: 2).

At least the original neorealists could still turn to the Italian Communist Party for affirmation that the miseries abound need not be so. Finding themselves on the brink of Obama's "changed" America, these indie filmmakers carry a deep skepticism towards the mass-manufactured hope in electoral politics as a catalyst for the redistribution of wealth and the creation of a more egalitarian society. In marked opposition to the dominant ideology of Hollywood cinema from the same era, these films suppose the futility of hope, and even critique hope's strategic mobilization by hegemonic forces to indefinitely delay the hoped-for's realization. In an intriguing artist-to-artist interview with Gus Van Sant in 2008, Kelly Reichardt candidly sums up the situation: "We were watching a lot of Italian neorealism and thinking the themes of those films seem to ring true for life in America in the Bush years," she says. "These haven't been optimistic times" (Reichardt and Van Sant 2008: n.p.). Based on the films that Reichardt went on to make in Obama-era America, it's clear that she didn't suddenly acquire a taste for populist optimism.

A.O. Scott's term "Neo-Neo Realism" is useful for connecting Reichardt's body of work to a cluster of filmmakers who also traffic in stock neorealist themes at the same historical moment, and for identifying this significant trend in American independent cinema that has tackled real life social issues without the sensationalism and spectacle of Hollywood-style realism. However, Reichardt's relationship to this film movement is a complicated one, because she arguably stands as both its most emblematic and most anomalous director. Of all the filmmakers who could be included in the movement, Reichardt is undoubtedly the most critically acclaimed and has proven to be the most prolific over the years (with seven feature length films to date). The themes of her films tend to fit with the movement's persistent focus on the quotidian lives of the economically disadvantaged, and her anti-sensationalist ethos coupled with a pared-down film style evoke its overall sensibility. But to frame her work solely in terms of adherence to the neorealist tradition runs the risk of occluding her deep indebtedness to the cinema of poetry and its aesthetic creation of the psychosocial image which proves so indispensible to her symptomatology of melancholy in contemporary America. In the following chapter, I invoke both filmmaking traditions on the premise that they are compatible categories: neorealism's focus on war-wrought poverty can coexist with the cinema of poetry's psychosocial images. Deleuze lends weight to this allying of neorealism and the cinema of poetry through the way he structures his cinema books. In *Cinema 2*, both neorealist and cinema of poetry auteurs are grouped together under the more general category of "modern cinema." Reference to all three of these overlapping categorizations will appear where appropriate in this chapter's reading of *Night Moves*, a film about believing in, and creating, the basis for collective action in the face of lost hope.

The three films that Kelly Reichardt directed leading up to *Night Moves* all play on the theme of hope, particularly as it fades in the face of increasingly dire situations. In *Old Joy* (2006), two long-lost friends whose lives have lead them down very different paths attempt to reconnect by taking a road trip to nearby hot springs. Kurt (Will Oldham) and Mark (Daniel London) couldn't be more different. Kurt is a vagabond without a stable job or relationship. Clean-cut Mark feels trapped in a stressful domestic situation. Both sense that a meeting with the other could provide some insight into how to find the joy that seems to elude them both. In what can only be a disappointement for the both of them, the film ends on the same melancholic note that it began, with the two characters thrust back into the norms of their respective lives—Mark in his home and Kurt wandering the streets—without any noticeable change to speak of. The little hope that they had for their encounter proves to be in vain. *Wendy and Lucy*, Reichardt's follow-up film, is quite similar in this regard. Unemployed and out of cash, Wendy's future is fairly grim. To make matters worse, her dog has gone missing and her car has broken down, barring her from leaving for Alaska, a place that she fantasizes as a sort of promised land. Even though she manages to find a helping hand from a cash-strapped security guard who musters just enough change for her to buy some gas and get on her way, the film concludes with Wendy in just as precarious of a position as she started in, with little promise that she will find the economic security and peace of mind that she is looking for. The 2010 period piece *Meek's Cutoff* is even more dour, and it follows an ill-fated caravan of settlers led across the Oregon desert by frontier guide Stephen Meek in 1845. To their demise, the supposed shortcut that he takes turns out to be inhospitable and without the necessities to support life. Reichardt's most recent film *Night Moves* starts out in another hopeless situation, present day Oregon plagued by the ecological degradation that comes with encroaching industrialization. Faced with a loss of confidence in the prospect that small-scale green actions could cumulatively make a significant difference when up against industrial capital's systematic expropriation of the earth and unceasing disregard for ecological health and sustainability, a group of radicalized—and hopeless—activists are left with nothing but belief as the basis for their activism. The belief which moves their activism and overcomes their loss of hope gives birth to a common world of experience that Reichardt aesthetically articulates through free indirect perception.

Belief Contra Hope

Belief, in the sense that it accrues across Deleuze's later works, couldn't be more different than hope. Whereas belief affirms this world's relevance and stages an encounter with it, hope unconsciously wishes this world away in the name of a transcendental ideal; the ideal of another world or utopian endpoint. There is a cruel irony to hope. What hope hopes for is fated to never arrive, since by hoping and waiting, instead of believing and acting, hope implicitly accepts the status quo instead of finding a way to change it. As an implicit acceptance of the existing state of affairs, it is fair to say that hope is a politically coopted comportment that perpetuates the dominant institutions, ideologies, and modes of subjectivity production within a given society.[2] In just about all of the films mentioned above,

2 In interview with Mary Zournazi, Brian Massumi points to this problem with hope, particularly when it is future oriented and connected to expected success. He opts for the concepts of

including Kelly Reichardt's, the film world is hopeless, even if some of the protagonists naively hold out hope for an economic miracle that will lift them out of their entrenched class position.[3] Next to hope's political naiveté, hopelessness seems politically astute, and perhaps even the only sound state of mind, given the unrelenting hold of capitalist realism. Perhaps this is one of the reasons why the hopelessness of American Neo-Neorealist films has resonated so well with left-wing critics. Hopelessness may indeed be a sober-minded response to the present state of the world, but in and of itself, it really doesn't offer any way out, or any avenues for action that could bring about therapeutically political change in the fabric of everyday life. Political astuteness is not always politically enabling.

Hopefulness and hopelessness each carries a beneficial and limiting quality. Hopefulness may ward off a despairing and nihilistic melancholy, but it often proves to be a naïve and misplaced optimism that negates this world in favour of a transcendental ideal, further cementing the existing status quo. Hopelessness, on the other hand, is undoubtedly liberating, since it lets go of a false consciousness, yet once hope is lost, very little is left to dispel the melancholy that exhausts so many activist milieus.[4] The total absence of hope closely parallels Andrew Solomon's account of depression, wherein "you cannot remember a time when you felt better, at least not clearly; and you certainly cannot imagine a future time when you will feel better" (Solomon 2001: 55). Even though hopelessness has the benefit of washing away political naiveté, it is not fix-all antidote to the shortcomings of hope, since it mirrors a depressive state of mind. How then is it possible to escape both the political naiveté of misplaced hopefulness and the melancholic stasis of a politically warranted hopelessness, and stage an encounter with the world rather than wish it away in the name of an unattainable ideal? Deleuze's concept of belief offers a way out of this deadlocked dialectic of hopefulness and hopelessness.

belief and affect that allow for a lived immersion and belonging in the world. See their interview in the book: Zournazi, Mary. *Hope: New Philosophies for Change.* New York: Routledge, 2003.

3 It is no coincidence that American Neo-Neorealism came to fruition at the very same moment that Obama rode a carefully manufactured wave of populist hope right into the White House. Looking back, this film movement offers a sober skepticism towards American macropolitics that anticipates how Obama's presidency failed to resolve the economic, and especially racial, injustices that his campaign promised to address.

4 The growth of depression, melancholy and exhaustion within activist milieus, and activist responses to this phenomenon have inspired the writings in various online venues. For one high quality contribution to these discussions that received a lot of attention in 2014 is the *Plan C* collective's "We Are All Very Anxious."

In *Cinema 2*, Deleuze lauds the modern cinema for its ability to restore a lost faith when confronted with the "modern fact that we no longer believe in *this* world" (171, my emphasis). He goes on to write: "The link between the human and the world is broken. Henceforth, this link must become an object of belief: it is the impossible which can only be restored within a faith. [...] The cinema must film, not the world, but belief in this world, our only link" (172, translation modified). To be intelligible, Deleuze's argument that the link between human and world has been broken, and can only be restored through belief must be read in light film history. The division between his two cinema books is telling in this regard. The first book on the "movement-image" begins to expound a taxonomy of signs in the pre-WWII "classical cinema" whereas the second book on the "time-image" continues this project but with regards to the postwar "modern cinema." For Deleuze, the classical and modern cinemas are characterized by two different types of images, with two different relationships to movement and time. In classical cinema, what he calls a "sensory-motor schema" links the spaces of the film together through protagonist-driven action. In this stylistic tradition, film space is constructed around the agency and motoricity of an action-oriented protagonist. Distances are traversed, rooms are entered, and landscapes are conquered. Movement through these spaces serve the goals and desires of a male protagonist (solving a mystery, winning over a love interest, serving the nation, etc.). As a result, the film worlds neatly correspond to these goals and desires, and space becomes subservient to them and predetermined by them. These worlds are made for, and given to, human action. Due to this being the case, the aesthetics of the classical cinema are only ever able to produce "indirect images of time," or more simply "movement-images." The "indirect image of time" has nothing to do with the force of the free indirect that so many of the auteurs inspired by the cinema of poetry have harnessed to craft psychosocial images. By "indirect images of time," Deleuze is simply referring to how these images never make time felt in and of itself.[5] Instead, time is represented and implied by the chain of goal-oriented movements

5 Deleuze distinguishes between the movement-image and the time-image based on their relationship to the signaletic force of time. He writes: "As long as signs find their material in the movement-image, as long as they form the singular expressional features, from a material in movement, they are in danger of evoking another generality which would lead to their being confused with a language. The representation of time can be extracted from this only by association and generalization, or as concept. Such is the ambiguity of the sensory-motor schema, agent of abstraction. It is only when the sign opens directly on to time, when time provides the signaletic material itself, that the type, which has become temporal, coincides with the feature of singularity separated from its motor associations" (2007: 42-43).

performed by a volitional protagonist. The protagonist's actions dictate the construction of time (and space), rather than time conditioning his actions. In the movement-image, a causal chain links human to world, but makes the world conform to the scale and needs of human action.

The modern cinema breaks this aesthetic model apart from the inside by liberating the force of time from it subsumption to movement. As a result, "pure optical and sound situations," or "time-images" arise that confound the movement-image's reliance on character intentionality and action. No longer determined by these goal-oriented actions of the individual protagonist, time's force is made felt, leading to an amplification of indeterminacy and ambiguity: a cinema of wavering, aberrant movement. Once human action has ceased to determine time and space, then the classical cinema's link between human and world is broken. Instead, time makes action waver and falter, casting doubt on the human's link to the world that was assured by the aesthetic logic of the movement-image.

Deleuze's writing is free from even a hint of nostalgia for this classical link between human and world, because to restore it would be to deny the cinema's discovery of the force of time. But his ultimate disavowal of the movement-image's linking of human and world via volitional action should not be mistaken for an abandonment of the world in favour of a higher ideal, as is the case with hope, nor as a renunciation of the creative act. Instead, Deleuze turns to belief as a way affirm the world, *this* world, and its eventful and creative activity, even amidst the unsettling effects of time. Belief in this world is synonymous with the transindividual's creativity. Belief "precipitates events, however inconspicuous, that elude control," and "engenders new space-times, however small their surface or volume (Deleuze 1995: 176, translation modified). The phrase, "eludes control" warrants extra emphasis because, as was discussed in the previous chapter, one of the ways that the control societies of late capitalism function is through the reterritorializing function of social subjection that produces a sense of existential isolation. Belief's elusion of control, as we will see, has to do with its creation of a common world of experience that can overcome the melancholic confines of feeling like the individual that neoliberal power, together with psychiatric power, never ceases to produce.

Erin Manning builds on Deleuze's affirmative understanding of belief to further underscore its creative capacity. For Manning, "A belief in the world is about crafting the conditions to encounter the world differently each time" (2016: 93). Crafting the conditions for an encounter with the world is very different from acting on it, or making it conform to the human scale, as is generally the case in the classical cinema's linking of human and world through volitional action. Belief, in the sense that Deleuze and Manning give to it, is a belief in the potential immanent to the world for novel productions of subjectivity.

To reiterate, this is why belief is of an entirely different order than hope. Whereas belief affirms potential for an encounter with the world that can recompose subjectivity, hope negates it in favour of a far off utopia, effectively reifying reigning standardizations of subjectivity. Deleuze insists that the belief which modern cinema has the power to restore "does not address a different or transformed world" but simply "this world [...] as it is" (2007: 171, 172). Unlike the speculative pragmatic[6] gesture of belief which aims to grasp the world in its really existing conditions, in order to stage an encounter with it that opens the potential for subjective recomposition, hope negates the world in favour of an ideal that is never actualized because hope was never pragmatically invested in the potential of the world to begin with. Hope isn't of this world, but rather exists for the "different or transformed worlds" that Deleuze figured as having nothing to do with belief.

The stakes of this distinction between hope and belief are particularly high for activist praxes, since the most transformative examples of activism find a way out of the hopefulness-hopelessness dialectic that ossifies melancholy's seeming interminability and stifles an encounter with the world, to embrace the creative quality of belief. As believers, activists move with the world's creative potential for new manners of becoming and relating—of composing subjectivity—and to once again paraphrase Manning, of recreating the conditions through which the world can be encountered, along the lines of economic, ecological and affective well-being. In doing so, activists, like the ones at the centre of *Night Moves*, find themselves in the midst of a commons-in-the-making, a shared world of experience where belief meets belief.

The Common World of Experience

This common site where belief meets belief has a name: the plane of immanence, or what William James calls, "pure experience."[7] William James

6 Brian Massumi provides an authoritative and concise definition of speculative pragmatism in *Semblance and Event*. He writes: "The speculative aspect relates to the character of potential native to the world's activity, as expressed eventfully in the taking place of change. The pragmatic aspect has to do with how, in the taking-definite-shape of potential in a singular becoming, the relational and qualitative poles co-compose as formative forces" (Massumi 2011: 12).

7 In David Lapoujade's article on the presence of James in *What is Philosophy?*, he writes explicitly that "pure experience" "is the name that William James gives to the plane of immanence"

is widely regarded as the founding figure of American psychology, whose eclectic development of the pragmatic method spans topics such as the philosophy of experience, the reality of consciousness and the nature of truth. By building on relevant ideas from the essays gathered in the *Essays in Radical Empiricism* collection, such as "Does Consciousness Exist," "A World of Pure Experience," and especially "How Two Minds Can Know One Thing," this section explores how the melancholic sensation of isolation and hopelessness, as well as its therapeutic overcoming through the collective composition of a common world, is brought about by virtue of how belief composes with this world of pure experience. The rationale for undertaking this line of inquiry comes from the film itself, since pure experience is fundamental to understanding the two psychological compositions found in the halves of *Night Moves*'s diptych structure: the first being the creation of a common encounter with the world that enables political action, the second being the alienation from such a common world and the sense of melancholic isolation that it entails. In each of these two circumstances, belief performs a different function, linking human to the world of pure experience in diametrically opposed manners, with two diametrically opposed effects on well-being.

Pure experience is "the instant field of the present at all times" (James 2003: 12), "the only one primal stuff or material in the world" (James 2003: 2). As "plain, unqualified existence," pure experience knows "no self-splitting [...] into consciousness and what the consciousness is 'of' " (James 2003: 12). It exists anterior and immanent to all senses of self, whether melancholic or otherwise, and all individuals hold a share of pure experience in common. Or, more accurately, pure experience holds all individuals in common. In the words of David Lapoujade, pure experience "is no one's state or rather it is not given for anyone" (Lapoujade 2000: 191-192).

The concept of pure experience makes it possible to further nuance how the modern cinema exposes the need to film and affirm belief in the world. As recounted above, the link between human and world is broken by the modern cinema's discovery of the force of time. In the philosophy of William James, the very fact of being an individual subject implies having already broken from the world of pure experience to attain subjective consciousness of an object. This splitting of the immediately present field

(2000: 190). In that very book, Deleuze and Guattari make clear that belief takes place on the plane of immanence. They write: "It may be that to believe in this world, in this life, has become our most difficult task, the task of a mode of existence to be discovered on our plane of immanence today" (Deleuze and Guattari 1994: 75).

of pure experience into subject and object confirms that such a break has taken place. Deleuze refines this idea when he figures that to be constituted as an individuated subject is to break from the world of pure experience, because such a subject is endowed with reflection, and reflection is possible only when the plane of immanence (a "pure consciousness") is split up into a subject with "consciousness of" an object (Deleuze 2001: 26). Pure experience cannot be an object of subjective consciousness, because it is the immediately given field of experience that precedes the emergence of a conscious subject and its habit of saying 'I' (Deleuze 1991: x).[8] Radical empiricism—the variety of empiricism advanced by William James—refuses to create a value distinction between the all-encompassing nature of pure experience and singular subjective facts of consciousness. A radical empiricist perspective aims to take account of the "full facts" of experience, which includes the reflective 'I' that has broken from the world of pure experience, as much as pure experience itself. James describes the importance of accounting for these full facts of experience as follows:

> That unshareable feeling which each one of us has of the pinch of his individual destiny as he privately feels it rolling out on fortune's wheel may be disparaged for its egotism, may be sneered at as unscientific, but it is the one thing that fills up the measure of our concrete actuality, and any would-be existent that should lack such a feeling, or its analogue, would be a piece of reality only half made up. (James 1936: 489-490)

Subjects are birthed on the plane of immanence, and break from it to become subjects *of* knowledge, consciousness, and experience. To be a subject is to be broken from pure experience, and a radically empirical account of any experience, melancholy included, must account for pure experience as much as the singular, "unshareable feeling" of the subjective break from it.

Two types of belief can link the subject back to the world of pure experience: a terminal belief and a non-terminal belief. The terminus is a common site where vectors of belief—or streams of consciousness—meet, before continuing along their respective trajectories, having shared this terminal experience "in common." To meet at a terminus is to transcend the isolating threshold of the constituted self, to arrive at "the point at which one state of mind passes into another" (James 1936: 132). An encounter of this sort

8 The importance of habit to the production of subjectivity opens Deleuze's study of Hume and human nature. "We are habits, nothing but habits—the habit of saying 'I'. Perhaps there is no more striking answer to the problem of the Self." (Deleuze 1991: x.)

inflects both mental streams along the lines of this belief that they now hold in common, momentarily warding off the isolation of melancholy's singular breaks from this common world of experience. A terminal belief thus brings the subject's stream of consciousness to a terminus where it meets with the beliefs guiding other individuated subjects, creating a common world of experience and the capacity for collective action.

Conversely, non-terminal belief leads the individuated subject's stream of consciousness to a solitary zone of the plane of immanence where no other streams of consciousness lead. It is this second, non-terminal variety of belief that digs the solitary depths of melancholic isolation. Melancholy can thus be thought of as analogous to what James calls a "non-substitutional" stream of consciousness, in that it does not meet up with any other inhabited streams of consciousness or belief (James 2003: 34-35). Two melancholics in the depths of despair do not necessarily recognize the pain in one another, nor do they understand the reasons for each other's suffering, since their experiences never meet, but burrow back into irreconcilable zones of the plane of immanence.

In "Immanence: A Life," an ode to William James and the last text that Deleuze wrote before his death, he appeals for a commons of experience, the very sort that could alter a political climate engendered by the proliferation of singular, non-terminal breaks from the plane of immanence productive of neoliberal individualism and melancholy's isolated depths. "We need a new conception of society in which what we have in common is our singularities and not our individualities," he writes, "where what is common is 'impersonal' and what is 'impersonal' is common" (Deleuze 2001: 14). The impersonal in common is the plane of immanence or the world of pure experience on which belief can be shared or lived alone. Equipped with the free indirect and its ability to produce a psychosocial image of transindividual psychology, Kelly Reichardt's *Night Moves* attunes to how the relational play of beliefs active in a given event compose subjectivity, connecting humans to the world they have in common, and that hold them in common, both melancholically and therapeutically.

Belief in Common

"The cinema must film, not the world, but belief in this world, our only link" (Deleuze 2007: 172). Kelly Reichardt takes this a step further and films not only belief in the world, but shared belief in the world—or more accurately, shared activist beliefs for a changed world. To do so, she makes recourse to the cinema of poetry and its deployment of free indirect perception. What this film style offers Reichardt, like the auteurs discussed in the previous two chapters, is the possibility of creating a film image, and a film world, that is immediately psychosocial. Perhaps this is one of the fundamental prerequisites for the modern cinema to film belief in the world, since the play of beliefs active in a given event is also a psychosocial phenomenon. To recap, the transindividual relation that links the psyche and socius to produce a psychosocial event is what Simondon and Deleuze respectively call "psychology" or "the brain." Belief fills a similar role in the work of James and in the Jamesian-inspired pages of *Cinema 2* and "Immanence: A Life," since belief's relationality not only connects the subject to the world, as if they were pre-existing entities, but composes a singular assemblage inclusive of subject and world, bringing the uniqueness of their relational iteration into existence. It is in the pragmatics—in "the how"—of belief's believing, connecting and producing, that the event's psychology or brain either moves into the clutches of melancholy or wards it off entirely. Free indirect perception is put to two distinct uses over the course of *Night Moves*, a film which differs dramatically from the first to the second half. In the first half, it is used to articulate the creation of a common world of belief, and in the second half, to articulate the singular melancholic breaks from this world once held in common.

A brief rundown of the plot will help to contextualize these aesthetic techniques. *Night Moves* tells the story of a group of eco-activists who undertake a dangerous direct action, and when things go wrong, their belief in the world, and relations to each other, quickly crumble, leaving a deep sense melancholic isolation. The film takes place in rural Oregon and focuses on Josh (Jesse Eisenberg), who lives on an organic farm co-operative and Dena (Dakota Fanning), who works at her mom's New Age spa. The context of their relationship isn't entirely clear from the beginning of the film. They seem a bit awkward around one another and run strange errands together, such as going for walks on top of a hydroelectric dam and buying a used boat in cash. Once they meet up with Harmon (Peter Sarsgaard), a hermit-type figure who lives in a sequestered trailer in the woods, it becomes apparent that they are intent on exploding the dam, a direct action so big that, as Josh says, "people are gonna start to think." These three activists are brought together by the radical aspirations that they have in common. They live their militancy together and relate to each other through their rare conviction in a project of this variety, simultaneously binding them together and cutting them off from the rest of society.

The halfway point of the film contains a scene where the three of them drive the boat to the base of the dam in the middle of the night, and Harmon, the ex-military explosions expert sets the bomb amidst high tension. They manage to canoe away in just enough time, load into their vehicles and escape, with the promise that they are never to speak to one another again, since doing so could make them susceptible to law enforcement surveillance. The next morning, Josh overhears the other workers at his farm discussing the news. They all speak negatively about the action, deeming it futile and fanatical, and go on to say that a man who had been camping overnight by the river has gone missing. The rest of the film then deals with the activists' traumatic reaction to realizing that their well-intentioned eco-activism has turned out to inadvertently cause the death of an innocent person.

Josh gets a call from Harmon—breaking their pact of silence—to say that Dena isn't doing too well. Upon receiving this call, a seed of doubt is planted in Josh's mind, and he is no longer sure that the secrecy of what they did together will be respected. He begins trailing Dena, speaking to her clandestinely, trying to calm her down and convince her of the righteousness of the action in spite of its unintended consequences. Any influence that he once had over her seems to be lost. She is so disturbed by the news of the camper's death that she is no longer sure that she can keep her promise of silence to the group. Dena's being unwell becomes the talk of the community, and Sean (Kai Lennox), the head of the organic farm, even confronts Josh to say that him and Dena are suspected of involvement in the dam explosion.

Having all but realized that the bond connecting them has dissipated due to fear, anxiety and guilt, Josh shows up uninvited at Dena's health spa one night as she is on her way out. A violent struggle erupts. He eventually finds her hiding in a sauna where he chokes her to death, quits town the next morning, and then calls Harmon wanting to meet up. Harmon, the more seasoned activist, offers him some final words of advice, to "get lost, get real lost, and stay lost. That's it." The film ends with Josh in a sporting goods store—the very epitome of unabashed consumerism that he detests—filling out an application for a job with the knowledge that he has killed a good friend and is banished to a life in hiding. The common world that was ushered into existence by the belief in activism that he, Dena and Harmon shared has eroded, leaving him alienated both from those with whom he believed, and a society based on hope that he has long since abandoned.

In the first half of the film, these activists who have lost hope, but who are spurred by belief, find one another, and act together, constituting a common world that doubles as a therapeutic barrier by warding off the alienating depths of melancholy to which they are especially susceptible, given that radical activism is their last refuge of commonality. There are three free indirect techniques that Reichardt deploys to aesthetically articulate how belief precipitates the creation of a common world in the first half of the film as the activists come together to explode the dam: obsessive framing, semi-subjective perspectives, and stylized lighting and image composition.

One important scene that illustrates Reichardt's obsessive framing takes place when the three activists drive to acquire the additional ammonium nitrate fertilizer needed to complete their homemade explosives. With fake IDs in hand and a strong desire to remain undercover—to keep the beliefs that bind them imperceptible to the outside world from which they have broken—they stop at a diner for breakfast on the way to the farm supplies store. They are shot together in three-shot as their mealtime conversation develops.[9] Then a diner employee who recognizes Harmon from prison passes by, and they share some back and forth banter before the he continues along his way. This discovery leaves Josh and Dena furious because they were under the impression that Harmon was not known in the area and that he didn't have any past criminal convictions. Luckily for them, the character who invades the shot—the share of the world that they hold in common—was unable to blow their cover and detect their true purpose for being there together.

A similar scene occurs later as they eat lunch by the bank of the river leading to the dam. While sitting around a picnic table, a friendly stranger approaches them and tries to make light conversation about the weather and the campgrounds. Now only moments away from embarking on the direct action together, they are even more wary of this stranger and manage to act aloof enough in his presence so as to subtly encourage him move along. During this interaction, the three protagonists are again shown in three-shot with one another, at first separate from the stranger, and then alongside him as he eventually manages to invade their private shot. Nevertheless, they keep him at enough of a distance that he never suspects what could really be binding them together.

Reichardt's emphasis on putting these three figures in the same shot as one another goes to some creative lengths. In addition to more orthodox three-shots such as the three of them in the front seat of the truck, there are other more inventive shots that stress the aesthetic importance of framing these people together. For example, when they drive into the camp grounds with a boat and explosives in tow, Josh and Dena ride in a separate vehicle than Harmon, so that they will each have escape vehicles and can drive their separate ways after they complete the direct action. Even sitting in different vehicles, Reichardt manages to frame them in a three shot through the car's

9 A "three-shot" is a film studies term that refers to three people being framed by the same shot. "The terms *one-*, *two-*, and *three-shots* are used to describe shots framing one, two, or three people—usually in medium close-ups or medium shots" (Hayward 2000: 328).

passenger windows. By consistently framing them together, and by marking the invasiveness of others who enter their shared three-shots, Reichardt underscores how shared belief is productive of a common world of experience.

This half of the film also includes a couple of "semi-subjective" shots that confuse any clear-cut distinction that it would be possible to make between wholly objective and subjective perspectives. As discussed in Chapter One, an ambiguity of this sort is one of the chief characteristics of the free indirect style. These "semi-subjective" shots could emanate from any one of the three characters, or some undefined place between them, thus undoing any definitive distinctions between their perspectival positions. In *Night Moves*, three of these semi-subjective shots offer a de-personalized gaze through a car window or windshield. These shots have the effect of linking the characters even more closely together, since it is impossible to distinguish between the way that each of them sees the world, since after all, a shared world has been co-created through the belief that they hold in common, and that first and foremost, holds them in common. Enabled by free indirect aesthetic construction, Reichardt makes it possible to show how each of their individual perspectives on the world is confounded by a shared impersonal gaze that corresponds to their group subjectivity—the zone they have carved out together on the plane of immanence—rather than any one of them in specific.

The third, and perhaps most significant, free indirect technique that Reichardt uses to articulate the creation of a common world through belief in the first half of the film is stylized lighting and image composition. Reichardt goes to great lengths to show the three activists in a similar light, which is consistent with her strategy of framing them in the same shots and offering up perspective shots that are "semi-subjective" and could emanate from any one of their points of view, or somewhere in between. The most significant example of this occurs in the lead-up to the explosion, as Josh, Dena and Harmon ride their canoe down towards the dam in a sequence of long, methodical takes. Each one of them is shot in succession, almost completely engulfed by the pitch-black of night that shrouds their journey in secrecy and anonymity. The stylization encompasses the harrowing psychology that binds them together in this moment where they each decide to put their lives on the line for a cause that they have mutually agreed upon. What these images render aesthetic is the quality of the pure experience that individuated subjects can hold in common when prompted by pre-personal and transindividual force of belief. Their voyage is saturated by a grave darkness, yet it is a darkness that wards off melancholy, because it belongs to the group's shared experiential plane. As harrowing as these moments in the film certainly are, they are co-created through belief that leads to a common terminus, and thus offers a touch of comfort to those who have put their lives on the line—together.

Melancholic Breaks

Belief creates a common link between Josh, Dena, Harmon and the world of pure experience, a link that potentializes collective acts of creation. But once belief begins to whither, the collective fractures, and they find themselves living in entirely incompatible worlds, so much so, that they can no longer understand or feel for one another the way that they could before. The second half of the film is the polar opposite of the first. Whereas the film opens with belief's creation of a common world of experience and action, a world that wards of melancholic hopelessness, the latter portion details the melancholic breaks that each of the three activists make from this world that they once held in common. The transmutation of a belief that commons into a belief that isolates begins the morning after the dam explosion, when upon hearing the news, it becomes apparent that an innocent bystander has been inadvertently killed. Josh, Dena and Harmon each start to digest the event differently and respond to its effects in incompatible ways. After making this unfortunate discovery, the only thing that they hold in common is the faith that they have lost in one another and in the activist project that once inspired them so deeply. By betraying the belief that they once shared, and the pure experience that it led to, the melancholy that they had once succeeded in warding off finds its way into each of their lives, and they start to feel like isolated individuals. Remarkably, this shift happens in spite of their attempts to connect and communicate with one another, in defiance of their pact of silence. Communicate as they may, it only reinforces their sense of alienation and desperation, because the communications are actually betrayals of the common world that once held them together.

Speaking of her earlier film *Old Joy*, Kelly Reichardt makes a comment that also echoes true for *Night Moves*: "What this threadbare narrative really underscores," she says, "is the unspoken impossibility of their reconnection" (Reichardt and Van Sant 2008: n.p.). After the activists each go their separate ways, the film's aesthetics dramatically shift to account for this impossibility. Reichardt still mobilizes the free indirect subjective techniques found in the first half, but the key difference is that instead of them being used to articulate an experience held in common, they begin to articulate the incommunicability, non-substitutionality, and radical singularity of melancholic experience. A close analysis of some key scenes from this second half of the film will illustrate how the common world of experience that these three activists shared is undone, and how melancholy comes to characterize their link to the world.

The second half of the film shifts the focus onto Josh, who in the first half of the film was always flanked by at least Dena and was hardly ever depicted alone. In this later part of the film his companions have disappeared in an attempt to disguise the reality of their relations. Josh makes a serious attempt at keeping up his normal routine and fly under the radar of anyone who could be suspicious. Much like the lead up to the dam explosion, this whole second part of the film is very mundane and revels in the quotidian. But whereas Josh used to have company, with whom he could at least be honest, and honestly share belief, even if they had to mask their shared reality from those around them, now his entire existence is a deceit, and the most important psychological fact of his life—that he has just blown up a dam—must remain hidden from those with whom he spends his days. Keeping secrets is alienating, brooding business and his alienation is aesthetically expressed through free indirect subjective shots.

Two scenes in particular stand out. In the first of these, Josh decides to confront Dena about her having broken their pact of silence by calling Harmon. Apparently she is distraught, and Josh intends to calm her down and convince her to honour their secrecy. In a scene unlike any other in the rest of the film, a scene that could go unnoticed for its proximity to standard continuity editing, Josh and Dena sit in the front seats of his truck, just like they had many times before. Yet this time the image composition is completely different. Whereas in the first half of the film, Josh and Dena were repeatedly shot through the truck's window in two-shots that depicted them both in crystal-clear focus, in this later scene, they are never captured in focus at the same time.

Josh expresses his frustrations, and Dena her guilt and worry, each one at a time, without ever coming to any sort of mutual understanding. The common terminus of belief and its corresponding experiential qualities have eroded, leaving two alienated subjects who can communicate and connect, but not share in any experiential commonality. They may both have become alienated and melancholic, but they cannot share the singularities of their respective melancholy; they may say that they understand one another, but the image says otherwise. Josh and Dena are in totally incommensurate streams of melancholic consciousness that undoubtedly mirror one another, but never intersect. Their reactions to the event that they brought into existence together, and that brought them into existence together, follow different trajectories of subjectification, leading them further and further

Image 6 *Night Moves*, Kelly Reichardt, 2013

away from the non-melancholic terminus of belief they previously shared. Their common world of experience has eroded, spawning two melancholic singularities doomed to indefinite isolation.

In the film's penultimate scene, Josh breaks into Dena's spa afterhours to confront her yet again, enraged that she has been reaching out to members of the small community about what happened. He presses up close to her and says, "I just think it's important that we know what we feel" acting as if everything is OK and he genuinely cares about her well-being, right before the truth of their feelings comes out and she attacks him with rain stick. The lighting and image composition reflect the subjective coordinates of Josh and Dena at this moment of aggression, in a manner completely inverse to the shots on the boat that once articulated their belief in a common world. In those shots previously mentioned, they are surrounded by darkness, their faces barely illuminated from the boat's interior. Each of the activists is lit from the same source, and they are surrounded by exactly the same darkness. In this spa scene, Josh and Dena's figures turn to blacked-out silhouettes on an orange-red background. Instead of emerging from the world together, they are cut out from it separately, imaged as what they are: melancholic breaks from the common world of experience.

The Truth of Melancholy

Based on this close analysis of *Night Moves*' aesthetics, we can say that Kelly Reichardt's free indirect mode of perception discovers another event-based symptom of melancholy: the presence of non-terminal belief that produces totally singular streams of incommensurate consciousness. Like Schanelec, Reichardt's use of the free indirect to discover an event-based symptom of melancholy raises both a philosophical and aesthetic problem about the truth-value of experience. For how can the truth of a singular experience that is non-terminal and that belongs to an incommensurate zone of the plane of immanence ever possibly be verified? And furthermore, how could the cinema ever possibly conduct such a verification? Acquiring complete knowledge of another's melancholy is an impossible task, since it would require complete knowledge of another, to the extent of actually being this other. It is also worth noting that given that melancholy lies in the plastics of the event's assemblage, in the primacy of the transindividual, that nobody can ever have complete knowledge of "their own" melancholy either. However, it would be erroneous, or at least a deviancy from a radically empirical ethos, if the truth of melancholic experience was cast aside as being a personal hallucination insufficiently linked to the world, since after all, the "full fact" of experience includes singular breaks from the common world of experience, even ones that are impenetrable, like those of the melancholic variety. Writing of other impervious singularities, like "ether waves and your anger," James pragmatically insists that while he cannot "ever know them directly, perceptually terminate in them" he can be led to "their very next effects" (2003: 38). The inability to verify the truth of the experience as such, due to its highly singular nature that renders its experiential quality inaccessible, does not prevent James, armed with the pragmatic method, from considering such singular breaks from pure experience as true. James posits that it is possible to consider the unconscious, ether waves, or mystic states to be true by virtue of the reality of their "very next effects" (James 1932: 506-507; James 2003: 38). The same can be said of melancholy, which James also saw as true, in so far as it "constitutes an essential moment in every complete religious evolution" (1932: 25). James may never have known the religious melancholy (acedia) of figures like Tolstoy or St. Theresa of Avila, but he would not hesitate to consider these experiences, and the supernatural explanations for their overcoming, as true, given that they produced real effects.

If the truth of melancholy is tied to it having real effects, effects that are observable and that can be held in common, even if the first-hand experience of it is not, then the cinema is apt to corroborate such effects. There are two types of effects that emanate from singular experience, each of which lead to distinct ontological assumptions about the nature of melancholy and its relationship to the image: residual effects and immediate effects. With regards to melancholy, the residual effects are most often expressed through faciality traits, bodily markers, or verbal relay. These visible symptoms can be considered as residual effects of a melancholic experience because they never actually cue the (medical) observer to either the experiential quality of melancholy or to the existential conditions that precipitate it. Not uncoincidentally, this type of effect, which predominates western art history's iconography of melancholy, also lends itself unobstructed to psychiatry's clinical gaze and its corresponding diagnostic models and therapeutic methods.

In spite of the limitations that prevent us from ever possessing another's share of pure experience, there is a radically empiricist manner of analyzing psychology that considers its immediate effects.[10] This type of effect is much more difficult to grasp, and requires an abolishment of "professional distance" and the psychiatric regime of visibility that it clings to, since it takes place at the juncture of the individuated subject's singular break from the plane of immanence, rather than it's report of this break, as mediated through facial and bodily signs. To decipher the quality of a melancholic break from the world of pure experience requires a completely different mode of perception, one that cannot wait for the individuated subject to be constituted and then attest to the experience that it has had. Such a radically empiricist mode of perception must perceive the manner of the break that constitutes the subject and its singular melancholic experience, in and of itself. If the sought after "really next effects" of melancholic experience are to be "full" effects, or at least more fully articulate the experiential truth from which they emanate, then an engagement with the existential quality of the production of subjectivity, and the way that such productions relationally move the events in which they are engendered is of the utmost urgency.

Hence why the cinema must believe in this world. To film the world is to film the residual effects of an experience; to film belief in this world is to film both its residual effects and its immediate ones; to film how an experience matters to the world in which it takes place. The cinema can most easily, and has most usually, adopted a mode of perception that lends itself to capturing residual effects. Facial and bodily movements lend themselves quite naturally

10 This approach which I expound here, and which is enacted by the films discussed in this project, is a variance on the pragmatic type of analysis encouraged by William James. For James, there are two interrelated ways of studying every psychological state: "First, the way of analysis: What does it consist in? What is its inner nature? Of what sort of mind-stuff is it composed? Second, the way of history: What are its conditions of production, and its connection with other facts?" (James 2005a: 59). Both of these lines of inquiry are absent from the psychiatric gaze which has little to no interest in the qualities or histories of the assemblages animating psychological states, but solely in their visible and quantifiable residual effects—symptoms that can be supressed through psychiatric treatment.

to the cinematographic conventions and semantic narrative codes to which the film image has most often been rendered subservient. For Bazin, an art such as this that limits itself to showing reality, instead of rendering it aesthetic, is coarse and unworthy of the title neorealism (Bazin 2009: 226). Conversely, to film belief in the world is to film the immediate effects of (melancholic) experience. Even if melancholic experience cannot be directly filmed due to its singular non-substitutionality and non-terminality, it can be immediately "indexed" by the relations between beliefs that engender an event and its mode of subjectivity production.

The truth-value of the cinematographic image has most often been discussed in terms of its indexicality; its penchant to attest, in the worlds of Roland Barthes, that "this has been" and to "make permanent the truth" (Barthes 1981: 79, 110). Indexicality has proven an especially important concept for theories of cinematic realism—and the truth of the film image—ever since Bazin proposed an existential link between the film image and reality.

In his widely cited book on Bazin entitled *Change Mummified*, Phil Rosen argues that Bazin's conception of cinema is inherently indexical. An illustrative passage reads as follows:

> Bazin insists on the pregivenness of the universe to the human. The indexicality of mechanically produced images makes it possible to experience that pregivenness in the realm of representation, through the temporal relation of the profilmic to the camera. For Bazin the photographic or cinematic image always provides the spectator with absolute brute knowledge that the objects visible in the frame *were at one time* in the spatial 'presence' of the camera that they appear from an irrefutable past existence. (Rosen 2001: 29)

This indexical reading of Bazin has its roots in Peter Wollen and his seminal work of political modernism *Signs and Meaning in the Cinema*, where he argues that Bazin sees the "indexical aspect of the cinema as its essence" (120). Expounding this "indexical Bazin," Wollen writes:

> It was the existential bond between fact and image, world and film, which counted for most in Bazin's aesthetic, rather than any quality of similitude or resemblance. Hence the possibility—even the necessity—of an art that could reveal spiritual states. There was for Bazin a double movement of impression, of moulding and imprinting: first, the interior spiritual suffering was stamped upon the exterior physiognomy; then the exterior physiognomy was stamped and printed upon the sensitive film. (Wollen 2013: 113)

Wollen's citation sums up perfectly the cinema's capacity to index the residual effects of experience. Spiritual states, like melancholy, are non-substitutional experiences that can only ever be known through their really next effects. The route to knowledge of these effects, according to Wollen and his indexical Bazin, is via the exterior physiognomy's indexation on the sensitive film emulsion, whose representation is meant to index an experience about which some knowledge can finally be produced. The exterior physiognomy is a residual effect of the experience that it indexes, and the indexical operation as it is conceived here is a communicational means of mediating that unexperienaceable experience, by transducing it into a sign that stands in for that singular experience's unrepresentable complexity. Here, at the crossroads of the experience and the film image-as-index, the cinema reaches an artistic limit, and must content itself with finding exterior signs to represent the unrepresentable. As a result, a certain "lack" is invested into the image. In an indexical schema, the image points to an experience that it attests to, that it indexes, without ever sharing in the experience.

This indexical approach has become the standard reading of Bazin.[11] Yet some important objections have been made to the appraisal of Bazin's ontology of the image through the semiotic framework of indexicality. The most recognizable opponent to this semiotic reading of Bazin is the early cinema scholar Tom Gunning. In his article, "What's the Point of an Index?, or Faking Photographs" he draws on Bazin and Barthes to argue that thinking the photograph in terms of indexicality brackets off its experiential qualities and limits its ability to do more than signify. Gunning writes: "Barthes told us that photography was not a copy of reality but rather its emanation. [...] He shares Bazin's belief that a photograph puts us in the presence of something, that it possesses an ontology rather than a semiotics" (Gunning 2004: 46). He goes on to address Wollen directly, whose "translation of the ontology of photography into a semiotics involved a canny appropriation and transformation of Bazin (who never used the term index, although his terms of comparison with photography—death masks, fingerprints, moulds—certainly correspond to Peirce' s examples of indices)" (Gunning 2004: 46). And finally, Gunning takes his stand:

> For Bazin, the photograph is not a sign of something, but a presence of something, or perhaps we could say a means for putting us into the presence of something, since clearly Bazin realizes that a photograph differs from its subject. But is the indexical relation to a referent enough

11 For examples of other indexical readings of Bazin, see Brigitte Peucker's *The Material Image* and Francesco Casetti's "Style as site of negotiation: the case of realism and neo-realism."

> to truly explain what Bazin describes as photography's 'irrational power to bear away our faith'? An indexical relation falls entirely into the rational realm. Likewise Barthes describes the power of photography as, "A magic, not an art." (Gunning 2004: 46)[12]

More than just an index, Bazin imagines that "photography plays a real part in natural creation, rather than substituting for it" (Bazin 2009: 9).

This is exactly the notion that Daniel Morgan builds on in his critique of the tendency to yoke theories of indexicality onto the writings of Bazin. In a *Critical Inquiry* article, he makes the astute observation that rather than positing the film image as an index of reality, Bazin uses a much more evocative phrase: "transfer of reality." For Bazin, "photography transfers reality from the object depicted to its reproduction" (8). This leads Morgan to conclude that "the rhetoric of transfer suggests a fundamental incompatibility of Bazin's position with the index argument" (2006: 449). Thus if it is at all appropriate to say that the film image is capable of indexing the immediate, "really next effects" of melancholic experience, or that Kelly Reichardt's cinema does exactly this, then "index" must take on a different meaning. In this broader and contraventional sense, in line with Peirce's original formulation of the concept[13], the "index" refers not to an absent reality or experience that the image is lacking, but to a portion of the plane of immanence whose effects are registered, felt and "transferred" by the image that is adjacent to it. The cinema's fidelity has nothing to do with reproducing the world, or indexing the profilmic as it already is,[14] but with

12 Also see Gunning's "Moving Away from the Index" in *differences: Journal of Feminist Cultural Studies*. In this article Gunning builds on his critique of semiological approaches to film. "The index," he writes, "may not be the best way, and certainly should not be the only way, to approach the issue of cinematic realism" (Gunning 2007: 31).

13 It is worth noting that the Bazinian definition parallels how C.S Peirce defines the index, as not needing a mediator or interpreter. Peirce writes: "An Index is a sign which refers to the object that it denotes *by virtue of it being really affected* by that Object" (Peirce 1974: 143, my emphsasis). Wollen, Rosen and the standardized interpretation of the index, tends to miss this earlier emphasis found in Peirce's original writings on the topic. See Peirce's essay, "Division of Signs."

14 Étienne Souriau offers the founding definition of the profilmic: "The opposite of the *afilmic*: everything that really exists in the world (ie. The flesh and blood actor; the studio's art design, etc.), but which is specifically destined for cinematographic use; notably, everything found in front of the camera and impressed onto the films strip" (Souriau 1953: 8). The issue with this sort of conceptualization of the relationship between image and reality is that it mitigates the relational dynamic of the act of filming. The profilmic connotes a stable world of actuality that wholly lends itself to the recording apparatus. On the other hand, the plane of immanence is pure virtuality. Kelly Reichardt shows that the cinema of poetry is capable of composing with

inventing an aesthetic that will allow an engagement with the world of pure experience, on the basis of its (psychosocial) reality, even in the case of singular experiences—such as the melancholic ones—that can only ever be known through their really next transferred effects.

For James, "thoughts are concrete and made of the same stuff as things are," that "stuff" being pure experience (2003: 20). The same can be said of cinematic images. What allows for film images to point to melancholic experience, to "index" it (in the Bazinian and Peircian sense), to be true to it, is precisely this experiential constitution that they share. The film image points as an index by virtue of its own stylistics being truly informed by a melancholic experience existing on the same plane of immanence. It is a sign of experience, made up of experience.

The free indirect image of melancholy aesthetics takes its psychosocial form by caring for how a melancholic singularity—a non-terminal stream of consciousness burrowed by belief into an incommensurate zone of the plane of immanence—creates an immediate next effect on the plane of immanence that it shares with the image. Even if the singularity of melancholic experience may be non-terminal, its non-terminality impacts the plane of immanence on which the image does its aesthetic, compositional work. It takes a free indirect mode of perception to register this immediate effect of melancholy experience taking place on the same plane of immanence as the image because the singularity of the melancholic experience is engendered by the transindividual vectors of belief active in a given event. The cinema may not ever be able to film the melancholic experience proper, in its singularity, but it can free indirectly film this play of beliefs constituting a world in which such an experience is a fact that needs to be considered—and the image can be true to that transindividual event of beliefs-in-relation.

In rare moments such as these when a filmmaker wholeheartedly adopts a free indirect mode of perception and abandons the condemned endeavour of representing the unrepresentable, of representing the singularity of melancholic experience through its residual signifiers, the film image becomes true, in the same way that ideas do in radical empiricism. For James, "ideas, (which themselves are but parts of our experience) become true just in so far as they help us get into satisfactory relations with other parts of our experience" (James 2005c: 138). The truth of the melancholic image is the satisfactory relationship that it has to melancholic experience, and its satisfactory relationship is precisely the manner in which it uses

these virtual forces, as imperceptible, or *afilmic,* as they may be, and making them felt through the stylistic and temporal composition of the image, attesting to their truth.

the free indirect to perceive the play of beliefs that give rise to melancholic isolation—the dynamics of this play being none other then melancholy's immediately "indexed" effects and event-based symptoms. Having used free indirect perception to enter into such a satisfactory relationship to melancholic experience, even though the singularity of melancholic experience cannot be known directly, Kelly Reichardt is able to truly perceive a vital symptom of melancholy: non-terminal belief that breaks from a common world of experience, once again making people feel like the individuals they are only in abstraction, isolated from the event of subjectivity production in which they are actually and virtually, totally imbricated.

Numerous political consequences stem from the aesthetic discoveries of the past two chapters, wherein artistic truths about melancholy squarely challenge the monopolistic truths produced by the psychiatric apparatus of normalization. If melancholic symptoms no longer lie solely on the individual, but in the world's psychosocial transindividuality, then, at least according to a radical and speculative etiology-to-come, the same can be said for melancholy itself. Owing to these two artist-physicians, Angela Schanelec and Kelly Reichardt, such an etiology-to-come has two lines of inquiry upon which to advance. Either it can investigate the potential within an event's neuroplasticity, or assess the qualitative play of beliefs active in a given event. That task will need to be taken up at each singular juncture in defiance of a will towards standardized and consensual etiology, symptomatology and therapy. In both cases, this etiological inquiry, artistic symptomatology, and activist therapy will be inseparable from an analysis of the operations of power, and power's conditioning of the event of subjectivity production.

If power has a hand in the production of melancholic subjectivity, as these artist-physicians indeed say that it does, then there is no reason for activists to wait for a comprehensive etiology to be delineated before beginning to act on the problem, before beginning to experimentally recompose subjectivity in search of therapeutic effects. If there is one strategy that therapeutic activism must poach from psychiatry's therapeutic toolbox, it is its trial and error approach. Except instead of experimenting with psychotropics whose efficacy (or lack thereof) can only be found in the trial, the challenge facing therapeutic activism is to conduct radically empirical research into the recomposition of subjectivity, until, with enough experimentation, mixtures of relations that tend towards well-being are discovered. Such a process would be nothing less than a well-becoming—a collectively animated well-being whose therapeutic and political value lies in *the how* of its making. The following two chapters looks at films that begin to imagine the contours of what a therapeutic activism to come may look like, and may have to deal with, to welcome healing right where the profound hurting takes place: in the midst of the event of subjectivity production conditioned by power.

Bibliography

Barthes, Roland. *Camera Lucida: Reflections on Photography*. Trans. Richard Howard. New York: Hill and Wang, 1981.

Brody, Richard. "About 'Neo-Neo Realism'." *The New Yorker*. 19 March 2009. Online. http://www.newyorker.com/culture/richard-brody/about-neo-neo-realism

Casetti, Franceso. "Style as Site of Negotiation: The Case of Realism and Neo-Realism." *Francescocasetti.com*. Online. 23 April 2005. https://francescocasetti.files.wordpress.com/2011/03/style-as-site-of-negotiation.pdf

Deleuze, Gilles. *Cinema 2: The Time-Image*. Trans. Hugh Tomlinson and Robert Galeta. Minneapolis: University of Minnesota Press, 2007.

Deleuze, Gilles. "Control and Becoming." *Negotiations: 1972-1990*. New York and Chichester, West Sussex: Columbia University Press, 1995. 169-176.

Deleuze, Gilles. *Empiricism and Subjectivity: An Essay on Hume's Theory of Human Nature*. Trans. Constantin V. Boundas. New York: Columbia University Press, 1991.

Deleuze, Gilles. *Pure Immanence: Essays in A Life*. Trans. Anne Boyman. New York: Zone Books, 2001.

Deleuze, Gilles and Félix Guattari. *What is Philosophy?* New York: Columbia University Press, 1994.

Fisher, Mark. *Capitalist Realism: Is There No Alternative?* Winchester, UK and Washington, USA: o Books, 2009.

Gunning, Tom. "Moving Away from the Index: Cinema and the Impression of Reality." *Differences: A Journal of Feminist Cultural Studies* 18.1 (2007): 29-52.

Gunning, Tom. "What's the Point of an Index?, or Faking Photographs." NORDICOM Review 1-2 (2004): 39-49.

Hayward, Susan. *Cinema Studies: The Key Concepts, Second Edition*. London and New York: Routledge, 2000.

James, William. *Essays in Radical Empiricism*. Mineola, New York: Dover Publications, 2003.

James, William. "The Psychology of Belief." *James and Dewey on Belief and Experience*. Eds. John M. Capps and Donald Capps. Urbana and Chicago. University of Illinois Press, 2005a. 59-77.

James, William. *The Varieties of Religious Experience*. New York: The Modern Library, 1936.

James, William. "The Will to Believe." *James and Dewey on Belief and Experience.* Eds. John M. Capps and Donald Capps. Urbana and Chicago. University of Illinois Press, 2005b. 95-110.

James, William. "What Pragmatism Means." *James and Dewey on Belief and Experience.* Eds. John M. Capps and Donald Capps. Urbana and Chicago. University of Illinois Press, 2005c. 133-143.

Lapoujade, David. "From Transcendental Empiricism to Worker Nomadism: William James." *Pli* 9 (2000): 190-199. Trans. Alberto Toscano.

Manning, Erin. *The Minor Gesture.* Durham and London: Duke University Press, 2016.

Massumi, Brian. *Semblance and Event: Activist Philosophy and the Occurrent Arts.* Cambridge, Massachusetts and London, England: The MIT Press, 2011.

Peirce, Charles Sanders. "Division of Signs." *Collected Papers of Charles Sanders Peirce. Volume 2. Book 2.* Eds. Charles Hartshorne and Paul Weiss. Cambridge, Massachussets: Harvard University Press, 1974. 134-155.

Peucker, Brigitte. *The Material Image: Art and the Real in Film.* Stanford, California: Stanford University Press, 2007.

Plan C. "We Are All Very Anxious." *Plan C.* Online. www.weareplanc.org

Reichardt, Kelly and Gus Van Sant. "Kelly Reichardt by Gus Van Sant – Artists in Conversation." *Bomb* (Fall 2008). http://bombmagazine.org/article/3182/kelly-reichardt

Rosen, Philip. *Change Mummified: Cinema, Historicity, Theory.* Minneapolis and London: University of Minnesota Press, 2001.

Scott, A.O. "A.O. Scott Responds to New Yorker Blog on the Value and Definition of Neorealism." *Carpetbagger: The Hollywood Blog of The New York Times.* 29 March 2009a. http://carpetbagger.blogs.nytimes.com/2009/03/23/ao-scott-responds-to-a-new-yorker-blogger-about-the-value-and-definition-of-neo-realism/?_r=0

Scott, A.O. "Neo-Neo Realism: American Directors Make Clear-Eyed Movies for Hard Times." *The New York Times.* 22 March 2009b. MM38.

Solomon, Andrew. *The Noonday Demon: An Atlas of Depression.* New York: Scribner, 2001.

Souriau, Étienne. *L'univers filmique.* Paris: Flammarion, 1953.

Wollen, Peter. *Signs and Meaning in the Cinema. Fifth Edition.* London: Palgrave Macmillan and British Film Institute, 2013.

Zournazi, Mary. *Hope: New Philosophies for Change.* New York: Routledge, 2003.

4 Ecosophy and Peace

Abstract

Chapter Four reads Apichatpong Weerasethakul's film *Uncle Boonmee Who Can Recall His Past Lives* through Félix Guattari's schizoanalytic cartographies to complexify how therapeutic activism can recompose events of subjectivity production. Guattari's cartographies offer working models for exploring how the relational movements of an event can give life to novel compositions of subjectivity through an encounter with alterity. They consist of four quadrants, or "ontological functors" which this chapter maps onto the cinematic image through a close analysis of select scenes from *Uncle Boonmee*. By connecting the schizoanalytic cartographies to Apichatpong Weerasethakul's film work, this chapter shows how they both advance a shared ethico-political sensibility that is encapsulated by Guattari's work on ecosophy—a manner of thinking the production of subjectivity in tandem with the socius and the environment.

Keywords: Apichatpong Weerasethakul, ecosophy, schizoanalysis, Thai cinema

"We watch films instinctively,
as therapy for mental or emotional pain"
–Apichatpong Weerasethakul[1]

Ecosophy as a Call for Peace

The fantastically alterious population of Apichatpong's film worlds—the mystical creatures, benevolent ghosts and talking animals who repeatedly appear and disappear in their travelling of time—offer an oblique access point into Thailand's war-torn history, especially the American-backed

1 Quoted in Quandt p. 114.

Szymanski, A., *Cinemas of Therapeutic Activism: Depression and the Politics of Existence*. Taylor & Francis Group, 2020
DOI: 10.5117/9789463723121_CH04

military occupation and communist purging of Isaan province that took place from the 1960s through to the 1980s. As a child, Apichatpong became intimately familiar with the region and its history after his parents relocated their medical practices to the province out of solidarity with its leftist organizing. He witnessed that amidst the violence of the occupation, villagers threatened by the military fled their homes and hid in the jungle.[2] Many of them never returned. *Uncle Boonmee Who Can Recall His Past Lives* is set in Isaan,[3] and is premised on the affective-historical fact that the region's purging is still felt by the widows and descendants of the disappeared communists, despite the reigning royalist regime's attempts to silence and censor this history in the name of national unity.[4]

Isaan is thus a site of conflicted signification in Thai culture. As a principally rural and agricultural province it lends itself to signifying as "rural utopia" and "cornerstone of Thai heritage," two ideological discourses taken up by forces as opposed as left-wing intellectuals and royalist-nationalists (Boehler 2011: 293). In defiance of these national heritage discourses, the rural space of the Isaan jungle simultaneously signifies as anti-nation[5] because of the region's historical association with communist resistance (which itself is tied to various ethnic minorities in Thailand such as the Chinese and Laotians).[6] *Uncle Boonmee* does more than signify on one side of this

2 For an autobiographical account of Apichatpong's intimate relationship to the occupation and more anecdotes about the role that the jungle plays in Apichatpong's engagement with the Thai political unconscious, see "A Memory of Nabua. A Note on the *Primitive* Project" in Weerasethakul (2009a: 192-206).

3 Isaan is still today one of the most economically disadvantaged regions of Thailand, making it a bastion of red shirt sympathies with an antagonistic relationship to yellow shirt urbanites. In 2005–2006 the Thai People's Alliance for Democracy or colloquially, the Yellow Shirts, organized mass protests against former Prime Minister Thaksin Shinawatra resulting in a coup d'état. The pro- and anti-Thaksin tensions continue to dominate the Thai political landscape with a subsequent political crisis in 2008 and yet another coup d'état which deposed Thaksin's younger sister and business magnate Yingluck Shinawatra in 2014.

4 Censorship is an active challenge to politicized filmmaking in Thailand, and Apichatpong Weerasethakul is one of the nation's most prominent voices of opposition to the censorship legislation in place. The Motion Pictures and Video Act B.E. 2551 (2008) modified the 1930 Film Act and implemented a new rating system, yet it still allows for the state to ban films from being shown in the Kingdom if they are deemed by the National Film and Video Committee (which includes the nation's chief of police) to "undermine social order or moral decency, or that might have an impact on the security and pride of the nation" (Rithdee 2007). For Apichatpong's critique of the (then proposed) legislation, see Weerasethakul (2009b).

5 Philip Rosen (1996) sets up the nation/anti-nation dialectic in order to emphasize how there exists an anti-national component that always troubles national cinemas.

6 See Casella (1970) for a historical account of how communist insurgency in Thailand is tied to the political activities of Chinese and Vietnamese minorities based in Khon Kaen (the city

ideological conflict between nation and anti-nation, geopolitical centre and margin, royalist and communist. In defiance of censorship threats and distribution difficulties in Thailand, Apichatpong's cinema endeavours to bring back the disappeared peoples who were driven into the jungle and lost to military aggression and to make reverberate the ethos that the government tried to extinguish when it disappeared the people of Isaan. From the heart of the jungle—a blot on the Thai political unconscious—*Uncle Boonmee* recomposes the thresholds of the three ecologies, and in doing so, brings repressed cultural memories out of obscurity to bear on a society that has had great difficulty acknowledging the willed omissions of its history, including the peoples and values that have been lost.

The psyche, the socius and the environment together compose what Félix Guattari calls "the three ecologies." The practice of ethically-politically thinking the pragmatics of their co-composition is called "ecosophy," and its chief problematic "is that of the production of human existence itself in new historic contexts" (Guattari 2008: 24). It is possible to read Guattari's late works on ecosophy as a call for "peace," at least in the sense that A.N. Whitehead gives to the word. As process theologist Mary Elizabeth Mullino Moore points out, Whiteheadian peace "is not the absence of war and violence, but the presence of other relationships ([in Whitehead's words,] 'a broadening of feeling') with the wider world" (Mullino Moore 2006: 205). Finding more heteropoetic ways of living with the "other" in "other relationships" is central to the ethico-political task of ecosophy, and its therapeutic investment in the production of subjectivity.

The Three Ecologies concludes with an appeal for a revitalized relationship to alterity, "new social and aesthetic practices, new practices of the Self in relation to the other, to the foreign, the strange [...] new solidarities, a new gentleness. [...] Individuals must become both more united and increasingly different" (Guattari 2008: 45, 51). With a similar concern for the value of alterity, Isabelle Stengers builds on Guattari's ecosophy to define "peace as the ecological production of actual togetherness where 'ecological' means the aim is not toward a unity beyond differences, which would reduce those differences through a goodwill reference to abstract principles of togetherness, but toward the creation of concrete, interlocked, asymmetrical, and always partial graspings" (Stengers 2002: 248-249). To compose peace is to

where Apichatpong would later grow up). Alpern (1975) also outlines the ethnic and linguistic makeup of the northeast and its importance to the Communist Party of Thailand's guerrilla strategies in the 1950s–60s. Thomas (1986) traces the rise and decline of Communist Party organization in Thailand from the 1960s through to the 1980s.

compose togetherness-in-difference, to assemble a collective that holds, not in spite, but because of its differences in a way that broadens the affective range of collective experience.

Encounters with alterity are opportunities for surpassing established subject positions. The adventurous character of peace—its broadening of feeling—comes about through this encounter with alterity, where self and other cease to be what they were by bringing a novel event of relation into existence. Whitehead writes:

> Peace is a broadening of feeling due to the emergence of some deep metaphysical insight, unverbalized and yet momentous in its coordination of values. Its first removal is the stress of acquisitive feeling arising from the soul's preoccupation with itself. Peace carries with it a surpassing of personality. […] Peace is the removal of inhibition and not its introduction. It results in a wider sweep of conscious interest. It enlarges the field of attention. Thus Peace is self-control at its widest, at the width where the 'self' has been lost, and interest has been transferred to coordinations wider than personality. […] Peace is the barrier against narrowness. (Whitehead 1967: 285)

By broadening feeling to encompass the play of differences that engender an ecology, peace re-coordinates the values governing the production of subjectivity, resulting in a jouissance of collective resubjectification that recasts the world's quantum of potential for cohabitation.

Two scenes in *Uncle Boonmee* are particularly illustrative of how Apichatpong uses ecosophic aesthetics to visualize the processual emergence of such a therapeutic peace. The first alters its range of perceptibility—and feeling—to visualize various degrees of alterity under one ecologically sensitive image. It clears the way for one of the film's concluding scenes, which enacts peace's overcoming of reified personality through the aesthetic creation of an event that shocks the coordinates of selfhood; coordinates that had started to loosen as soon as this alterious collective from the first scene came into existence. Apichatpong's aesthetic composition with the imperceptible makes return a repressed ethico-political force that reconditions the ontological functors immanent to the three ecologies through what could be called an act of making peace.[7]

7 I use the term "repressed" here because it best articulates the psychic and social character of the targeted militarized purging seen in Isaan province. In Deleuze and Guattari's chapter "Social Respression and Psychic Repression" in *Anti-Oedipus* (1983) they detail how psychic

Encountering Alterity, Broadening Feeling

The first exemplary scene depicts the film's protagonist, Uncle Boonmee (Thanapat Saisaymar), an ill plantation owner, his sister-in-law Jen (Jenjira Pongpas), and his nephew Tong (Sakda Kaewbuadee) calmly eating dinner inside of a windowless veranda. Then, out of nowhere, a ghost materializes. It turns out to be Huay (Natthakarn Aphaiwonk), Boonmee's deceased wife. Overcoming their initial surprise, the three characters speak with her about Boonmee's illness and impending death, until they are joined by an even more surprising guest. This time it's (what the subtitles refer to as) a "monkey-ghost" with bright red eyes, covered head-to-toe in thick black hair. The monkey-ghost claims to be Boonsong (Geerasak Kulhong), Boonmee and Huay's long-lost son who went missing after taking a trip into the jungle many years ago.

This scene, like the entire film, is entirely devoid of point of view shots. In their absence, the various depersonalized forces active within the ecology of the film world come to guide the logic of the relationship between shots, constituting an ecosophic découpage (and corresponding editing structure).[8]

repression and social repression reproduce and reinforce one another, in order to prevent desire's revolutionary force from disrupting established social structures. This psychosocial conception of repression posits that both desiring production and repression are inherently collective acts which condition the life of an ecology and thus overrun the limits of Freud's individualized subject who possess a personalized unconscious of repressed desires. Thus my use of the term repression should not be confused with repression as used in the more limited Freudian sense, wherein repression is "an operation whereby the subject attempts to repel, or to confine to the unconscious, representations (thoughts, images, memories) which are bound to an instinct. Repression occurs when to satisfy an instinct—though likely to be pleasurable in itself—would incur the risk of provoking unpleasure because of other requirements" (Laplanche and Pontalis 1988: 390).

8 I use the term "découpage" here mostly in the Bazinian spirit of the term that Timothy Barnard evokes in his updated translation of *What is Cinema?* For Barnard's Bazin, découpage is "editing's corollary at the mise-en-scène stage of production" and a way of "organizing the profilmic" (2009: 265, 279). Bazin has also referred to découpage as "composition and camera movement" (2009: 264) and as "the aesthetic of the relationship between shots" (as they are conceived, Barnard tells us, not as they are edited) (2009: 264). Elsewhere, Noël Burch (1981: 4) has described découpage as the "underlying structure of the finished film", which Barnard argues should in fact be called "formal treatment" (2009: 264). In spite of Burch's apparent blindness to the fact that the process of découpage starts longs before the film is finished and can be used to discuss creative aspects of film production, Burch's notion of "underlying structure" best encapsulates how découpage can be seen and felt in a film. In the following analysis my use of the term then borrows from both Burch and Barnard as I use the term to speak simultaneously of the film's underlying formal structure (of which editing certainly plays a part in determining), its shot composition, as well as the aesthetic relationship between shots as they are conceived and then

There is action to propel the scene's formal organization, yet this action is as driven by memories, ghosts, far-off sounds and animals as it is by any human-centered drama. The logic of Apichatpong's cut is irrational from the point of view of the human subject and can only be accounted for through a consideration of the unknown and the unseen that are made felt in the broader ecology. The scene's découpage spatially situates the different characters within their broader environment and temporally situates them with regards to their past transformations. It opens with a long shot of a veranda, as seen from the surrounding jungle. The interior space marks the only source of light amidst the long shot of the dark rural area. The characters' voices are heard in the distance. Following a cut to inside the veranda, the cinematography squarely lines up within its box-shaped architectural form. The camera moves in closer to compose medium shots of the three characters sitting at a table. Then the film mounts a dark landscape shot with the veranda now completely out of frame, decentered in an unknown direction. The sound of an approaching storm rumbles across the soundtrack before the film cuts to an adjacent shot of bushes swaying and rustling. "What's that sound?" one of the characters asks, before a cut back inside, to the original medium shot of the table. The subsequent few shots show Boonsong's entrance. On the axis of spatiality, the cutaway shots of the mountain, bushes, and neon bug-zappers break from human-centered schemas of scopic organization that coordinate the ecology according to an anthropocentric hierarchy of value. The localized, character-driven action is fragmented and repositioned by the active presence of the adjacent environment just outside the veranda.

The scene also intensively channels Boonsong's mental history, his recollection of the events that have brought him to where he is today and made him what he has become. When he recounts the story of his past transformations, the camera takes on a new fluidity, which is abruptly juxtaposed with the scene's darkness and rigidity. Through a découpage equally sensitive to material and mental intensity, the past is made an ecological force. The film sees beyond the actuality of any given plane of temporality and instead renders visible their mutual co-composition of the film world. The present is coloured with a splash of pastness, as

edited in line with this guiding directorial vision. I opt to analyze the film's "découpage" rather than solely its "editing" because "découpage" holds onto the importance of shot composition (which is inextricable from how a film like this is structured and later edited) and also because it recognizes that the film's underlying structure is given birth in the filmmaker's mind before being shot, and that the editing of the film is then carried out in line with this original vision.

Boonsong's recollection interjects into the dinner table gathering and its environmental surround. In beginning to recount his story, Boonsong says, "There are many beings outside right now [...] spirits and hungry animals, like me." As a sensitive character in an equally sensitive film ecology, he can feel them, even if he can't see them. Boonsong's story recalls how he transformed from an ordinary human photographer to a red-eyed monkey-ghost after he became obsessed with finding the strange creature that had once appeared in the background of one of his landscape photographs. The images of the past that accompany Boonsong's recollection appear as a shared collective heritage. There are no clichéd wipes or dissolves, only an abrupt cut from a shot behind the back of Jen's head to Boonsong's human form inside of a dark room for photography development. The cut is prompted by his narration of the story, words that all of the characters hear. These images are not psychologized, residing inside of Boonsong's head. These images, as much as they make up Boonsong's experience and memory, are exteriorized and socialized—made a concrete part of the shared ecology (to the extent that they can even be affected by others in the scene). At one point in the recollection, Jen says "excuse me" and gets up from the table to go sit on a nearby bench. The recollection immediately stops and cuts back to the present. All of the characters at the table have access to the recollection and the ability to stop it, because the recollection doesn't belong solely to Boonsong, entrenched in an inaccessible past. It belongs to their shared ecology. Memories affect others, and in Apichatpong's ecosophical aesthetics, others can affect memories.

The ecosophic logic of the découpage described above diverges from *découpage en plan américain* (also called classical découpage), the logic of the relationship between shots that governs most classical Hollywood cinema.[9] Under the classical system, character-driven shot sequences advance a narrative that reproduces visual codes predicated on stock character behaviour, gaze, and movement. This shooting style is most often contrasted with *découpage en profondeur* (shooting in depth). In découpage en profondeur each plane of depth within the shot is in equally sharp focus and part of what excited André Bazin about this artistic development was its ability to "embrace the totality of the event" (Bazin 1997: 103, translation modified).

9 *Découpage en plan américain* refers to the logic of shot organization at work in classical Hollywood studio era productions. See the chapter on découpage in David Bordwell's *History of Film Style* (1997) for a discussion of this term (which contrasts quite sharply with Timothy Barnard's later usage of the term découpage in his footnotes to the translation of *What is Cinema?*).

In the oft-cited Wellesian vein of découpage en profondeur, background planes of action complexify and enrich the story and allow for an expanded number of associations between elements in a single shot to be drawn by the spectator, all without recourse to montage. *Uncle Boonmee* is exemplary of découpage en profondeur, but with a key exception: it has no background in or out of focus. It has an "outside", a blacked-out zone of metamorphosis[10] without concrete form that puts the foreground of character drama into contact with the indetermination of pure opacity.[11] Ghosts (who used to be human) emerge from this zone of opacity where the jungle lies, and they come out into the light. They are made visible and their memories are depersonalized and made equally accessible to all, provoking a shift in the scene's ontological consistency.

Guattari's *Schizoanalytic Cartographies* advances the theory that each assemblage of enunciation, or event, is composed of four ontological functors that together give the assemblage its ontological consistency. These functors include existential Territories (T), Fluxes of materiality (F), machinic Phyla of diagrammatic organization (Θ) and incorporeal Universes of value (U). In a passage from *Guattari's Diagrammatic Thought* worth quoting at length, Janell Watson provides a useful summary of the functors that undergird the myriad cartographies of Guattari's schizoanalytic thought experiments:

> *Fluxes* include physical matter and physical signals; these are subject to the coordinates of energetic quanta, space, and time. The abstract machinic *Phyla* comprise evolution; Guattari's deterritorializing abstract machines; and blueprints, plans, diagrams, rules and regulation (in the cybernetic sense of control mechanisms). Existential *Territories* include subjective identity, the sense of self, and existential 'apprehension.' The incorporeal *Universes* of reference are made up of values, nondiscursive references, and virtual possibility; these 'escape the energetic, legal, evolutionary, and existential coordinates of the three preceding domains.' (Watson 2009: 99)

Cinematographic images, like any other event of perception, are assemblages of enunciation produced through the co-composition of each of the four

10 For Deleuze, the outside is "always an opening onto a future [where] nothing ends, since nothing has begun, but everything is transformed" (Deleuze 1988: 89).

11 While the opacity of the outside may not be a background, it nevertheless "re-introduces ambiguity into the structure of the image," which for Bazin is one of the defining traits of *découpage en profondeur* (1997: 101).

ontological functors. Firstly, images have a material basis in the Fluxes: signifying and asignifying visual and aural material made up of colours, bodies, movements, landscapes, and text. These cinematic Fluxes function in the realm of sensuous perceptibility. The machinic Phyla can be read as the set of organizing principles at work in an image. Depending on the image, there could be many of these operating at once, in sync or in opposition to one another. Organizing principles can refer to generic and industrial standards, national cinema traditions, and intertextual references, in addition to the social norms and conventions that may be relayed through a film's dissemination. Both Fluxes and Phyla lie on the side of the actual. Incorporeal Universes and existential Territories contribute to the image virtually. The Territories inform how characters within the filmic world are positioned, often through the granting or denying of scopic agency via point-of-view shots. Finally, Universes of value inflect the image's horizon of references and the coordination of value, giving sense to character subjectivities (T), image intensities (F), and the governing structures of the film (Θ). Together, the four ontological functors co-compose the filmic reality.[12]

For the sake of clarity, the ontological functors have been described separately, but an assemblage of enunciation is dynamically composed out of the reality of the relation immanent to its functioning. In Guattari's own words: "They will only be able to sustain their own configurations through the relations that they entertain with each other; they will be required to change state and status as a function of their overall Assemblage" (Guattari 2013: 27). In order live up to its name, a functor must indeed function—it must move. Starting from a movement in any one of these quadrants, an entire ecology can be reworked (for an ecology is fundamentally an assemblage of enunciation). Or rather, an entire ecology can't help but be

12 Reality is here understood in a different sense than it often acquires within film studies discussions of realism. In these discussions, what scholars who use the term reality really mean, is a more specialized notion of the term that could be called "profilmic reality". Profilmic reality is a term that comes from the work of Étienne Souriau and refers to the world that exists before the camera, which the camera then records (see Souriau's *L'Univers filmique* (1953; 8). When I use the term reality here, I am speaking of an entirely different relationship between image and reality. What interests me is not how the camera adheres to a profilmic reality, or even how the camera is productive of reality (which studies of direct cinema documentaries have so frequently pointed out), but that the reality of the image is informed by ontological functors. The Fluxes of the image are really the only domain that exists in a reciprocal relationship with the profilmic reality. Values, Phlya, and the existential Territories of the self remain sensuously imperceptible, yet all still go into producing the reality of the image—what it really contains, what it really expresses, what it really does, and what effects it may really produce in the world.

reworked by one of the functors' very functioning, precisely because the functioning of a functor is simultaneously a relational movement between the four.[13]

Uncle Boonmee's dinner table scene offers an idiosyncratic take on depth of field (nourished by the opacity of the outside) to invite consideration of its ontological depth. From this perspective, whole domains of desire imperceptible on the surface of the image are if not "brought to light" and rendered sensuously perceptible then at least brought nonsensuously to thought, in their opacity. Each of the four ontological functors is active in the cinematographic image, but only the Fluxes are sensuously perceptible. The domain of Fluxes is both actual and real, whereas the machinic Phyla, incorporeal Universes of value and existential Territories are all inflected by either the nonsensuous realms of the possible or the virtual.[14] The aesthetic strategy of this scene makes the ontological depth of Apichatpong's film world felt, without needing to visually represent all that is virtually active yet out of sight.[15] The spontaneous arrival of alterity is certainly registered by the Fluxes, as the image alters its range of perceptibility in order to accommodate the bodies that emerge from the darkness of the jungle. Huay's translucent ghost body is registered right next to Boonsong who is covered in pitch-black fur. This feat in découpage completely alters the semiotic arrangement (F) of the image in a manner that allows for diverse forms of life and modes of existence (ghosts, animals, disappeared peoples) to be convoked by the very same image. If this actual semiotic arrangement is to be thought of as an index, it is an index of the virtual movements of the four ontological functors in the process of recomposition, and not an index of a pre-existing reality (the profilmic). With the collective

13 Erin Manning deploys the term relational movement to emphasize movement's metastable and creative quality of "worlding". For Manning, the relational movement of bodies in space literally creates the world in which the movement happens (creates the world *through* movement). For a discussion on relational movement, see Manning (2009). I use the term here to emphasize how the creative act of bringing a world into existence emerges immanent to the movement of the ontological functors at work in a given event, and how the body always carries these functors into the event via the very fact of its existence, and its potential for prompting movements in others that can invoke resubjectifying affects.

14 For Guattari's original chart that lays out the co-compositions between actual and real, and virtual and possible in the ontological quandrants, see page 28 of *Schizoanalytic Cartographies* (2013).

15 Thus Apichatpong's ecosophic aesthetic composition reflects what Brian Massumi has to say about how the entirety of the event always contains a nonsensuous component. "Even if the event's conditioning elements and culmination are actual, the entirety of the event is virtual: doubly nonlocal, nonsensuously present, registering only in effect, and on all three counts really abstract" (Massumi 2011: 24).

emergence convoked, the abstract machine (Θ) governing the possibility of the event's actual development is different than it was before. The table that originally arranged the characters around it in the act of eating together has become a locus for the emergence of difference harboured by opacity. The real virtual domain of diegetic subjectivity (T) is also altered by the unlikely appearances of Huay and Boonsong—the group subjectivity shifts in composition, as two others fold into the scene. Through this mutual inclusion, notions of family, togetherness, and collectivity take on meanings that extend across species and the divide between life and death. In conjunction with all of this movement, which creates a new ontological consistency, Boonmee comes to regret his anti-communist violence and attributes his liver disease to the bad karma of these past actions. The family's relational dynamics are renewed and they take on a new collective character, accommodating alterious forms of life and modes of existence along with memories and premonitions, and whole virtual universes of value that these degrees of difference bring into the scene. The renewal is so profound as to constitute a "group subject," in that it becomes a group "that respects the heterogeneity of its component parts, and does not try to subsume them under an illusion of unity; that it is a group in process that explores and changes as conditions change, instead of hardening into a paralytic hierarchy of mutually exclusive terms with assigned value" (Massumi 1988: 440). Values (U), qualities of virtual possibility, are also modified in the recomposition of group subjectivity, because when Boonsong and Huay emerge from the jungle they carry a repressed set of political values and cultural memories with them. The jungle—a space of hiding, fleeing and taking cover for the communists liquidated by the military invasion of Isaan province—is here a point of emergence. Boonsong and Huay are different when they come out of the jungle, having been transformed by the unrepresentable horrors that took place within it. Emerging and asserting the difference of one's metamorphosis is an unrepresentable historical testimony that demands to be accommodated in the scene of presence. Shifting to accommodate the expressive presence of the repressed is a relational movement of the four ontological functors that alters the assemblage of enunciation, resingularizing the three ecologies. A small group's subjective orientation shifts, making peace with the alterious re-emergence of remnants from an opaque past made virtually active and nonsensuously perceptible. The schizoanalytic cartography demands to be redrawn once more, to account for this broadening of feeling, this burgeoning peace.

Disappearing/Reappearing: Surpassing Personality

Uncle Boonmee and short films and installations from Apichatpong's *Primitive* project[16] extensively use images of male teenage youth from Nabua, a "town of widows", that suffered immensely at the hands of the military occupation and communist purging.[17] The choice of teenage boys is significant since they are the descendants of the disappeared men and are orphans of the town of widows. Their presence carries the legacy of their disappeared fathers and widowed mothers along with the story of their past struggles for communism. In another important scene that facilitates the peace process, Boonmee has a nightmarish "dream of the future" where "past people are made to disappear." The scene uncannily invokes what Walter Benjamin has to say about the ephemerality of historical images: "Every image of the past that is not recognized by the present as one of its own concerns threatens to disappear irretrievably" (Benjamin 2007: 255). *Uncle Boonmee* shows how Benjamin's observation is true yet incomplete. Yes, the present carries a selective function; selecting presence—or what Whitehead calls the actual occasion[18]—out of the possibilities that a given process has made available to it. Yet what *Uncle Boonmee* adds to this account is that the present not only chooses which images to remember and forget based on its own concerns, but that the presence of an image, or a remembering, can doubly conceal a disappearance, an active forgetting. The forced disappearance of Isaan communists during the Thai military invasion is a prime example. As a people made to disappear, their image is charged with that very disappearance, to the extent that in order to maintain the status quo, such an image must be concealed and censored, even to the point of the image's (and not just the people's) disappearance. The disappearance of the image of Isaan communists in Thailand cannot at all be accounted for

16 Some of these other films that use similar imagery as found in Boonmee's dream sequence include two shorts from *The Primitive Project, A Letter to Uncle Boonmee* and *Phantoms of Nabua*.

17 Apichatpong explains the pertinence of his cinematic intervention into the contemporary Thai mediascape as follows: "The story of Nabua undeniably has echoes of the current political turmoil in Thailand. Institutions involved in those events of the past, along with new ones, are the key players in the ongoing chaos. Just as in the past, they manipulate the public psyche, instilling it with faith and fear" (Weerasethakul 2009a: 198). In the same piece he provides a further account of how he encountered the stories of Nabua's military occupation while filming his *Letter to Uncle Boonmee* for the *Primitive* project.

18 Actual occasions are the "final real things of which the world is made up," they are "drops of experience, complex and interdependent" (Whitehead 1978: 27). Actual occasions emerge from process, and thus carry a selective function, for they never actualize all of the possibilities offered by the processual flow from one set of actual occasions to another.

based on the fact that the present does not see it as one of its own concerns. Conversely, the very fact of the communists' disappearance, along with the disappearance of their image, can be attributed to them being a pressing concern to the current Thai political context. The present, so concerned that such an image could usher in a new ethico-political consistency that calls for making peace with this lingering past, restricts the conditions for its appearance. Maybe after long enough the present will no longer need to repress this image if the social landscape has changed to such a degree that its reappearance loses the power to shock subjectivity. In any case, Apichatpong's work is a high-stakes wager on the chance that the reappearance of the disappeared, this making active of the past, can prompt ecological recomposition.[19]

Boonmee's "dream of the future" enacts this wager. On the eve of his death, Boonmee, the ghost of his ex-wife Huan, his sister-in-law Jen, and Tong (the same characters from the dinner table scene) make a pilgrimage to an enormous cave where Boonmee enters a divinatory reverie. The dream is conveyed through ten still photographs that disrupt the film's live-action flow. Boonmee's voiceover monologue reads as follows:

> Boonmee: What's wrong with my eyes. They are open but I can't see a thing? Or are my eyes closed?
> Jen: Maybe you need time for your eyes to adjust to the dark.
> Boonmee: This cave is like a womb, isn't it? I was born here in a life I can't recall. I only know that I was born here. I don't know if I was a human or an animal, a woman or a man.
> [Dream sequence of ten still photographs begins]
> Boonmee: Last night, I dreamt of the future. I arrived there in a sort of time machine. The future city was ruled by an authority able to make anybody disappear. When they found 'past people,' they shone a light at them. That light projected images of them onto the screen. From the past, until the arrival in the future. Once those images appeared, these 'past people' disappeared. I was afraid of being captured by the authorities because I had many friends in this future. I ran away. But wherever I ran, they still found me. They asked me if I knew this road. I told them I didn't know. And then I disappeared.

19 Whitehead might have even considered *Uncle Boonmee* a historical adventure film, given its activation of the past: "[A]dventures are to the adventurous [...] a passive knowledge of the past loses the whole value of its message" (Whitehead 1967: 279).

Image 7 *Lung Bunmi Raluek Chat (Uncle Boonmee Who Can Recall His Past Lives)*, Apichatpong Weerasethakul, 2010

The monologue is interlaced with ten still photos which can be briefly described as follows:

Photo one: In a straw coloured open field, a person in an ape suit with a rope tied around its neck is led by a young man in paramilitary attire.

Photo two: A medium close-up shot of three young soldiers laying on the grass. The pattern of the shadows that cover them resemble the pattern of their camouflage uniforms.

Photo three: An eaten away tree leaf takes on the texture of the camouflage pattern and hangs in-between the faces of three young soldiers and the chest of another.

Photo four: Again, two soldiers lying on the ground amidst the bushes with the rifles resting beside them. They camouflage into their green and brown surroundings.

Photo five: A large group of military men dispersed throughout a field similar to the one seen in the first photo. A mysterious orange (human? animal?) figure walks in the background.

Photo six: Medium straight-on shot of the ape figure roped up by the neck, held by the soldier seen in the first photo. They are still in the same field.

Photo seven: The same young men, now dressed in civilian attire, throw stones out of frame to the right. Is the ape figure the target?

Photo eight: The ape figure with his arms around a group of six armed soldiers, looking directly at the camera as if posing for a group photo.

Photo nine: Five of the young men take a photo of a shirtless sixth laying out on the ground. Is he dead or alive?

Photo ten: Crop circles on a dirt path.

Image 8 *Lung Bunmi Raluek Chat (Uncle Boonmee Who Can Recall His Past Lives)*, Apichatpong Weerasethakul, 2010

The phrasing of Boonmee's voiceover suggests that he is the ape figure—possibly a man inside of an ape suit—who arrives in the future "wearing" a different body. However, this is merely one possible interpretation. He could very well be one of the soldiers, one of the civilians, the group as a whole, or even the photographer of the images. There is a real uncertainty as to where to locate him in his own dream, which fits in completely with the ecosophic logic of the dinner table scene's découpage. Boonmee's dream is not really *his* dream at all. The sunny photographs of the dream rip through the slowly paced and opacity filled images of the present in a manner that parallels Boonsong's earlier recollection. The dream is not localized within Boonmee's psyche, cordoned off from the world. It surpasses Boonmee's personality, enters into the shared ecology. Boonmee is not even identifiable in "his own" dream; he can barely recognize himself in it. It makes little difference whether Boonmee is in fact the ape, the soldiers, or the photographer taking the pictures of these characters—Boonmee cannot find himself in the future. The impossibility of being identified in a dream of one's "own" future proves unbearable to one's self.

Boonmee sees the future as a time where a pervasive conflict plays out between the people of the future and the people of the past. Even if it remains undetermined exactly where he figures in the dream, or what body he identifies with, he is nevertheless there, as are Jen, Tong and Huay. They are enmeshed in a future where they do not have a defined place, and yet they are implicated in its inter-generational and inter-species violence. The prospect of living in a future completely incompatible with one's notion of both "self" and "future" instigates a reappraisal of them both. The future becomes a site in dire need of reconfiguration along the lines of a new ontological consistency of peace, to make room for the appearance of the self. Yet the very notion of self will need to become other than it presently is to fabricate the future condition for its own habitability. For it is largely humankind's unyielding will to dominate difference that led to the prospect of a future where alterity is suffocated to begin with (in other words, a future not so different from the past). Boonmee and his companions are caught in a double bind: cease to exist or exist amidst the uninhabitable. Making this realization shocks their subjectivity (T). Having shaken the existential territory of the self, the future needs to be re-speculated, accounting for this quality of functional alterity that has rendered the ecology slightly more accommodating and less self-assured.

Now that Boonmee's sense of self has been rattled by the shock of the dream, new possibilities for the organization of ontological consistency have been ushered in. Peace is given a chance. Here, in Apichatpong's cinema, the sons of the "town of widows," marginalized and invisible in the Thai political landscape, claim a presence that defies their historical disappearance. Diegetically, Boonmee is shocked and this visual confrontation forces him to reassess his very sense of self on the eve of his death. He can no longer rationalize and justify the actions of his past (which included purging the communists of Isaan), now that he sees a future in which his fate could be as arduous as theirs. *Uncle Boonmee* has made the absent present and the ontological consistency of the film's images has broadened feeling to accommodate the disappeared, in all of their alterity. Apichatpong uses aesthetic experimentation to more fully perceive the movement of the ecology in order to make peace with those whose existence has been denied, whose way of life has been extinguished and whose values have been denigrated. *Uncle Boonmee* has listened to the disappeared—those who were killed and whose memory has been excluded from official nationalist discourse—and has given them presence by expanding its range of perceptibility. The speculative risk of the film, which brings back the disappeared in defiance of the powers-that-be, is that such a modulation on the plane of the image, a modulation that brings the disappeared to perceptibility and enunciation can, when seeded in the world and into the Thai mediascape, provoke a similar type of modulation. Putting the ontological functors immanent to the film image in touch with the functors of the world in which the film lives and circulates: the force of art in life. As such, *Uncle Boonmee* carries the potential to broaden feeling towards an ethico-political paradigm of peace that surpasses personality yet respects the right to singularity, and cares for the alterious contrasts of the world, even the ones which have not yet been made to (re)appear.

Bibliography

Alpern, Stephen I. "Insurgency in Northeast Thailand: A New Cause for Alarm". *Asian Survey* 15.8 (August 1975): 684-692.

Bazin, André. *What is Cinema?* Trans. Timothy Barnard. Montreal: Caboose, 2009.

Benjamin, Walter. "Theses on the Philosophy of History". in *Illuminations*. New York: Schocken Books, 1969: 253-264.

Boehler, Natalie. "The Jungle as Border Zone: The Aesthetics of Nature in the Work of Apichatpong Weerasethakul". *ASEAS – Austrian Journal of South-East Asian Studies* 4.2 (2011): 290-304.

Bordwell, David. *On the History of Film Style*. Cambridge, MA: Harvard University Press, 1997.

Casella, Alessandro. "Communism and Insurrection in Thailand". *The World Today* 26.5 (May 1970): 197-208.

Deleuze, Gilles and Félix Guattari. *Anti-Oedipus: Capitalism and Schizophrenia*. Trans. Robert Hurley, Mark Seem, and Helen R. Lane. Minneapolis: University of Minnesota Press, 1983.

Deleuze, Gilles. *Foucault*. Trans. Seán Hand. Minneapolis: University of Minnesota Press, 1988.

Guattari, Félix. *Schizoanalytic Cartographies*. London and New York: Bloomsbury Academic, 2013.

Guattari, Félix. *The Three Ecologies*. London and New York: Continuum, 2008.

Laplanche, Jean and J.-B. Pontalis. *The Language of Psychoanalysis*. Trans. Donald Nicholson-Smith. London: Karnac Books, 1988.

Manning, Erin. *Relationscapes: Movement, Art, Philosophy*. Cambridge and London: The MIT Press, 2009.

Massumi, Brian. "Deleuze and Guattari's Theories of the Group-Subject, Through a Reading of Corneille's *Le Cid*". *Discours Social/Social Discourse* 1.4 (Winter 1988): 423-440.

Massumi, Brian. *Semblance and Event: Activist Philosophy and the Occurrent Arts*. Cambridge, Massachusetts and London, England: The MIT Press, 2011.

Mullino Moore, Mary Elizabeth. "Imagine Peace: Knowing the Real—Imagining the Impossible. Ed. Jay B. McDaniel and Donna Bowman. *Handbook of Process Theology*. St. Louis, MO: Chalice, 2006. 201-216.

Quandt, James. *Apichatpong Weerasethakul*. Vienna: Synema Publikationen, 2009.

Rithdee, Kong. "Thailand passes controversial film act." *Variety*. 20 December 2007. Online. http://variety.com/2007/film/news/thailand-passes-controversial-film-act-1117978081/

Rosen, Philip. "Nation and Anti-Nation: Concepts of National Cinema in the 'New' Media Era". *Diaspora* 5.3 (1996): 386-391 and 391-393.

Stengers, Isabelle. "Beyond Conversation: The Risks of Peace". *Process and Difference: Between Cosmological and Poststructuralist Postmodernisms*. Ed. Catherine Keller and Anne Daniell. Albany: State University of New York Press, 2002. 235-255.

Souriau, Étienne. *L'univers filmique*. Paris: Flammarion, 1953.

Watson, Janell. *Guattari's Diagrammatic Thought: Writing Between Lacan and Deleuze*. London and New York: Continuum, 2009.

Weerasethakul, Apichatpong. "The Memory of Nabua: A Note on the Primitive Project". *Apichatpong Weerasethakul*. Ed. James Quandt. Vienna: Synema Publikationen, 2009a. 192-206.

Weerasethakul, Apichatpong. "The Folly and Future of Thai Cinema Under Military Dictatorship". *Apichatpong Weerasethakul*. Ed. James Quandt. Vienna: Synema Publikationen, 2009b. 178-181.

Whitehead, Alfred North. *Adventures of Ideas*. New York and London: The Free Press, 1967.

Whitehead, Alfred North. *Process and Reality: An Essay in Cosmology*. New York and London: The Free Press, 1978.

5 Healing and Decolonization

Abstract
Chapter Five makes a claim for the therapeutic value of Indigenous cinemas by drawing on the body of Indigenous scholarship which conceives of decolonization as healing process. This chapter foregrounds Barry Barclay's theory of Fourth Cinema which emphasizes the centrality of traditional Indigenous values to Indigenous filmmaking, and asks how such values can be affectively embedded in a film for political and therapeutic effect. Kanakan Balintagos' film *Palawan Fate* serves as an intercessor for thinking about cinema's contribution to social projects for healing and decolonization across the Fourth World, from Canada to the Philippines and beyond.

Keywords: Kanakan Balintagos, Fourth Cinema, Indigenous Cinema, decolonization

"I make films to heal my people."
–Kanakan Balintagos[1]

The Soul of Fourth Cinema

In a 2002 lecture given at the Auckland University Film and Media Studies department, Maori filmmaker Barry Barclay announced the arrival of Fourth Cinema, a feature-length cinema made by and for Indigenous peoples. At that point in time, eleven Indigenous features had been released worldwide.[2] The canon of Fourth Cinema has now grown and diversified

1 Quoted during a personal discussion with the filmmaker at the Cinemalaya Film Festival in August, 2015.

2 In his address, Barclay describes the emerging body of Fourth Cinema as follows: "*Bedeviled* (1993), by Aborigine film maker Tracey Moffatt; *The Pathfinder*, by Nils Gaup (1987), the Saami director of Norway. *Smoke Signals* (1998) has been out here fairly recently, directed by Chris

Szymanski, A., *Cinemas of Therapeutic Activism: Depression and the Politics of Existence.* Taylor & Francis Group, 2020
DOI: 10.5117/9789463723121_CH05

since its relatively recent emergence. When Barclay first spoke of Fourth Cinema, he identified a couple of organizational principles that brought together geographically, culturally and stylistically diverse films. He inferred that Fourth Cinema attested to Indigenous presence and existed outside the national orthodoxy of colonial nation-states. For Barclay, Fourth Cinema at its strongest fundamentally embodies core Indigenous values—values that often clash with those of the colonizer. As he states in his now-seminal lecture,

> If we as Maori look closely enough and through the right pair of spectacles, we will find examples at every turn of how the old principles have been reworked to give vitality and richness to the way we conceive, develop, manufacture and present our films. [...] It seems likely to me that some Indigenous film artists will be interested in shaping films that sit with confidence within the First, Second and Third cinema framework. While not closing the door on that option, others may seek to rework the ancient core values to shape a growing Indigenous cinema outside the national orthodoxy. (Barclay 2003b: 11)

In order for a film directed by an Indigenous filmmaker to truly embody the spirit of Fourth Cinema as Barclay conceives it, the film must revitalize the ancient core values of his or her Indigenous culture, values which exist outside, and even challenge, the national orthodoxy of the nation-state in which the film was made, distinguishing it from the First, Second and Third "invader cinemas," as Barclay refers to them.

More so than blood, language, identity or geography, Indigenous values are the essential characteristic of Fourth Cinema. They form what Barclay, following Maori scholar Rangihiroa Panoho, refers to as the "interiority" of a Fourth text. Barclay identifies numerous core values at the heart of the very influential Maori feature filmmaking tradition that helped to initiate today's global renaissance of Indigenous cinema. The values include:

Eyre of the Cheyenne and Arapaho peoples of Oregon in the USA; From producer and director Zacharias Kunuk of the Inuit peoples, we have *Atanarjuat* (The Fast Runner) (2001). There's the feature of young Aborigine director, Ivan Sen: *Beneath Clouds* (2002). And a film just completed and released, a feature titled *The Business of Fancy Dancing* (2002), written and directed by Sherman Alexie of the Coeur d'Alene tribe of Indians. [...] In this country [New Zealand], we have *Mauri* (1988), written and directed by Merata Mita; *Once Were Warriors* (1994), director Lee Tamahori; and released this year, *Te Tangata Whai Rawa O Weneti* (the Maori Merchant of Venice) (2004), directed by Don Selwyn, and the first of them *Ngati*, written by Tama Poata and directed by myself, released in 1985. And *Te Rua* (1992) which I wrote and directed" (Barclay 2003b: 7).

"whanaungatanga" (family, kinship, relationship; rights and obligations that strengthen the ties of a kin group), "wairua" (soul or spirit), "mana" (pride, power, effectiveness, prestige; a supernatural force in a person, place or object) and "aroha" (to love, feel compassion or pity, to emphasize).[3] As much as the previous definitions evoke the meaning of these core Maori values, they are inherently incomplete because Indigenous values are lived, shared and embodied, and thus stretch far beyond the limits inherent to a linguistic definition. By thinking of values not as abstract ideals but as collectively lived, and thus as having concrete effects in the world, the political import of Fourth Cinema starts to appear. As was analyzed in the previous chapter on the ontological quadrants of schizoanalysis, values condition what is possible in a given event; films that embody different values will effectuate diverging effects.

This counter-power to condition an event of subjectivity production has been invested in Indigenous practices of storytelling. In her book, *Dancing on Our Turtle's Back: Stories of Nishnaabeg Re-Creation, Resurgence and a New Emergence*, Leanne Simpson (Michi Saagiig Nishnaabeg) shares Nishnaabeg creation stories with the reader to transmit traditional values such as "gentleness, re-balancing and love" that the stories—like the Elders who kept them alive—embody (Simpson 2011: 19 & 74). The embodiment of values also plays a foremost role in Taiaiake Alfred's (Kanien'kehá:ka) influential writings on Indigenous liberation. Alfred's *Peace, Power and Righteousness: An Indigenous Manifesto* advances with clarity and force the idea that contemporary and future Indigenous political leaders must come to embody traditional Onkwehonwe[4] values to radically change the relationship that First Nations have with the colonial nation-states that legislate over them. For Alfred, traditional Indigenous values carry a resurgent, decolonizing force capable of reconfiguring the social reality of Onkwehonwe that is currently dictated in so many ways by neocolonialism's coercive powers of state and "free market." Alfred understands Indigenous values as the "the heart and soul of indigenous nations: a set of values that challenge the destructive and homogenizing force of Western liberalism and

3 These definitions come from the online Maori dictionary. For each one of these terms to be understood in their complexity, a more intimate familiarity with the workings of Maori culture is needed. However, I use the translations above to offer at least some insight into the sorts of values that Barry Barclay imagines as essential to the Maori incarnation of Fourth Cinema. Each Indigenous cinema will embody its own culturally specific values. Over the course of this chapter I will present two of these values—"ingasiq" and "busong"—specific to the film *Palawan Fate* and the people of Palawan.

4 Onkwehonwe: "the real and original people" (Alfred 1999: xv).

free-market capitalism; that honour the autonomy of individual conscience, non-coercive authority, and the deep interconnection between human beings and the other elements of creation" (Alfred 1999: 60). In order to activate their transformative power, values must be embodied, they must be made the "heart and soul" of the Indigenous nation. Once embodied, they affirmatively challenge neocolonialism, not in the sense of being its negation or deconstruction, but in actively creating the conditions for an Indigenous resurgence on its own terms, collectively informed by traditional values operating at the core of Indigenous social and ecological life.

By emphasizing the role of values in Fourth Cinema, Barclay shifts the lens through which Fourth Cinema must be viewed to perceive the soul stirring beneath its plastic composition. After all, core values belong to what Barclay calls the film's "interior," and the burnished surface of a film's "exterior" can be quite deceiving. The popular New Zealand film *Whale Rider* (2003) is a good example, and Barclay takes issue with this film in an open letter to its producer John Barnett. *Whale Rider* is based on a story "unique to the descendants of the tribe Ngati Porou whose lands are centered on the East Coast of the North Island of Aotearoa, (New Zealand) and was written by Maori author Witi Ihimaera." However, the film was adapted for the screen, directed, and produced without the involvement of Maori, by an all-white team (Barclay 2003: 33). In his open letter, Barclay condemns Barnett's public justification for appropriating the Maori story. Barnett claimed that the film's themes are "absolutely international" and that white New Zealanders have the right to use the story in the name of overcoming what Barnett—offensively—calls "cultural apartheid" (Barclay 2003: 33). The film reaped big profits for Barnett, and launched the successful career of director Niki Caro who has gone on to direct feel-good Hollywood films about other racialized groups,[5] all while sidelining the production of Maori films at the New Zealand Film Commission, where, as Barclay points out, an entire decade passed without one Indigenous film being produced by the commission (Barclay 2003: 36). All of these problems characterize the production and exhibition of *Whale Rider*, despite the fact that on the representational level alone, the film could very well be mistaken for an authentically Maori film.

Whale Rider is based on a traditional Maori story about a young girl who challenges the patriarchal orthodoxy within her tribe to emerge as the new

5 Caro's film *McFarland, USA* (2015) exemplified this trend in her work. The film was produced by Disney and focuses on a high school cross-country team of Mexican-American youth who, with the help of a white All-American coach and a dose of determination and discipline, manage to overcome their marginal socio-economic status.

leader of her people. The film is populated with images of Maori, and Maori actors are cast to play the lead characters of the film. The film's representation of Maori people is largely positive: they are dynamic, fleshed-out human characters and the Maori community functions as a source of inspiration for audiences. The film even positions the Maori as a people that international, non-Indigenous audiences can both applaud and learn from, because the film celebrates gender equality in positions of political leadership. *Whale Rider* looks like a work of Fourth Cinema, but closer investigation reveals that its values, at best, are emblematic of liberal feminism (in its pro-gender equality message), and at worst, are emblematic of neocolonial cultural appropriation keen at turning a hefty profit for a layer of cultural elite. *Whale Rider* looks Maori, but has a colonial soul.

Anticipating the continued cultural appropriation of Indigenous images, Barclay was careful to insist on the presence of Indigenous values for a film to be considered as constitutive of Fourth Cinema. He says quite clearly that Fourth Cinema consists of something more than an Indigenous "exteriority." By "exteriority" Barclay is referring to surface-level, plastic elements of the image, such as its "language, posturing, décor, use of elders, presence of children, attitudes to land, and rituals of a spirit world" (Barclay 2003b: 7). He goes on to assert his belief "that in Fourth Cinema—at its best—something else is being asserted which is not easy to access" (Barclay 2003b: 7). The "something else" is the "interiority," the embodiment of Indigenous values, and Barclay himself is reluctant to say exactly how to tell if these "interior" values are present. As he admits, they're not easy to access. Reaching the "heart and soul" of a film requires more than analyzing what it represents, but encountering the values that justify its creation. If a film is indeed found to embody Indigenous values, and not just represent Indigenous people or narrate Indigenous stories, then it is going to function very differently than a film like *Whale Rider*, even if it looks quite similar. Armed with Indigenous values at its core, Fourth Cinema enables therapeutic subjective recompositions that facilitate healing from and resurging against the weighty legacy of colonialism and its continued aggressions.

Decolonization and Healing

In the recent efforts to theorize strategies of decolonization, especially in Canada, for reasons I will explain, Indigenous political activism is regularly framed by the concept of "healing." This section of the chapter will present some of the various ways in which this concept has been elucidated in the discourse on decolonization produced by Indigenous academics, and will subsequently examine the complex stakes of healing for Indigenous nations. As we will see, healing can be made to function in two contradictory ways, one that forwards the decolonization movement's focus on "resurgence" or cultural flourishing, and another that subjects Indigenous communities to the laws of the neocolonial market in contempt of their well-being. Faced with this predicament, that healing can work to advance the project of global decolonization or further entrench the neocolonial hold over Indigenous communities, Dian Million (Tanana Athabasca) insists that we consistently pose the question: "What kind of order does healing serve?" (2013: 144). The following analysis will first highlight healing's conceptual significance to select Indigenous theorists, before moving to elucidate how healing also carries the latent risk of being coopted by neocolonial interests if not undertaken in line with traditional Indigenous values.

Healing is an important concept because it can be made to acknowledge the under-recognized reality that Indigenous nations are the survivors of genocide,[6] and connects this historical violence to the elevated rates of Indigenous suicide, depression, alcoholism and substance abuse worldwide.[7] A number of influential Indigenous authors on the topic of decolonial resurgence advance this two-pronged understanding of healing as both historical and medical to articulate how rebuilding strong Indigenous nations capable of redressing the countless effects of genocidal colonial policy necessarily entails restoring holistic wellness through mental, physical, emotional and spiritual renewal.

One of these authors is Ann N. Dapice (Lenape-Cherokee), who turns to the medicine wheel and the holistic sense of health it diagrams to show how colonial violence has precipitated losses in each of the wheel's quadrants: the mental, physical, emotional and spiritual realms. For example, she cites the loss of language and elders' teachings (mental), the loss of identity (emotional), the loss of strong bodies (physical), and the loss of religious ceremonies (spiritual) as particularly damaging aspects of the colonial legacy (Dapice 2006: 256). Dapice offers tactics for healing from these losses that specifically address each of these four areas, a selection of which include

6 In their stunning article "Genocide and Indian Residential Schooling: The Past is Present," Roland Chrisjohn et al. present a detailed history of how the Canadian government lobbied the United Nations to change its proposed definition of genocide in the aftermath of World War II in an effort to prevent the Indian residential school system in Canada from qualifying as an act of genocide.

7 For example, see Ernst Hunter and Desley Harvey's "Indigenous Suicide in Australia, New Zealand, Canada and the United States" and Ann N. Dapice's "The Medicine Wheel."

elder-led experiential pedagogy (mental), culturally competent psychotherapy (emotional), outdoor exercise (physical), and ceremony participation (spiritual) (2006: 259). These remedies work to address concrete health problems as much as the historical injustices that continue to precipitate them. For instance, the revitalization of religious ceremony brings about spiritual healing while at the same time strengthening connections to the land and pre-colonial ancestry, making the practice an overtly political act that may disrupt both the colonial imaginary of *terra nullius* as well as neocolonial resource extraction interests. Furthermore, acting on the spiritual domain affects the three other domains of the medicine wheel. A ceremony can also be a time for the sharing of traditional food (physical), enacting land-based pedagogy (mental), and nurturing family relationships (emotional). To act on one of the four areas of health found in the medicine wheel is to create an opening for acting on them all and for strengthening the resolve of Indigenous nations in their self-defence against continued neocolonial encroachment.

Taiaiake Alfred's work builds on this connection between the medicine wheel's four elements of health and overtly politicizes it by staging how it can further the decolonization movement. In an emblematic line that alludes to the holistic conception of Indigenous health, he rhetorically asks, "How can anyone confront the depressing, disintegrating reality of this world without the restorative strength of spirituality?" (2005: 250). Spirituality saturates his political writings and one of his books is even organized around the leitmotif of "wasáse," an ancient war ritual known in English as the Thunder Dance. This specific dance calls Indigenous warriors to serve their nations by adopting the necessary customs and ethics. Alfred goes so far as to offer an entire checklist of qualities that a resurgent nation of warriors should put into practice, may of which put an emphasis on reclaiming health through temperance and moderation: "Simple lifestyles, disciplined surroundings, and a healthy existence characterized by cleanliness and organization are the traits of a warrior [...] as opposed to the slovenly and poisoned lives expected of colonized beings" (2005: 88). This celebration of health's political dimension should not be lost. The Thunder Dance interpolates warriors, and offers them the restorative strength of spirituality, which in turn encourages the self-discipline necessary to live a healthy lifestyle, which subsequently makes Indigenous nations stronger and better able to contest neocolonial power. In this scholarship, healing works equally as a concept of subjective recomposition and political transformation whereby recovering from past trauma enables the conditions for resurging into a decolonized future with undeniable macropolitical consequences, such as land title transfers.

Thinkers such as Waziyatawin and Michael Yellow Bird in *For Indigenous Minds Only* contribute to the activist discourse on healing by foregrounding how the mental makeup of Indigenous peoples constitutes a battleground in the struggle for decolonization. Their work "reflects an understanding that decolonizing actions must begin in the mind, and that creative, consistent, decolonized thinking shapes and empowers the brain, which in turn provides a major prime for positive change." Building yet again on the connectedness of the medicine wheel, they argue, "Undoing the effects of colonialism and working toward decolonization requires each of us to consciously consider to what degree we have been affected by not only the physical aspects of colonization, but also the psychological, mental and spiritual aspects" (2013: 2). In their paradigm of decolonization, healing is a process of undoing belief systems that have been instilled by the colonial imagination, and replacing them with decolonial ways of thinking in line with traditional Indigenous values. According to their theorization, decolonizing actions capable of bringing about a more just relationship between Indigenous peoples and settler states are unfathomable without first healing the mind by unlearning the colonial thought patterns that have shaped it.

One of the ways to overcome this "mental imperialism," as Leanne Simpson refers to it, is through pedagogical storytelling. Simpson's work consistently reactivates her nation's ancestral stories, and the rich cultural heritage and traditional values that they embody, to promote the flourishing of Indigenous life. Her strategy for doing so can be read as equally therapeutic and political. Stories enact a healing function by immersing people in a collective heritage from which they have traditionally been alienated, offering the strength of community, belonging and cultural pride. At the same time, they implicitly dispute colonial myths, and reclaim the freedom of Indigenous peoples to narrate their past, present and future existence along the trajectory of their desired political resurgence.

Dance, storytelling, land-based pedagogy, language learning, traditional feasts, sweat lodges, sacred fires and drumming circles are some of the healing practices cited by grassroots Indigenous activist initiatives. The authors discussed above repeatedly emphasize how healing activities such as these advance the decolonization movement. To summarize, healing techniques prove themselves to be a vital component of decolonization strategies for a number of important reasons: They challenge colonial myths, strengthen the relational fabric within communities, increase the physical health of peoples who may find themselves in direct confrontation with colonial police and military, fortify title claims over contested land and help to bring a decolonized future into the Indigenous cultural imagination.

Hence the political efficacy of healing, and why these healing techniques double as therapeutic activism. Yet in spite of what a word like "healing" connotes, healing in the age of neocolonialism is a double-edged sword that is burdened by the risk for political cooption with detrimental consequences for Indigenous nations.

The political ambivalence of healing is illustrated by the work of Glen Coulthard (Yellowknives Dene) and Dian Million who each offer a critique of "state bio-political programs for healing" which subtly abnegate Indigenous self-determination efforts (Million 2013: 6). Their critiques focus on the specific relationship between First Nations and the Canadian government, since this official relationship has engendered a discourse and set of policy initiatives that embraces "healing" as a way to reconcile the history of abusive treatment towards First Nations, Métis and Inuit peoples.[8] In 1998, the Canadian government responded to the Royal Commission on Aboriginal Peoples (1996) with its policy document *Gathering Strength: Canada's Aboriginal Action Plan* and the allocation of a $350 million dollar fund for healing from the abuses suffered in the residential school system. This allocation of moneys was used to establish the Aboriginal Healing Foundation (AHF), an organization that provided health services up until 2014 when its programming was discontinued. The goal of the AHF was to "help create, reinforce and sustain conditions conducive to healing, reconciliation, and self-determination" and it "committed to addressing the legacy of abuse in all of its forms and manifestations, direct, indirect and intergenerational, by building on the strength and resilience of Aboriginal peoples."[9]

According to Indigenous studies scholars Julian Robbins (Mi'kmaq) and Jonathan Dewar (Huron-Wendat), this "positive development" was remarkable for its willingness to flow government funds to an Indigenous-run arms-length organization, and marks "unprecedented support for community-based approaches to healing" (2011: 11). The healing initiatives

8 A similar discourse and set of policy initiatives has appeared in the Australian Aboriginal context as well. *Bringing them Home, a Report of the National Inquiry Into the Separation of Aboriginal and Torres Strait Islander Children from Their Families* was tabled in parliament in 1997, and over a decade later, after the National Apology to the Stolen Generations took place in 2008, the government allotted funds for the creation of the Healing Foundation, which was established in 2009. The foundation was established to "address the harmful legacy of colonization, in particular the history of child removal that continues to affect Aboriginal and Torres Strait Islander people" (Healing Foundation: n.p.).

9 This statement of objective comes from the Aboriginal Healing Foundation cached website, www.ahf.ca.

that were funded by the program were truly grassroots in orientation, and bottom-up in structure, as each community was able to choose their own healing strategies. A glance through the AHF's archived website shows that different nations chose to enact their healing through different techniques, geared towards their specific needs and traditions, often blending Western, traditional, and alternative therapeutic methods.[10] The healing enabled by the AHF is undoubtedly commendable, and has positively affected the lives of tens of thousands Indigenous peoples in Canada.[11] One AHF report even suggests that around 98% of abuse survivors who accessed its services had never before participated in a similar healing program (2003: 89).

How could such grassroots healing possibly raise the suspicion of Indigenous scholars? The answer lies in how the *Gathering Strength* report frames "reconciliation" and "self-determination." Coulthard and Million raise three serious concerns. The first concern cited in Coulthard's work is that the political discourse that gave rise to the AHF effectively denies the reality of the colonial present, and situates colonial wrongdoing as firmly in the past: "*Gathering Strength* begins with a 'Statement of Reconciliation' in which the Government of Canada recognizes 'the mistakes and injustices of the past' in order 'to set a new course in its policies for Aboriginal peoples.' [...] The result," he suggests, "is an approach to reconciliation that goes out of its way to fabricate a sharp divide between Canada's unscrupulous 'past' and the unfortunate 'legacy' this past has produced for Indigenous people and

10 For example, Wasekun House in Cree nation, Quebec (Saint-Alphonse-Rodriguez), used the AHF support for "therapeutic techniques such as the Healing Circles, Drumming Ceremonies, Sacred Fired, the Cleansing Ceremonies, the Sweat Lodges and Traditional Feasts; and the Cognitive-Behavioural Techniques used by the Psychologists and the staff of the program such as relaxation training, systematic desensitization, assertion training, self-management and meditation are all used in accordance with standard practice in the field." The Nunavik Regional Board of Health and Social Sciences provided sexual abuse training and a healing gathering of elders to address the issue in fourteen communities in the Nunavik region. To offer yet another example, the McLeod Lake Indian Band in British Columbia created a family development program to help recover the loss of parenting skills due to the residential school system's separation of families. The AHF website includes a description of every project that it funded over the course of its history, so it is possible to see the different foci and approaches of different communities who accessed the fund. For a specific list of the different Western, traditional and alternative therapeutic techniques used, see page 68 of the Aboriginal Healing Foundation's *Third Interim Evaluation Report of the Aboriginal Healing Foundation Program Activity*.

11 Levi Nowdlak, a sexual abuse survivor and client of the Mamisarvik Healing Centre in Ottawa, testified to the positive impact that AHF programs have had on her life: "It changed things for me dramatically. I started loving myself more" (Zerehi: n.p.).

communities in the present" (Coulthard 2014: 121).[12] By situating colonial wrongdoing solely in the trauma of the past, the state is able to advance its settlement of Indigenous lands without acknowledging the hardship that such actions are causing in the present. Made to function in this light, "healing" can assist an ideological sleight of hand that distracts from the intensification of colonial control over Indigenous land and life.

The second objection that Coulthard makes to *Gathering Strength* is that this strategic move to situate colonial wrongdoing in the past buoys the state's rhetoric of reconciliation. Using the funds it has allocated for healing as an alibi, the colonial state clams the injustice to have been "reconciled" as a way to avoid true "restitution,"[13] which would entail the transfer of significant portions of occupied lands back to Indigenous peoples. Coulthard sums up this position as follows: "Rather than affirm Aboriginal title and substantially redistribute lands and resources to Indigenous communities through a renewed treaty process, or recognize Indigenous autonomy and redistribute political authority from the state to Indigenous nations based on the principle of Indigenous self-determination, *Gathering Strength* essentially reiterates, more or less unmodified, its present policy position as evidence of the essentially just nature of the current relationship between Indigenous peoples and the state" (2014: 122).

The third major objection to colonial state sponsored healing programs, as expressed by Dian Million, is that they can be made to lend themselves to the free marketization of Indigenous nations. For Million, "Indigenous cultures may represent the only living models for different economic and social systems on the planet, ways of life that have the power to challenge capital cultures, even when they are not pure or untouched by capitalism" (Million 2013: 161). But having undergone government-sponsored healing, "reconstituted, 'self determining' Aboriginal nations are envisioned in part as a form that might be prepped to compete in the marketplace" (Million 2013: 133). Her critique aptly questions the government's supposed goodwill in supporting healing programs, and demonstrates how they can

12 Coulthard builds on the work of Stephanie Irlbacher-Fox, whose book *Finding Dahshaa: Self-Government, Social Suffering, and Aboriginal Policy in Canada* also argues that the discourse on reconciliation denies the present colonial reality. Roland Chrisjohn et. al further this argument with respect to how the reconciliation discourse is used to obscure the historical reality of genocide in Canada.

13 The concept of restitution has been most forcefully advanced by Taiaiake Alfred. For a detailed account of its what it entails and how it dramatically differs from the liberal ideology of "reconciliation," see Taiaiake Alfred's "Restitution is the Real Pathway for Justice of Indigenous Peoples."

actually be made to serve the interests of colonial capitalism. "Healing," for the neocolonial state, is a financial investment in human development that seeks to make "self determining"[14] communities seeking government recognition more easily incorporated into a resource development economy and hierarchical colonial governance structure that really only benefits colonial interests and inherently contradicts Indigenous ways of valuing land and labour.

Yet in spite of attempts to render healing in the service of the neocolonial project, Million still insists that "colonized communities actively perform healing as liberatory practices" (Million 2013: 155). Parsing out the difference between a resurgent, decolonizing healing and reconciliatory, neocolonial healing is no easy task because these competing political interests overlap over the very same healing practices. A decolonizing act of community resurgence through a healing ceremony may very well be funded by the state seeing to advance its own colonial objectives, and this contradiction is very difficult to escape. But nor would it necessarily be a beneficial strategy to try and resolve this contradiction outright. If there is to be any criteria for whether or not healing can constitute a decolonizing act, I propose that it is useful to transpose the criteria that Barclay uses to define Fourth Cinema. For Barclay, above all else, it is the presence of traditional Indigenous values that determine whether or not a film is indeed "Indigenous" and whether it will challenge colonial orthodoxy. The same can be applied to healing: methods that are undertaken wholeheartedly in line with traditional Indigenous values will inherently function to heal in a manner that contests neocolonialist modes of valuation. The efficacy of healing, and what prevents its cooption, even when it must bear the contradiction of being funded by a colonial state with an antithetical political investment, lies in its unfurling of value systems that animate people and the many relationships which engender their lives, so that when these values brush up against colonial demands, they win out.

14 For Glen Coulthard the problem with self-determination as it is presently practiced in Canada is that it is "a conciliatory form of settler-state recognition for Indigenous nations […] that seeks to 'reconcile' Indigenous assertions of nationhood with settler state sovereignty via the accommodation of Indigenous identity claims in some form of renewed legal and political relationship with the Canadian state" (Coulthard 2014: 24, 3). According to these "politics of recognition," as Coulthard calls it, building on the work of Richard Day, First Nations "self-determination" still incarnates a hierarchical relationship where First Nations are subservient to the colonial state. Expressing a parallel concern, Taiaiake Alfred convincingly advances the idea that "sovereignty" is an "inappropriate concept" when thinking about Indigenous liberation struggles because it pre-determines the ends of such struggles by attaching it to the state-form. See pages 55-72 of "Sovereignty—An Inappropriate Concept" in *Peace, Power, Righteousness.*

Palawan Fate's Core Values

This section turns to analyze a work of Fourth Cinema that not only represents healing practices, but actually seeks to heal by transmitting core Indigenous values and the modes of relationality that they engender. For director Kanakan Balintagos (also known as Auraeus Solito) who is cited in this chapter's epigraph, filmmaking is a healing practice and he makes films for no less of a reason than to heal his people. For this reason, I engage with his film *Busong* (*Palawan Fate*) (2011) to articulate how Fourth Cinema can play a vital role in a decolonizing politics of resurgence that incorporates healing in accordance with traditional values. The reader will undoubtedly remark that the bulk of the analysis on healing above references Canadian, American and to a lesser extent, Australian colonial contexts, but that this film comes from the island of Palawan in the Philippines. Furthermore, in contextualizing the film's healing motifs, this section will offer examples from films that take place in very geographically diverse locations. I permit this potentially disorientating shift because it responds to Fourth Cinema's—like the Fourth World's[15]—geographic dispersal across the global North as much as the global South, and the East as much as the West. Certainly, the decolonization movement within every country must contend with a unique set of state institutions, legal frameworks and occupation strategies. However, there are many traumatic experiences that the world's Indigenous peoples hold in common, especially when it comes to displacement from ancestral lands, and it is no coincidence that Indigenous cinema from around the world—a global constellation of Indigenous flourishing—is punctuated by images of healing, and images that aim to heal.

Growing up in the mainland Philippines, Auraeus Solito's Palawan heritage was kept in the closet because of anti-Indigenous sentiment in Filipino society. In his young adult life, Solito began to investigate his family origins more deeply and discovered that he is the descendant of a long line of shaman-kings.[16] In an effort to discover these long repressed facts of his

15 The term "Fourth World" was coined in George Manuel and Michael Poslun's 1974 book *The Fourth World: An Indian Reality*. Manuel defines the Fourth World as the "indigenous peoples descended from a country's aboriginal population and who today are completely or partly deprived of the right to their own territories and its riches" (40). The term actually originated in conversation between Manuel and Mbuto Milando, who stated that "When Native peoples come into their own, on the basis of their own culture and traditions, that will be the Fourth World" (McFarlane 1993: 160).

16 The film's producer Raymond Lee mentions that Solito's Palawan heritage was hidden from him in a podcast by the Centre for Southeast Asian Studies Lecture Series at the University of Hawaii.

mother's ancestry and become the Palawan he didn't know he could be, Solito changed his name to Kanakan Balintagos and decided to make a film on the island of Palawan, with the Palawan people. The result is *Palawan Fate*, the first Indigenous Palawan feature film ever made.

The island of Palawan is considered the "last frontier" of the Philippines and has attracted many resource developers interested in Palawan lumber, minerals, and especially pearls (Eder 85). The contemporary Indigenous peoples of Palawan have lived as the ancient stewards of the trees, water and mountains since time immemorial, in harmony with the natural surroundings. The traditional Palawan way of life is highly imbricated with the richness of the land and Palawan regularly live off the wild food that grows, and that they grow, on the island. These staples include rice, coconuts, local fruits and to a lesser extent, various sorts of fish and game (Macdonald 2007: 46). Since the Palawan way of life is so directly imbricated in the vitality of the ecological surrounds, Palawan livelihood is in constant threat from the expansion of industrial powers onto the island whose impacts are registered directly in the environment. The intimate relationship between the Palawan and their land has come under increasing duress over the past 115 years with the number of inhabitants on Palawan island increasing 25-fold between 1900 and 1980 due to lowland migration (Eder 87). This influx of non-Palawan to the island has resulted in wage labour becoming the increasingly dominant mode of survival, and Palawan peoples are frequently employed to work for lowland farmers. The result is what anthropologist of the Palawan James Eder calls a "subsistence economy consisting of a desultory combination of hunting and gathering, shifting cultivation, collection and sale of forest products, and wage labour, all underwritten by a heavy reliance on credit and clientage" (Eder 1989: 88). The intensification of neocolonialist presence on the island of Palawan also continues to have a severe impact on tribal culture, including its ritual healing practices. In reference to the Batak tribe, Eder explains that "the incorporation of the Batak of Palawan into wider social and economic systems has eroded traditional ritual life, particularly shamanistic curing ceremonies" (1989: 81) and that "such processes of 'deculturation' and 'detribalization' can be destructive of the welfare of contemporary tribal people," (1989: 82) including the non-Batak peoples of Palawan.

Kanakan Balintagos inserts himself into the midst of these ecologically destructive developments on the island (for the Palawan, the land and the people are completely inextricable), to fulfill the dual role of shaman-king and storyteller that had been long denied to him due to separation from his people. In his director's statement accompanying the film, Balintagos draws an evocative connection between the storytelling tradition of the Palawan people and his independent filmmaking practice.

> My mother told me stories about her hometown in South Palawan to put me to sleep when I was a child. She used to tell me that the Tultol, or epic chants that were sung from twilight till dawn, were her 'movies.' She would imagine each myth in her mind and wait each night for another myth to be retold. Perhaps now, as a modern filmmaker with an ancient lineage, it is my turn to retell these stories and visualize them through film. (Solito 2011: n.p.)

Taking his turn at retelling these stories, Solito crafts a film that embodies traditional Palawan values and revitalizes ancient Palawan stories as a way to confront the resource development projects destroying the island's environmental, social, and psychic ecologies, long expertly maintained by its Indigenous inhabitants.

In keeping with Barclay's Fourth Cinema criteria, two traditional Palawan values guide the film's narrative structure and aesthetic composition: "bu-song," the Palawan concept of instant karma or fate, which serves as the film's original language title, and "ingasiq," a term that translates roughly as "giving disposition, empathy, sympathy, compassion, and pity, which infers a sharing of one's resources [...] an expression of solidarity" (Macdonald 2011: 135). Through an investigation of how these two values are narratively and aesthetically articulated in *Palawan Fate*, Barry Barclay's notion of "interior-ity"—the inherently Indigenous quality of Fourth Cinema—starts to come to perceptibility, because the film form emerges organically from ancient Palawan values, so that the "soul" of the film and its aesthetic expression are consistent with one another.

Palawan Fate focuses on the title characters of the Palawan epic "Punay and Angkadang": Punay (Alessandra de Rossi), a woman who is covered in skin lesions so painful that she is unable to walk, and her brother Angkadang (Rodrigo Santikan), who wraps her body in a hammock and carries her around the island in search of a shaman who can heal her wounds. The film opens with the call of the sap-od bird whose squawk warns of the sadness that saturates the three Palawan landscapes (forest, mountain and sea) that Punay and Ang-kadang move through in their search for healing. The film foregrounds major resource development projects currently taking place in each of these locales that are detrimental to Palawan livelihood: illegal logging (forest), mining (mountain), and dynamite fishing and pearl hunting (sea). The film's serial narrative structure puts the protagonists into contact with three consecutive strangers who help them locate a shaman capable of healing Punay's wounds.

The serial narrative emerges immanently from the influential presence of "ingasiq" in Palawan life. Charles Macdonald, in his anthropological work on the Palawan, points out that "ingasiq" gives life to a mode of relationality predicated on "weak ties."[17] A weak tie "is not only a tie that is not strong (and thus disposable); it is a tie that is always available (or, rather, reusable). It is a transferable tie. Weak ties may be a fundamental characteristic of human gregariousness" (Macdonald 2011: 128). In all of their gregariousness and transferability, "weak ties" break from the sense of duty encompassing "strong ties," wherein the burden of care in times of healing is distributed according to familial and professional duty. Weak ties are not about duty or "being committed," since "to be committed is completely alien to the Palawan ethos. This is why Palawan people cannot really commit themselves to any program, leader, or cause, a situation that baffles indigenous rights activists" (Macdonald 2011:138). "Ingasiq" conditions Palawan society in such a way that there is a collective appetite for care that extends beyond familial or professional duties (or even the duties embedded in dominant structures of Indigenous rights activism), so that care, which may very well be expressed through traditional healing, is available to anyone in the ecology, simply by virtue of being a part of it.

The mode of relationality catalyzed by the value of "ingasiq" intersects with the workings of "busong." As both a value and cosmological law, "busong" functions to immediately manifest the karmic consequences of actions. As Punay and Angkadang encounter the helpful strangers, each one of them recounts a tale, told in flashbacks, that shows the mystical force of "busong's" fatal retribution. Cutting the sacred Amugis tree leaves one character's husband dead, and privatizing a Palawan beach causes an Australian businessman to step on a poisonous stonefish. Yet in one of the film's most politically potent and aesthetically daring scenes, "busong" is constructed as more than a retributive karmic force, punishing wrongdoers. It takes on a distributive force that makes acts of healing felt across the fields of relation that compose the ecology.

The film concludes with a climactic scene of traditional healing. By this point in the story, Punay and Angkadang have encountered a character named Aris (Clifford Bañagale). He is a mixed-race Palawan who has just abandoned his shamanistic training. Aris is upset with himself for failing

17 The concept of weak ties originates in the influential sociology essay by Mark Granovetter "The Strength of Weak Ties." Granovetter focused on how weak ties (relationships to friends and acquaintances) factored into employment searches. Charles Macdonald points out how weak ties are fundamental to the spirit of cooperation in Palawan economic, ritual and communal life.

Image 9 *Busong (Palawan Fate)*, Kanakan Balintagos, 2011

his apprenticeship and the film recounts his failed attempts to heal a young child who ultimately dies. In spite his supposed inadequacy, the sound of the sap-od bird leads Punay to believe that Aris could be the healer that she needs. Then, Aris enacts a healing ceremony in a concluding scene that intensifies the mystical moments of "busong." The first part of the traditional healing ritual shows Aris holding bunches of dried grass, dancing, and entering a trance.

The film aesthetics shift dramatically here to signal that the healing ritual is opening up onto a supernatural realm. Aurally, disembodied voices accompany fast-paced tribal music that have no on-screen source. The image's colour scheme shifts as the intensity of the ceremony rises, and the island becomes a shade of grey. A triangle mask abruptly appears over the image. The intensity of the ceremony continues to rise, past its breaking point, and as the fast-paced music gives way, the film abruptly cuts to a calming, tender shot of Punay in front of a waterfall—a shot with no aesthetic resemblance to the former. In a long take that moves the film into a mytho-poetic register infused with magic, and breaking completely from the struggles of the Palawan reality under neocolonialism, Angkadang delicately moves his hand over Punay's face, removing the fleshy lesions and turning them into butterflies. In reaching out to one another in gestures of mutual care reflective of "ingasiq," the Palawan of *Palawan Fate* meet their "busong," in an event of healing so intense that it literally transcends the coordinates of the known reality. In a full embrace of the mystical, the film astonishingly concludes on the plane of a truly decolonized future governed by ancient core Palawan values and healed from the scars left by the ongoing history of colonialism.

Image 10 *Busong (Palawan Fate)*, Kanakan Balintagos, 2011

Mystic Healing in a Time of War

It is through this recourse to mysticism that *Palawan Fate*'s images of healing become healing images in their own right. This final section of the chapter examines Fourth Cinema's healing potential. By invoking Henri Bergson's little-used concept of mystic intuition, I suggest that Fourth Cinema should be regarded as a healing art that contributes to the decolonization movement's resurgent flourishing of Indigenous life, and acts as a tool for resisting healing's cooptation into a neocolonial politics of recognition and reconciliation. Fourth Cinema can be thought of in this healing light because its mystic quality incarnates traditional values, making them felt as an affective force that prompts subjective recomposition in the grasping for a decolonized future. By catalyzing subjective recompositions in line with core Indigenous values, values that brush up against those propagated by colonial-capitalism, Fourth Cinema has a key role to play in the conflict between these two inherently contradictory value systems and the politics they engender.

As a way to express the deep antagonism of this conflict and burst any fantasies about the colonial state's benevolence in a "post-reconciliation" era, Taiaiake Alfred has declared, "the war is not over yet" (Alfred 1999: xv).[18]

18 A similar idea is advanced by Mike Mitchell, former chief of the St. Regis Mohawks (Akwesasne) in the seminal work of early First Nations documentary, *You Are on Indian Land*. In the film, he confronts an Indian agent, and says "We never broke a treaty. That Jay Treaty, stated in there, that as the Indians we obliged to seize making wars on the white man. [...] When that

Why this recourse to war, especially a war that cleaves along more-or-less ethnic lines, in the era of multiculturalism? There comes a moment when one community's flourishing is impinged upon by a predatory colonizing community and to consider this sort of offence as anything less than an act of war and outright hostility, even if it comes couched in ideologies of multiculturalism or "Aboriginalism,"[19] would be to fall prey to the mystifying traits of Eurocentric ideology that Robert Stam and Ella Shohat point out in their seminal book on the topic.[20] Some value-systems are so utterly incompatible that to invoke "peaceful coexistence" in their moments of conflict is tantamount to espousing the extinction of one of the parties, the one with the more fragile value-system under attack. In the midst of a war that doubles as a what Guattari calls a "war of subjectivity," the therapeutically political import of Fourth Cinema lies in the fact that films subject—they subject along the lines of the values immanent to them; values that defy neocolonial norms and expectations.

One of the most important attempts at theorizing the cinema's production of subjectivity appears in *Cinema 2*'s passages on fabulation. Fabulation is a term originally mobilized by Henri Bergson, and later taken up in an overtly political usage by Gilles Deleuze to theorize the creative force of fiction that convokes "a people to come" (in political cinemas responding to

treaty was broken, that meant that we must again have been at war with the white man. Because when you break a treaty, this is what it signifies."

19 According to Taiaiake Alfred, Aboriginalism equals death for Indigenous peoples; it is a colonial ideology of assimilation that is being sold to Indigenous communities through comprador politicians that aim to turn Indigenous culture and land into cultural and natural resources (Alfred 2005: 129). Aboriginalism aims to marketize everything about and belonging to Indigenous peoples that has not yet been assimilated. In this regard, we can see why colonial governments around the world are so at ease in abandoning the policies of complete cultural assimilation that characterized colonial policy up until the mid-20th century, and was embodied by legislation prohibiting religious and cultural practices of Indigenous peoples, the forced conversion to Christianity, and adoption of colonial languages. Now, neocolonial governments view Indigenous languages, songs, dances, ceremonies and arts as marketable commodities of national prestige and as perfectly acceptable cultural products, as long as they do not interfere with the ongoing colonial project of converting Indigenous lands into "natural resources."

20 The five main aspects of Eurocentrism according to Stam and Shohat are: 1. It projects a linear historical trajectory leading from classical Greece to metropolitan capitals to Europe and the USA, and it renders history a series of empires from Pax Romana to Pax Americana; 2. It attributes to the West an inherent progress towards democracy; 3. It elides non-European democratic traditions, while obscuring manipulations within Western democracies and masking their part in manipulating/subverting non-Western democracies; 4. It minimizes the West's oppressive practices by viewing them as contingent, accidental, exceptional; and 5. It appropriates the cultural and material production of non-Europeans while negating both their achievements and its own appropriation, in that way consolidating its own sense of self (Shohat and Stam: 2-3).

a colonial relationship).[21] Writing on filmmakers such as Ousmane Sembene, Pierre Perrault and Glauber Rocha, Deleuze uses the concept of fabulation to account for individual speech-acts (legending, "storytelling") that cross the boundary separating private business from politics in the production of collective utterances that call forth "the lines of potential collective development that are immanent within the present [psycho]social field" (Bogue 2007: 98, my modification). Deleuze's focus on the fabulatory speech-act as an immediately collective utterance productive of a revolutionary people to come has proven particularly useful for analyzing political cinemas of orality. It may even seem like a well-suited theory for conceptualizing the healing force of Fourth Cinema, given that it grows out of the world's most ancient oral traditions. Yet in dwelling on this final, wordless scene of *Palawan Fate*, and thinking about the most visceral moments that punctuate the Fourth Cinema canon, there seems to be "something else," to paraphrase Barclay, at work in its method of fabulatory subjectification beyond the oral tradition.

Many of Fourth Cinema's most poignant moments are literally speechless scenes filled with mystical healing. These are the moments of another—decolonized—world being birthed out of the present colonial reality. A brief gloss of the canon springs the following examples to mind: The childhood fantasies of a boy whose family overcomes its history of separation through magic in Taiaka Waititi's *Boy* (2010); the brooding Maori statues, angered over being stolen from their people and trapped in a Berlin museum whose magnetism produces an international social movement, in Barry Barclay's *Te Rua* (1991); the concluding scene of Sterlin Harjo's *Barking Water* (2009) when the elder protagonist must announce the death of her best friend to a family member, yet the death is too grave to be spoken of on film, so she silently kisses a baby on the top of the head; the non-diegetic inserts in Sherman Alexie's *The Business of Fancydancing* (2002) where poet protagonist Seymour Polatkin performs a shawl dance in front of a blacked out background, in an act that fully embraces the contradictions of the two worlds that

21 It is worth pointing out the important differences between fabulation in Deleuze and Bergson. What for Deleuze is a revolutionary act constructive of "a people to come" that defies colonial mythology, originally appeared in Bergson as the reactionary function of society *par excellence*. For Bergson, fabulation "attaches man to life, and consequently individual to society, by telling him tales on par with those with which we lull children to sleep" (1935: 179). Fabulation is a necessity of social cohesion, a necessary fiction, that prevents man, who has been endowed with intelligence and can thus think of his own individual interests and foresee his own death, from acting egotistically or from being overwhelmed by his mortality. Fabulation ensures a moral order that keeps man socially productive. For these reasons, fabulation is a fundamental operation of religion in what Bergson terms "closed societies." To consult Bergson's use of the concept of fabulation see the chapter "Static Religion" in *The Two Sources of Morality and Religion*.

he straddles; and *Samson & Delilah* (Warwick Thornton, 2009), a feature length film almost entirely devoid of dialogue, where in a bout of gasoline induced hallucination, Samson's girlfriend Delilah appears to him as an angel who, in an unexpected, decolonizing détournement of *terra nullius*, whisks him off to a wide-open, seemingly unpopulated, land of limitless possibility and mutual recovery.

These non-discursive moments, pulled from some of the most significant Indigenous feature films ever made, shows that the values constitutive of Fourth Cinema's "interiority" come to expression, and convoke a people to come, in ways other than just the speech-act. Rather than orally convoking a new social condition, these moments excavate the affective tonality of a possible world through a technique that approximates what Bergson calls "mystic intuition." For Bergson, the mystic's intuition delves into a virgin plane of ecstatic experience never previously felt, which is then shared with humankind, interpolating it into that affective quality of rapture: "William James used to say he had never experienced mystic states; but he added that if he heard them spoken of by a man who had experienced them 'something within him echoed the call'" (Bergson 1935: 210). Great mystics, by making their experiences reverberate in the world "lift the soul to another plane," (Bergson 1935: 182) and by uplifting the soul, an affective image is awakened that anticipates what is to come:

> When the darkest depths of the soul are stirred, what rises to the surface and attains consciousness takes on there, if it be intense enough, the form of an image or an emotion. The image is often pure hallucination, just as the emotion may be meaningless agitation. But they both may express the fact that the disturbance is a systematic readjustment with a view to equilibrium on a higher level: the image then becomes symbolic of what is about to happen, and the emotion is a concentration of the soul awaiting transformation. (Bergson 1935: 196)

If Fourth Cinema can be endowed with a healing capacity, and not merely be recognized as representing or narrating healing, it is precisely because its mystic intuition firmly holds onto core Indigenous values (assuring it has a soul) while at the same time speculatively entering into the affective plane of a decolonized world-to-come where these values have won out in the war of subjectivity and are granted the freedom to proliferate. By entering into this fabulatory, decolonized future, absorbing what it feels like, and bringing that feeling back to the colonial present, Fourth Cinema offers itself up as a healing presence to an Indigenous present bearing the wounds of systematic harm. According to Bergson, the method of the mystics consists in supposing possible what is actually impossible in a given society (1935: 63), and this is exactly what Fourth cinema does. Fourth Cinema's mysticism, the non-discursive analogue of Deleuze's fabulation, makes echo a decolonized way of feeling that beckons a response—a mode of subjectification that defies, and in defying, that attacks—the neocolonial appropriation of Indigenous health and resurgence.

The mystic intuition of Fourth Cinema's therapeutically speculative images explains, finally, why Barry Barclay had such a hard time putting his finger on his own invention, and identifying the "interiority" of Fourth Cinema as anything more than an ambiguous notion of ancient values. For inside of the ancient values transported to new generations, lands and peoples through cinema, there is an affective stirring—a mystic intuition—that eludes stable form, precisely because it does not yet know the collective future that it echoes forth. This mystic intuition which spills out from the Fourth Cinema's interior—the seat of its core values, or soul— is at once an act of resurgent flourishing and act of political antagonism, an act of healing and act of war. Indigenous filmmakers are thus what we could call "therapeutic activists," at once artists and storytellers, clinicians of a neocolonial wartime reality and speculators of a decolonial health.

Bibliography

Aboriginal Healing Foundation. *Third Interim Evaluation Report of the Aboriginal Healing Foundation Program Activity*. Ottawa: Aboriginal Healing Foundation, 2003.

Alfred, Taiaiake. *Peace, Power, Righteousness: An Indigenous Manifesto*. Don Mills, Ontario: Oxford University Press Canada, 1999.

Alfred, Taiaiake. "Restitution is the Real Pathway for Justice of Indigenous Peoples." *Response, Responsibility, Renewal: Canada's Truth and Reconciliation Journey*. Eds. Gregory Younging, Jonathan Dewar, Mike DeGagné. Ottawa: Aboriginal Healing Foundation, 2009. 179-187.

Alfred, Taiaiake. *Wasáse: Indigenous Pathways of Actions and Freedoms*. Peterborough, Ontario: Broadview Press, 2005.

Alpern, Stephen I. "Insurgency in Northeast Thailand: A New Cause for Alarm". *Asian Survey* 15.8 (August 1975): 684-692.

Barclay, Barry. "An Open Letter to John Barnett." *Oceania in the Age of Global Media*. Ed. Peter Britos. Special Issue of *Spectator* 23:1 (Spring 2003a) 33-36.

Barclay, Barry. "Celebrating Fourth Cinema." *Illusions: New Zealand Moving Image and Performing Arts Criticism* 35 (Winter 2003b): 7-11.

Bergson, Henri. *The Two Sources of Morality and Religion*. Trans. R. Ashley Audra and Cloudesley Brereton with the assistance of W. Horsefall Carter. London: MacMillan and Co., Limited, 1935.

Bogue, Ronald. *Deleuze's Way. Essays in Transverse Ethics and Aesthetics*. Aldershot & Burlington: Ashgate, 2007.

Chrisjohn, Roland D., Tanya Wasacase, Lisa Nussey, Andrea Smith, Marc Legault, Pierre Loiselle and Mathieu Bourgeois. "Genocide and Indian Residential Schooling: The Past is Present." *Canada and International Humanitarian Law: Peacekeeping and War Crimes in the Modern Era*. Eds. R.D. Wiggers and A.L. Griffiths. Halifax: Dalhousie University Press, 2002.

Coulthard, Glen Sean. *Red Skin White Masks: Rejecting the Colonial Politics of Recognition*. Minneapolis and London: University of Minnesota Press, 2014.

Dapice, Ann N. "The Medicine Wheel." *Journal of Transcultural Nursing*. 17.3 (July 2006): 251-260.

Deleuze, Gilles. *Cinema 2: The Time-Image*. Trans. Hugh Tomlinson and Robert Galeta. Minneapolis: University of Minnesota Press, 2007.

Department of Indian Affairs and Northern Development. *Gathering Strength: Canada's Aboriginal Action Plan*. Ottawa: Minister of Public Works and Government Services Canada, 1998.

Department of Indian Affairs and Northern Development. "Notes for an Address by the Honourable Jane Stewart, Minister of Indian Affairs and Northern Development, on the Occasion of the Unveiling of Gathering Strength—Canada's Aboriginal Action Plan." Ottawa, 1998. http://www.aadnc-aandc.gc.ca/eng/1100100015725/1100100015726

Eder, James F. "Economic Change and the Demise of Curing Ceremonies Among the Batak of Palawan". *Changing Lives, Changing Rites: Ritual and Social Dynamics in Philippine and Indonesian Uplands*. Eds. Susan D. Russell and Clark E. Cunningham. Ann Arbor: Center for South and Southeast Asian Studies at the University of Michigan, 1989: 81-102.

Granovetter, Mark S. "The Strength of Weak Ties." *American Journal of Sociology* 78.6 (May 1973): 1360-1380.

Irlbacher-Fox, Stephanie. *Finding Dahshaa: Self-Government, Social Suffering, and Aboriginal Policy in Canada* (Vancouver: University of British Columbia Press, 2009).

Macdonald, Charles. "Kinship and Fellowship among the Palawan". *Anarchic Solidarity: Autonomy, Equality, and Fellowship in Southeast Asia*. New Haven, Connecticut: Yale University Southeast Asia Studies, 2011. 119-140.

Macdonald, Charles. *Uncultural Behaviour: An Anthropological Investigation of Suicide in the Southern Philippines*. Honolulu: University of Hawaii Press, 2007.

Manuel, George and Michael Posluns. *The Fourth World: An Indian Reality*. Don Mills, Ontario: Collier-Macmillan Canada, 1974.

Million, Dian. *Therapeutic Nations: Healing in an Age of Indigenous Human Rights*. Tucson: University of Arizona Press, 2013.

Robbins, Julian A. and Jonathan Dewar. "Traditional Indigenous Approaches to Healing and the modern welfare of Traditional Knowledge, Spirituality and Lands: A critical reflection on practices and policies taken from the Canadian Indigenous Example." *The International Indigenous Policy Journal* 2.4 (2011): 1-17.

Shohat, Ella and Robert Stam. *Unthinking Eurocentrism: Multiculturalism and the Media*. London and New York: Routledge, 1994.

Simpson, Leanne. *Dancing On Our Turtle's Back: Stories of Nishnaabeg Re-Creation, Resurgence and a New Emergence*. Winnipeg: Arbeiter Ring Publishing, 2011.

Waziyatawin and Michael Yellow Bird, Eds. *For Indigenous Minds Only: A Decolonization Handbook*. Santa Fe: School for Advanced Research Press, 2013.

Solito, Auraeus. "Director's Statement". *Busong (Palawan Fate) Press Kit*. 2011.

UHM Center for Southeast Asian Studies Lecture Series Podcast. "Raymond Lee". *University of Hawaii*. Podcast.

Zerehi, Sima Sahar. "Plight of Inuit Healing Centre in Ottawa Highlights North's Lack of Mental Health Care." *CBC News*. 15 February 2016. Online. https://www.cbc.ca/news/canada/north/plight-of-inuit-healing-centre-in-ottawa-highlights-north-s-lack-of-mental-health-care-1.3448218

For Therapeutic Activisms

"The work of art, for those who use it, is an activity of unframing, a rupture of sense [...] which leads to a recreation and a reinvention of the subject itself"
–Félix Guattari[1]

How is therapeutic activism? It remains to be developed, but by challenging the psychiatric consensus around depression's etiology, symptomatology, and therapy, filmmakers like Apichatpong Weerasethakul, Kanakan Balintagos, Kelly Reichardt and Angela Schanelec create the intellectual conditions for its proliferation, and legitimize the sorts of grassroots practices that have historically grown in response to pandemics.

In response to the cataclysmic events of the 1980s, Paula A. Treichler turned to visual culture and art to protest the hegemonic discourse of "scientists, physicians and public health authorities who argued repeatedly that AIDS represented 'an epidemic of infectious disease and nothing more'" (1999: 1). Defying their authoritative consensus on the matter, she asserts, "AIDS is more than an epidemic disease, it is an epidemic of meanings" (1999: 1). Once the authority of the disease model was contested through recourse to visual culture, it became possible to reimagine the nature of the pandemic and initiate ways of acting in and on the crisis. In the 1980s-90s, HIV/AIDS activists seized the opportunity offered by the crisis in which they lived and loved to prompt a collective reimagining of modes of relationality. Much of the activism that arose utilized the media of the time, especially VHS tapes, but independently published magazines as well, to change the narrow set of meanings that network television's fear mongering stapled onto the pandemic. New images and perspectives that constructed the subjective cartography of life with HIV/AIDS in a much different light than

1 Quoted in *Chaosmosis* p. 134.

Szymanski, A., *Cinemas of Therapeutic Activism: Depression and the Politics of Existence.* Taylor & Francis Group, 2020
DOI: 10.5117/9789463723121_CONC

either science or the mainstream media vacated a role for non-professional involvement.

Acting therapeutically in the grips of the AIDS crisis came to imply a multiplicity of relational practices, such as collective quilting, gatherings and vigils to mourn the mounting deaths, caring for the sick, sharing knowledge about different treatment methods and their side effects, and promoting overall health. These collective acts ultimately became as indispensible for well-being as going to the doctor or taking one's medication. Even when these collective practices were primarily catalyzed by concern for well-being, they undoubtedly doubled as activism, since they intervened in a crisis perpetuated by political negligence, and refused to let the brokers of power dictate the subjective coordinates of those at at risk. Carrying on this tradition today, therapeutic activism ceases to relinquish subjectivity to power's dominant modelizations, and works on the premise articulated by Erin Manning, that "it is impossible to abstract conditions of well-being from the relational field" (2016: 128).

Working therapeutically on the relational field is exactly what the auteurs discussed in the preceding pages make possible, because their critical acts of perception have discovered the relational field to be the eventful site where melancholy is produced. Limit-cases of minor cinema such as these lend support to the growing wave of politicized mental health activism that, building on the tradition of HIV/AIDS activism, has begun to experiment with recomposing subjectivity without waiting for the sanction of medical authorities. A living example of this is Sheffield-based *Designing Out Suicide*, an open submission zine that holds workshops on suicide prevention. "The workshops that support the making of the zine are a means of peer support in a non-hierarchical environment," says founder Lisa O'Hara. "It's good to share experiences or just get together to talk with no experts present" (Bedei: n.p.). The zine is one of many activist-oriented "DIY resources for self-care, support and intersectional debate" which include the *Doll Hospital Journal*, *Black Women & Self Care: Thoughts on Mental Health, Oppression, and Healing*, and *Bad Therapy/Rad Therapy*, among others.

Grassroots initiatives to support mental health have also manifested a strong presence online. One particularly active online community is called the *Bunz Mental Health Zone*, a closed Facebook group with over four thousand members mostly based in the Toronto area. The group is a place where people ask for advice, share their experiences navigating the city's mental health system and make friends who encourage their wellness efforts, usually by checking-in or organizing shared activities. It is also a regular occurrence for people on *Bunz* to announce their suicidal intentions, and for other members to offer support in the most urgent of moments by extending sympathy, compassion and shared presence. Whether it be a zine workshop or an online group devoted to suicide prevention, these platforms of relation carry the seeds for a more sustained and concerted therapeutic activism premised on the subjective contingency of the encounter. In addition to working interpersonally by connecting individuals based on their mutual mental health needs, these platforms also work through the transindividual, by prompting spontaneous collective formations (whether in-person or online) based on a mutual concern for well-being which leave no parties unaffected. To respond to another's call for help in a time of crisis is to encounter alterity and to move with some of the most ancient values known to humankind. Psyches and socius are bound to be affected, recomposed into novel, and perhaps therapeutic, assemblages. Contemporary cinema's aesthetic mapping of melancholy justifies these sorts of activist praxes by affirming the therapeutic value of tending to the relational field's conditions of subjectivity production. Cinemas of therapeutic activism offer a perceptual *optique*, a symptomatology of civilization, through which these collective experiments can be seen as more than supplements to medical treatment, but the very basis of a radically relational and experimental therapeutics based on the ethos of schizoanalysis.

The cinema's relationship to the burgeoning therapeutic activisms-to-come is partially one of inspiring and legitimizing initiatives such as these. To conclude on an even more speculative note though, I would like to propose a line of inquiry for future research: that we take these filmmakers at their word, or at least extend to them a hypothetical sympathy,[2] when they espouse faith in the healing potential of cinema. When Kanakan Balintagos explains how he makes films to heal his people and Apichatpong Weerasethakul says that film viewing functions as therapy for mental or emotional pain, they are not speaking metaphorically. Nor is Guattari, who echoes their faith with conviction when he asserts, "It is even possible for a film to upset our whole existence" (2009a: 266).

The cinemas of therapeutic activism that populate the pages of this study are comprised of images that perceive the therapeutic potential of encountering alterity, creating common planes of experience, and building alterious relationships predicated on sustainable and mutually beneficial Indigenous values. They broaden perception from the limits of the clinical gaze to critically re-envision a speculative and eventfully-contingent

2 This attitude is inspired by Bertrand Russell, who writes: "In studying a philosopher, the right attitude is neither reverence nor contempot, but first a kind of hypothetical sympathy" (58).

etiology, symptomatology and therapy of depression embedded in the dynamism of diverse relational fields of subjectivity production. In turn, as these films are folded into the world's assemblages at large, their images offer themselves up as "vectors of subjectification" (Guattari 1995: 25) on the chance that they may catalyze the sorts of subjective recompositions that they go to such lengths to picture.

How these types of images are taken up remains to be seen, and the effects of these artists' concern for melancholy and investment in the therapeutic potential of the relational encounter cannot yet be assessed. Nevertheless, one thing is for certain: through aesthetic experimentation, they have initiated a process of re-existentializing and re-politicizing the depression pandemic, and made it possible to act, politically and therapeutically, in the midst of a crisis whose subjective dimension has been obscured by psychiatric power.

Bibliography

Bedei, Cristina. "The Mental Health Zines Filling the Gap that Therapy Doesn't." *Dazed*. July 2016. Online. www.dazeddigital.com/artsandculture/article/32004/1/the-mental-health-zines-filling-the-gap-that-therapy-doesn-t

Manning, Erin. *The Minor Gesture*. Durham and London: Duke University Press, 2016.

Guattari, Félix. *Chaosmosis: An Ethico-Aesthetic Paradigm*. Trans. Paul Bains and Julian Pefanis. Bloomington and Indianapolis: Indiana University Press, 1995.

Guattari, Félix. *Chaosophy: Texts and Interviews 1972-1977*. Ed. Sylvère Lotringer. Trans. David L. Sweet, Jarred Becker, and Taylor Adkins. Los Angeles, CA: Semiotext(e), 2009a.

Treichler, Paula A. *How to Have Theory in an Epidemic: Cultural Chronicles of AIDS*. Durham and London: Duke University Press, 1999.

Bibliography

Abel, Marco. *The Counter-Cinema of the Berlin School.* Rochester, New York: Camden House, 2013.

Aboriginal Healing Foundation. *Third Interim Evaluation Report of the Aboriginal Healing Foundation Program Activity.* Ottawa: Aboriginal Healing Foundation, 2003.

Alfred, Taiaiake. *Peace, Power, Righteousness: An Indigenous Manifesto.* Don Mills, Ontario: Oxford University Press Canada, 1999.

Alfred, Taiaiake. "Restitution is the Real Pathway for Justice of Indigenous Peoples." *Response, Responsibility, Renewal: Canada's Truth and Reconciliation Journey.* Eds. Gregory Younging, Jonathan Dewar, Mike DeGagné. Ottawa: Aboriginal Healing Foundation, 2009. 179-87.

Alfred, Taiaiake. *Wasáse: Indigenous Pathways of Actions and Freedoms.* Peterborough, Ontario: Broadview Press, 2005.

Alpern, Stephen I. "Insurgency in Northeast Thailand: A New Cause for Alarm". *Asian Survey* 15.8 (August 1975): 684-692.

American Psychiatric Association. *Diagnostic and Statistical Manual of Mental Disorders. Third Edition. DSM-I.* Washington, DC: American Psychiatric Association, 1952.

American Psychiatric Association. *Diagnostic and Statistical Manual of Mental Disorders. Fifth Edition. DSM-5.* Washington, DC and London, England: American Psychiatric Association, 2013.

Andrew, Dudley. "Foreward." *Global Art Cinema: New Theories and Histories.* Eds. Rosalind Galt and Karl Schoonover. Oxford and New York: Oxford University Press, 2010. v-xi.

Angell, Marcia. "The Epidemic of Mental Illness: Why?" *The New York Review.* 23 June 2011a. Online. www.nybooks.com/articles/2011/06/23/epimeic-mental-illness-why/?pagination=false

Angell, Marcia. "The Illusions of Psychiatry." *The New York Review.* 14 July 2011b. Online. http://www.nybooks.com/articles/2011/07/14/illusions-of-psychiatry/

Baer, Hester. "Affectless Economies: The Berlin School and Neoliberalism." *Discourse* 35.1 (Winter 2013): 72-100.

Balázs, Béla. *Theory of the Film: Character and Growth.* Trans. Edith Bone. New York, Dover Publications, 1970.

Barclay, Barry. "An Open Letter to John Barnett." *Oceania in the Age of Global Media.* Ed. Peter Britos. Special Issue of *Spectator* 23:1 (Spring 2003a) 33-36.

Barclay, Barry. "Celebrating Fourth Cinema." *Illusions: New Zealand Moving Image and Performing Arts Criticism* 35 (Winter 2003b): 7-11.

Barthes, Roland. *Camera Lucida: Reflections on Photography.* Trans. Richard Howard. New York: Hill and Wang, 1981.

Baute, Michael, Ekkehard Knrer, Volker Pantenberg, Stefan Pethke, Simon Rothler. "The Berlin School – A Collage." *Senses of Cinema* 55 (July 2010): n.p. Online. http://sensesofcinema.com/2010/feature-articles/the-berlin-school-%E2%80%93-a-collage-2/

Bazin, André. *Bazin and Italian Neorealism.* Ed. Bert Cardullo. New York: Continuum, 2011.

Bazin, André. *Qu'est-ce que le cinéma?* Paris: Éditions du Cerf, 1997.

Bazin, André. *What is Cinema? Volume Two.* Trans. Hugh Gray. Berkeley and Los Angeles: University of California Press, 2005.

Bazin, André. *What is Cinema?* Trans. Timothy Barnard. Montreal: Caboose, 2009.

Bedei, Cristina. "The Mental Health Zines Filling the Gap that Therapy Doesn't." *Dazed.* July 2016. Online. www.dazeddigital.com/artsandculture/article/32004/1/the-mental-health-zines-filling-the-gap-that-therapy-doesn-t

Benjamin, Walter. "Theses on the Philosophy of History". in *Illuminations.* New York: Schocken Books, 1969: 253-264.

Bensmaïa, Réda. "Foreward: The Kafka Effect." *Kafka: Toward a Minor Literature.* Trans. Terry Cochran. Minneapolis: University of Minnesota Press, 1986.

Berardi, Franco 'Bifo'. *After the Future.* Edinburgh, Oakland, Baltimore: AK Press, 2011a.

Berardi, Franco 'Bifo'. *Le Ciel Est Enfin Tombé Sur La Terre.* Paris: Le Seuil, 1978.

Berardi, Franco 'Bifo'. *Félix Guattari: Thought, Friendship, and Visionary Cartography.* Trans and Eds. Guiseppina Mecchia and Charles J. Stivale. Hampshire and New York: Palgrave MacMillan, 2008

Berardi, Franco 'Bifo'. "Re-Assessing Composition: 40 Years After the Publication of Anti-Oedipus." *Subjectivity* 5.1 (2012): 111-119.

Berardi, Franco 'Bifo'. "Repression, Expression, Depression." *The Guattari-Effect.* Ed. Éric Alliez and Andrew Goffey. London and New York: Continuum, 2011b.

Berardi, Franco 'Bifo'. *The Soul at Work: From Alienation to Autonomy.* Trans. Francesca Cadel and Guiseppina Mecchia. Los Angeles: Semiotext(e), 2009.

Berardi, Franco 'Bifo'. *The Uprising: On Poetry and Finance.* Los Angeles: Semiotext(e), 2012.

Bergson, Henri. *The Two Sources of Morality and Religion.* Trans. R. Ashley Audra and Cloudesley Brereton with the assistance of W. Horsefall Carter. London: MacMillan and Co., Limited, 1935.

Beugnet, Martine. *Cinema and Sensation: French Film and the Art of Transgression.* Edinburgh: Edinburgh University Press, 2007.

Blankenship, Janelle. "Preface to Holes, Burrows, Lines of Flight: Media and Spatiality in Deleuze and Guattari." Ed. Janelle Blankenship. *Polygraph: An International Journal of Culture and Politics* 14 (2002): 3-15.

Boehler, Natalie. "The Jungle as Border Zone: The Aesthetics of Nature in the Work of Apichatpong Weerasethakul". *ASEAS – Austrian Journal of South-East Asian Studies* 4.2 (2011): 290-304.

Bogue, Ronald. *Deleuze's Way. Essays in Transverse Ethics and Aesthetics*. Aldershot & Burlington: Ashgate, 2007.

Boltanski, Luc and Even Chiapello. *The New Spirit of Capitalism*. London: Verso, 2005.

Bondanella, Peter. *A History of Italian Cinema*. New York and London: Continuum, 2009.

Bordwell, David. "Contemporary Film Studies and the Vicissitudes of Grand Theory." *Post-Theory: Reconstructing Film Studies*. London: The University of Wisconsin Press, 1996. 3-36.

Bordwell, David. *Narrative in the Fiction Film*. London: Methuen, 1985.

Bordwell, David. *On the History of Film Style*. Cambridge, MA: Harvard University Press, 1997.

Bordwell, David. "The Art Cinema as Mode of Film Practice." *Film Theory and Criticism: Introductory Readings. Sixth Edition.* Eds. Leo Braudy and Marshall Cohen. New York and Oxford: Oxford University Press, 2004: 774-782.

Bordwell, David and Kristin Thompson. *Film History: An Introduction*. New York: McGraw-Hill, 2010.

Bordwell, David, Janet Staiger, and Kristin Thompson. *The Classical Hollywood Cinema: Film, Style & Mode of Production to 1960*. London: Routledge, 2006 [1985].

Brody, Richard. "About 'Neo-Neo Realism'." *The New Yorker*. 19 March 2009. Online. http://www.newyorker.com/culture/richard-brody/about-neo-neo-realism

Brüggeman, Dietrich. "Fahr zur Hölle, Berliner Schule." *D-Trick*. 11 February 2013. http://d-trick.de/blog/fahr-sur-holle-berliner-schule

Burcasa, Stephanie L. and William G. Iacono. "Risk for Recurrene in Depression." *Clinical Psychology Review* 27.8 (December 2007): 959-985.

Burch, Noël. *Theory of Film Practice*. Trans. Helen R. Lane. Princeton, NJ: Princeton University Press, 1981.

Burkeman, Oliver. "Therapy wars: the revenge of Freud." *The Guardian*. 7 January 2016. Online. https://www.theguardian.com/science/2016/jan/07/therapy-wars-revenge-of-freud-cognitive-behavioural-therapy

Burton, Robert. *The Essential Anatomy of Melancholy*. Mineola, New York: Dover Publications, 2002.

Butler, Judith. *The Psychic Life of Power: Theories in Subjection*. Stanford, California: Stanford University Press, 1997.

Campbell, Denis. "NHS Mental Health Services Failing Young People, Say Psychiatrists." *The Guardian*. 26 December 2016. Online. https://www.theguardian.com/society/2016/dec/26/nhs-mental-health-services-failing-young-people-say-psychiatrists

Carlat, Daniel. *Unhinged: The Trouble with Psychiatry. A Doctor's Revelations About a Profession in Crisis.* New York: Free Press, 2010.

Carterine, James. "Can Computer-Guided Cognitive Behaviour Therapy Improve Depression Treatment?" *Harvard Health Blog.* 17 December 2015. www.health.harvard.edu/blog/computer-guided-cognitive-bahviour-therapy-can-it-improve-depression-treatment-in-primary-care-201512178856

Casella, Alessandro. "Communism and Insurrection in Thailand". *The World Today* 26.5 (May 1970): 197-208.

Casetti, Franceso. "Style as Site of Negotiation: The Case of Realism and Neo-Realism." *Francescocasetti.com.* Online. 23 April 2005. https://francescocasetti.files.wordpress.com/2011/03/style-as-site-of-negotiation.pdf

Child, Ben. "Apichatpong Weerasethakul: I won't censor my work for Thailand." *The Guardian.* Online. https://www.theguardian.com/film/205/2015/oct/16/apichatpong-weerasethakul-cemetery-of-splendour-cannes

Chrisjohn, Roland D., Tanya Wasacase, Lisa Nussey, Andrea Smith, Marc Legault, Pierre Loiselle and Mathieu Bourgeois. "Genocide and Indian Residential Schooling: The Past is Present." *Canada and International Humanitarian Law: Peacekeeping and War Crimes in the Modern Era.* Eds. R.D. Wiggers and A.L. Griffiths. Halifax: Dalhousie University Press, 2002.

Clair, Jean. *Mélancolie: génie et folie en Occident.* Paris, Gallimard, 2005.

Clarke, David. "'Capitalism Has No More Natural Enemies': The Berlin School." *A Companion to German Cinema.* Eds. Terri Ginsberg and Andrea Mensch. West Sussex, UK: Wiley-Blackwell, 2012.

Cloud, Dana L. *Control and Consolation in American Culture and Politics: Rhetoric of Therapy.* Thousand Oaks: Sage Publications, 1998.

Combes, Muriel. *Gilbert Simondon and the Philosophy of the Transindividual.* Trans. Thomas LaMarre. Cambridge and London: The MIT Press, 2013.

Cook, David A. *A History of Narrative Film.* Fourth Edition. New York and London: W.W. Norton & Company, 2004.

Coulthard, Glen Sean. *Red Skin White Masks: Rejecting the Colonial Politics of Recognition.* Minneapolis and London: University of Minnesota Press, 2014.

Crimp, Douglas. *Melancholy and Moralism: Essays on AIDS and Queer Politics.* Cambridge, Massachusetts: MIT Press, 2002.

Curry, Bill. "Philpott warns premiers she won't budge on effort to expand mental-health funding." *The Globe and Mail.* 20 December 2016. Online. https://beta.theglobeandmail.com/news/politics/philpott-warns-premiers-she-womt-budge-on-effort-to-expand-mental-health-funding/article33397386/

Cvetkovich, Ann. *Depression: A Public Feeling.* Durham and London: Duke University Press, 2012.

Dapice, Ann N. "The Medicine Wheel." *Journal of Transcultural Nursing*. 17.3 (July 2006): 251-260.

Day, Richard. *Multiculturalism and the History of Canadian Diversity*. Toronto: University of Toronto Press, 2000.

De Guia, Katrin. *Kapwa: The Self in the Other. Worldviews and Lifestyles of Filipino Culture-Bearers*. Quezon City: Anvil Publishing, 2005.

Deleuze, Gilles. *Cinema 1: The Movement-Image*. Trans. Hugh Tomlinson and Barbara Habberjam. Minneapolis: University of Minnesota Press, 2006.

Deleuze, Gilles. *Cinema 2: The Time-Image*. Trans. Hugh Tomlinson and Robert Galeta. Minneapolis: University of Minnesota Press, 2007.

Deleuze, Gilles. "Control and Becoming." *Negotiations: 1972-1990*. New York and Chichester, West Sussex: Columbia University Press, 1995. 169-176.

Deleuze, Gilles. *Difference and Repetition*. New York: Columbia University Press, 1994.

Deleuze, Gilles. *Empiricism and Subjectivity: An Essay on Hume's Theory of Human Nature*. Trans. Constantin V. Boundas. New York: Columbia University Press, 1991.

Deleuze, Gilles. *Essays Critical and Clinical*. Trans. Daniel W. Smith and Michael A. Greco. London and New York, 1998.

Deleuze, Gilles. *Foucault*. Trans. Seán Hand. Minneapolis: University of Minnesota Press, 1988.

Deleuze, Gilles. "How Do We Recognize Structuralism?" *Desert Islands and Other Texts: 1953-1974*. Los Angeles and New York: Semiotext(e), 2004.

Deleuze, Gilles. "Immanence: A Life." *Two Regimes of Madness: Texts and Interviews 1975-1995*. Ed. David Lapoujade. Trans. Ames Hodes and Mike Taormina. New York: Semiotext(e), 2006. 384-389.

Deleuze, Gilles. "Mediators." *Negotiations: 1972-1990*. Trans. Martin Joughin. New York and Chichester, West Sussex: Columbia University Press, 1995. 121-134.

Deleuze, Gilles. *Pure Immanence: Essays in A Life*. Trans. Anne Boyman. New York: Zone Books, 2001.

Deleuze, Gilles. "The Brain is the Screen: An Interview with Gilles Deleuze." *The Brain is the Screen: Deleuze and the Philosophy of Cinema*. Ed. Gregory Flaxman. Minneapolis and London: University of Minnesota Press, 2000. 365-373.

Deleuze, Gilles. *The Logic of Sense*. New York: Columbia University Press, 1990.

Deleuze, Gilles and Félix Guattari. *A Thousand Plateaus: Capitalism and Schizophrenia*. Trans. Brian Massumi. Minneapolis: University of Minnesota Press, 1987.

Deleuze, Gilles and Félix Guattari. *Anti-Oedipus: Capitalism and Schizophrenia*. Trans. Robert Hurley, Mark Seem, and Helen R. Lane. Minneapolis: University of Minnesota Press, 1983.

Deleuze, Gilles and Félix Guattari. *Kafka: Toward a Minor Literature*. Trans. Dana Polan. Minneapolis and London: University of Minnesota Press, 1986.

Deleuze, Gilles and Félix Guattari. *What is Philosophy?* New York: Columbia University Press, 1994.

Department of Health. *IAPT three-year report: The first million patients*. Department of Health. November, 2012.

Department of Indian Affairs and Northern Development. *Gathering Strength: Canada's Aboriginal Action Plan*. Ottawa: Minister of Public Works and Government Services Canada, 1998.

Department of Indian Affairs and Northern Development. "Notes for an Address by the Honourable Jane Stewart, Minister of Indian Affairs and Northern Development, on the Occasion of the Unveiling of Gathering Strength—Canada's Aboriginal Action Plan." Ottawa, 1998. http://www.aadnc-aandc.gc.ca/eng/1100100015725/1100100015726

Doidge, Norman. *The Brain that Changes Itself: Stories of Personal Triumph from the Frontiers of Brain Science*. London: Penguin, 2007.

Dosse, François. *Gilles Deleuze and Félix Guattari: Intersecting Lives*. Trans. Deborah Glassman. New York: Columbia University Press, 2010.

Eder, James F. "Economic Change and the Demise of Curing Ceremonies Among the Batak of Palawan". *Changing Lives, Changing Rites: Ritual and Social Dynamics in Philippine and Indonesian Uplands*. Eds. Susan D. Russell and Clark E. Cunningham. Ann Arbor: Center for South and Southeast Asian Studies at the University of Michigan, 1989: 81-102.

Fisher, Mark. *Capitalist Realism: Is There No Alternative?* Winchester, UK and Washington, USA: 0 Books, 2009.

Flaxman, Gregory. "Introduction." *The Brain is the Screen*. Ed. Gregory Flaxman. Minneapolis and London: University of Minnesota Press, 2000.

Foucault, Michel. *Discipline and Punish: The Birth of the Prison*. Trans. Alan Sheridan. New York: Vintage Books, 1995.

Foucault, Michel. "Preface." *Anti-Oedipus: Capitalism and Schizophrenia*. Minneapolis: University of Minnesota Press, 1983.

Foucault, Michel. *Psychiatric Power: Lectures at the Collège de France 1973-1974*. Eds. Jacques Lagrange, François Ewald, Alessandro Fontana and Arnold I. Davidson. Trans. Graham Burchell. Basingstoke and New York: Palgrave Macmillan, 2006.

Foucault, Michel. *The Birth of Biopolitics: Lectures at the Collège de France, 1978-1979*. Trans. Michel Sennelart. Basingstoke: Palgrave MacMillan, 2008.

Foucault, Michel. *The Birth of the Clinic: An Archeology of Medical Perception*. Trans. A.M. Sheridan. London and New York: Routledge, 2003.

Foucault, Michel. "The Discourse on Language." *The Archaeology of Knowledge*. Trans. Rupert Sawyer. New York: Pantheon, 1982. 215-237.

Fournier, Jay C., Robert J. DeRubeis, Steven D. Hollon et al. "Antidepressant Drug Effects and Depression Severity: A Patient-Level Meta-analysis. *JAMA* 303.1 (2010): 47-53.

Fraser, Nancy. "Introduction: Revaluing French Feminism." *Revaluing French Feminism: Critical Essays on Difference, Agency, and Culture.* Eds. Nancy Fraser and Sandra Lee Bartky. Bloomington and Indianapolis: Indiana University Press, 1992.

Freud, Sigmund. "The Ego and the Id." *The Standard Edition of the Complete Psychological Works of Sigmund Freud, Volume XIX (1923-1925): The Ego and the Id, and Other Works.* London: Penguin (Vintage Classics), 2001.

Freud, Sigmund. *The Interpretation of Dreams.* Trans. James Strachey. Eds. James Strachey, Alan Tyson and Angela Richards. London: Penguin, 1991.

Freud, Sigmund. "Mourning and Melancholia." *The Standard Edition of the Complete Psychological Works of Sigmund Freud, Volume XIV (1914-1916): On the History of the Psycho-Analytic Movement, Papers on Metapsychology and Other Works.* London: The Hogarth Press and The Institute of Psycho-Analysis, 1957. 237-258

Galt, Rosalind and Karl Schoonover. *Global Art Cinema: New Theories and Histories.* Oxford and New York: Oxford University Press, 2010.

Gansera, Rainer. "Glücks-Pickpocket." *Süddeutsche Zeitung.* 4 November 2001, 14.

Gaudreault, André and Philippe Morion. *The End of Cinema? A Medium in Crisis in the Digital Age.* New York: Columbia University Press, 2015.

Genosko, Gary. *Félix Guattari: A Critical Introduction.* London: Pluto, 2009a.

Granovetter, Mark S. "The Strength of Weak Ties." *American Journal of Sociology* 78.6 (May 1973): 1360-1380.

Guattari, Félix. *Chaosmosis: An Ethico-Aesthetic Paradigm.* Trans. Paul Bains and Julian Pefanis. Bloomington and Indianapolis: Indiana University Press, 1995.

Guattari, Félix. *Chaosophy: Texts and Interviews 1972-1977.* Ed. Sylvère Lotringer. Trans. David L. Sweet, Jarred Becker, and Taylor Adkins. Los Angeles, CA: Semiotext(e), 2009a.

Guattari, Félix. "Cracks in the Street." *Flash Art* Summer 135 (1987): 82-85.

Guattari, Félix. "Institutional Practice and Politics." *The Guattari Reader.* Ed. Gary Genosko. Oxford and Cambridge, Mass: Wiley-Blackwell, 1996a. 121-140.

Guattari, Félix. *The Machinic Unconscious: Essays in Schizoanalysis.* Trans. Taylor Adkins. Los Angeles: Semiotext(e), 2011.

Guattari, Félix. "The Postmodern Dead End." *Flash Art* May/June 128 (1986): 40-41.

Guattari, Félix. "Project for a Film by Kafka." *Deleuze Studies* 3.2 (2009b): 150-161.

Guattari, Félix. *Les années d'hiver: 1980-1985.* Paris: Les Prairies Ordinaires, 2009c.

Guattari, Félix. "Le Cinéma: Un art mineur." *La révolution moléculaire.* Fontenay-sous-bois: Recherches (Encres), 1977: 203-238.

Guattari, Félix. "The Schizoanalyses." *Soft Subversions: Texts and Interviews 1977-1985*. Ed. Sylvère Lotringer. Trans. Chet Wiener and Emily Wittman. Los Angeles, Semiotext(e), 2009d. 204-225.

Guattari, Félix. *Schizoanalytic Cartographies*. London and New York: Bloomsbury Academic, 2013.

Guattari, Félix. "Subjectivities, For Better or for Worse." *The Guattari Reader*. Ed. Gary Genosko. Cambridge and Oxford: Blackwell Publishers, 1996b. 193-203.

Guattari, Félix. *The Three Ecologies*. London and New York: Continuum, 2008.

Guattari, Félix and Suely Rolnik. *Molecular Revolution in Brazil*. Trans. Karel Clapshow and Brian Holmes. Cambridge and London: Semiotext(e), 2007.

Guattari, Félix and Toni Negri. *Communists Like Us: New Spaces of Liberty, New Lines of Alliance*. New York: Semiotext(e), 1990.

Gunning, Tom. "Moving Away from the Index: Cinema and the Impression of Reality." *Differences: A Journal of Feminist Cultural Studies* 18.1 (2007): 29-52.

Gunning, Tom. "What's the Point of an Index?, or Faking Photographs." NORDICOM Review 1-2 (2004): 39-49.

Hayward, Susan. *Cinema Studies: The Key Concepts, Second Edition*. London and New York: Routledge, 2000.

Healing Foundation. "Our History." *Healing Foundation*. Online. www.healing-foundation.org.au

Higgins, Edmund S. "Is Mental Health Declining in the U.S.? *Scientific American Mind*. January 2017. Online. https://scientificamerican.com/article/is-mental-health-declining-in-the-u-s/

Hochäusler, Christoph. "On Whose Shoulders: The Question of Aesthetic Indebtedness." *The Berlin School: Films From the Berliner Schule*. New York: The Museum of Modern Art, 2013. 20-29.

Hongisto, Ilona. *Soul of the Documentary: Framing, Expression, Ethics*. Amsterdam: University of Amsterdam Press, 2015.

Horton, Justin. "Mental Landscapes: Bazin, Deleuze, and Neorealism (Then and Now)." *Cinema Journal* 52.2 (Winter 2013): 23-45.

Hunter, Ernst and Desley Harvey. "Indigenous Suicide in Australia, New Zealand, Canada and the United States." *Emergency Medicine* 14.1 (March 2002): 14-23.

Irlbacher-Fox, Stephanie. *Finding Dahshaa: Self-Government, Social Suffering, and Aboriginal Policy in Canada* (Vancouver: University of British Columbia Press, 2009).

James, William. *Essays in Radical Empiricism*. Mineola, New York: Dover Publications, 2003.

James, William. "The Psychology of Belief." *James and Dewey on Belief and Experience*. Eds. John M. Capps and Donald Capps. Urbana and Chicago. University of Illinois Press, 2005a. 59-77.

James, William. *The Varieties of Religious Experience*. New York: The Modern Library, 1936.

James, William. "The Will to Believe." *James and Dewey on Belief and Experience*. Eds. John M. Capps and Donald Capps. Urbana and Chicago. University of Illinois Press, 2005b. 95-110.

James, William. "What Pragmatism Means." *James and Dewey on Belief and Experience*. Eds. John M. Capps and Donald Capps. Urbana and Chicago. University of Illinois Press, 2005c. 133-143.

Johnsen, Tom J. and Oddgeir Friborg. "The Effects of Cognitive Behavioural Therapy as an Anti-Depressive Treatment is Failing: A Meta-Analysis." *Psychological Bulletin* 141.4 (July 2015): 747-768.

Kirsch, Irving. *The Emperor's New Drugs: Exploding the Antidepressant Myth*. New York: Basic Books, 2010.

Klibansky, Raymond, Erwin Panofsky and Fritz Saxl. *Saturn and Melancholy: Studies in the History of Natural Philosophy, Religion and Art*. London: Nelson, 1964.

Kluge, Alexander, Edgar Reitz, et al. "The Oberhausen Manifesto." *Film Manifestos and Global Cinema Cultures: A Critical Anthology*. Ed. Scott Mackenzie. Berkeley, Los Angeles and London: University of California Press, 152.

Köhler, Ulrich. "Why I don't Make Political Films." *Cinema Scope* 28 (Spring 2009): 10-13.

Kolker, Robert. *The Altering Eye: Contemporary International Cinema*. Oxford: Oxford University Press, 1983.

Knudtson, Peter and David Suzuki. *Wisdom of the Elders*. Toronto: Stoddart Publishing, 1992.

Kracauer, Sigfried. *From Caligari to Hitler: A Psychological History of the German Film*. Princeton: Princeton University Press, 1947.

Lacan, Jacques. *Écrits: The First Complete Edition in English*. Trans. Bruce Fink. New York and London: W.W. Norton and Company, 2006.

Laplanche, Jean and J.-B. Pontalis. *The Language of Psychoanalysis*. Trans. Donald Nicholson-Smith. London: Karnac Books, 1988.

Lapoujade, David. "From Transcendental Empiricism to Worker Nomadism: William James." *Pli* 9 (2000): 190-199. Trans. Alberto Toscano.

Lazzarato, Maurizio. *Signs and Machines: Capitalism and the Production of Subjectivity*. Trans. David Joshua Jordan. Los Angeles: Semiotext(e), 2014.

Lim, Dennis. "Moving On: The Next New Wave." *The Berlin School: Films from the Berliner Schule*. New York: The Museum of Modern Art, 2013. 88-97.

Luzzi, Joseph. "Rossellini's Cinema of Poetry: *Voyage to Italy*." *Adaption* 3.2 (September 2010): 61-81.

Macdonald, Charles. "Kinship and Fellowship among the Palawan". *Anarchic Solidarity: Autonomy, Equality, and Fellowship in Southeast Asia*. New Haven, Connecticut: Yale University Southeast Asia Studies, 2011. 119-140.

Macdonald, Charles. *Uncultural Behaviour: An Anthropological Investigation of Suicide in the Southern Philippines*. Honolulu: University of Hawaii Press, 2007.

Mackay, Robin and Armen Avenessian, Eds. *#Accelerate: The Accelerationist Reader.* Falmouth, United Kingdom: 2014.

Malabou, Catherine. *What Should We Do with our Brain?* Foreword by Marc Jeannerod. Trans. Sebastian Rand. New York: Fordham University Press, 2008.

Manuel, George and Michael Posluns. *The Fourth World: An Indian Reality*. Don Mills, Ontario: Collier-Macmillan Canada, 1974.

Manning, Erin. *Always More Than One: Individuation's Dance*. Durham and London: Duke University Press, 2013a.

Manning, Erin. "In the Act: The Shape of Precarity." *|П| Magazine for Live Arts Research* 2 (November 2013b): 10-15. Special issue: "Melancholy and Politics."

Manning, Erin. "Introduction." *Nocturnal Fabulations: Ecology, Vitality and Opacity in the Cinema of Apichatpong Weerasethakul*. London: Open Humanities Press, 2017.

Manning, Erin. *Relationscapes: Movement, Art, Philosophy*. Cambridge and London: The MIT Press, 2009.

Manning, Erin. *The Minor Gesture*. Durham and London: Duke University Press, 2016.

Marazzi, Christian. *Capital and Affects: The Politics of the Language Economy*. Trans. Guiseppina Mecchia. Los Angeles and Cambridge, Massachusetts: Semiotext(e), 2011.

Massumi, Brian. "Deleuze and Guattari's Theories of the Group-Subject, Through a Reading of Corneille's *Le Cid*". *Discours Social/Social Discourse* 1.4 (Winter 1988): 423-440.

Massumi, Brian. *Parables for the Virtual: Movement, Affect, Sensation*. Durham and London: Duke University Press, 2002.

Massumi, Brian. *Power at the End of the Economy*. Durham and London: Duke University Press, 2015.

Massumi, Brian. *Semblance and Event: Activist Philosophy and the Occurrent Arts*. Cambridge, Massachusetts and London, England: The MIT Press, 2011.

Massumi, Brian. "Sensing the Virtual, Building the Insensible." *Architectural Design* 68.5/6 (May/June 1998): 16-24.

McFarlane, Peter. *Brotherhood to Nationhood: George Manuel and the Making of the Modern Indian Movement*. Toronto: Between the Lines, 1993.

Merzenich, Michael. "The Brain Plasticity Revolution." *"On the Brain" with Dr. Michael Merzenich*. http://www.onthebrain.com/2009/07/brain-plasticity-revolution/

Million, Dian. *Therapeutic Nations: Healing in an Age of Indigenous Human Rights*. Tucson: University of Arizona Press, 2013.

Morgan, Daniel. "Rethinking Bazin: Ontology and Realist Aesthetics." *Critical Inquiry* 32 (Spring 2006): 443-481.

Mullino Moore, Mary Elizabeth. "Imagine Peace: Knowing the Real—Imagining the Impossible. Ed. Jay B. McDaniel and Donna Bowman. *Handbook of Process Theology*. St. Louis, MO: Chalice, 2006. 201-216.

Munsterberg, Hugo. *The Film: A Psychological Study*. Trans Richard Griffith. Mineola, New York: Dover Publications, 1970.

Neale, Steve. "Art Cinema as Institution." *Screen* 22.1 (1981): 11-40.

Nord, Christina. "Man stürzt, steht wieder auf und latscht weiter." *taz*, 18 February 2006. http://www.taz.de/1/archiv/archiv/?dig=2006/02/18/a0189.

Orr, John. *Contemporary Cinema*. Edinburgh: Edinburgh University Press, 1998.

Pasolini, Pier Paolo. "The 'Cinema of Poetry'". *Heretical Empiricism*. Trans. Ben Lawton and Louise K. Barnett. Washington, DC: New Academia Publishing, 2005. 167-186.

Peirce, Charles Sanders. "Division of Signs." *Collected Papers of Charles Sanders Peirce. Volume 2. Book 2*. Eds. Charles Hartshorne and Paul Weiss. Cambridge, Massachussets: Harvard University Press, 1974. 134-155.

Peucker, Brigitte. *The Material Image: Art and the Real in Film*. Stanford, California: Stanford University Press, 2007.

Pignarre, Philippe. *Comment la depression est devenue une épidémie*. Paris: Éditions la découverte, 2012.

Plan C. "We Are All Very Anxious." *Plan C*. Online. www.weareplanc.org

Polan Dana. "Translator's Introduction." *Kafka: Toward a Minor Literature*. Trans. Dana Polan. Minneapolis and London: University of Minnesota Press, 1986.

Quandt, James. *Apichatpong Weerasethakul*. Vienna: Synema Publikationen, 2009.

Radden, Jennifer. *The Nature of Melancholy: From Aristotle to Kristeva*. New York: Oxford University Press, 2000.

Rafanell i Orra, Josep. *En finir avec le capitalism thérapeutique: soin, politique, communauté*. Paris: Éditions la Découverte, 2011.

Reichardt, Kelly and Gus Van Sant. "Kelly Reichardt by Gus Van Sant – Artists in Conversation." *Bomb* (Fall 2008). http://bombmagazine.org/article/3182/kelly-reichardt

Rhodes. John David. "Pasolini's Exquisite Flowers: The 'Cinema of Poetry' as a Theory of Art Cinema." *Global Art Cinema: New Theories and Histories*. Eds. Rosalind Galt and Karl Schoonover. Oxford and New York: Oxford University Press, 2010. 142-163.

Rithdee, Kong. "Thailand Passes Controversial Film Act." *Variety*. 20 December 2007. Online. http://variety.com/2007/film/news/thailand-passes-controversial-film-act-1117978081/

Rivette, Jacques. "Letter on Rossellini". *Cahiers du Cinéma: The 1950s: Neo-Realism, Hollywood, New Wave*. Ed. Jim Hillier. Cambridge, Massachusetts: Harvard University Press, 1985: 192-204.

Robbins, Julian A. and Jonathan Dewar. "Traditional Indigenous Approaches to Healing and the Modern Welfare of Traditional Knowledge, Spirituality and Lands: A Critical Reflection on Practices and Policies Taken from the Canadian Indigenous Example." *The International Indigenous Policy Journal* 2.4 (2011): 1-17.

Rodowick, D.N. *The Crisis of Political Modernism: Criticism and Ideology in Contemporary Film Theory.* Berkeley, Los Angeles and London. University of California Press, 1994.

Rodowick, D. N. *The Virtual Life of Film.* Cambridge, Massachusetts and London, England: Harvard University Press, 2007.

Rose, Nikolas. "Brain, Self and Society." Andrew F. Holmes Dean of Medecine Distinction Lectures. McGill University. Montreal, Canada. 27 October 2016. Public Lecture.

Rose, Nikolas and Joelle M. Abi-Rached. *Neuro: The New Brain Sciences and the Management of the Mind.* Princeton and Oxford: Princeton University Press, 2013.

Rosen, Philip. *Change Mummified: Cinema, Historicity, Theory.* Minneapolis and London: University of Minnesota Press, 2001.

Rosen, Philip. "Nation and Anti-Nation: Concepts of National Cinema in the 'New' Media Era". *Diaspora* 5.3 (1996): 375-402.

Rosen, Philip. "The Politics of the Sign and Film Theory." *October* 17 "The New Talkies" (Summer 1981): 5-21.

Roy, Rajendra. "Introduction." *The Berlin School: Films from the Berliner Schule.* New York: The Museum of Modern Art, 2013. 10-13.

Royal Commission on Aboriginal Peoples (Canada), Rene Dussault and Georges Erasmus. *Report of the Royal Commission on Aboriginal Peoples.* Ottawa: The Commission, 1996.

Sarris, Andrew. "Notes on Auteur Theory in 1962." *Film Culture* 27 (Winter 1962/3):1-8.

Schwartz, Jeffrey and Sharon Begley. *The Mind and the Brain: Neuroplasticity and the Power of Mental Force.* New York: Regan Books, 2002.

Scott, A.O. "A.O. Scott Responds to New Yorker Blog on the Value and Definition of Neorealism." *Carpetbagger: The Hollywood Blog of The New York Times.* 29 March 2009a. http://carpetbagger.blogs.nytimes.com/2009/03/23/ao-scott-responds-to-a-new-yorker-blogger-about-the-value-and-definition-of-neo-realism/?_r=0

Scott, A.O. "Neo-Neo Realism: American Directors Make Clear-Eyed Movies for Hard Times." *The New York Times.* 22 March 2009b. MM38.

Seligman, Martin. *Flourish: A Visionary New Understanding of Happiness and Well-Being.* New York: Free Press, 2011.

Shaviro, Steven. *The Cinematic Body.* London and Minneapolis: University of Minnesota Press, 1993.

Shaviro, Steven. "Cognitive Capitalism?" *The Pinnochio Theory.* 3 February 2008. http://www.shaviro.com/Blog/?p=620

Shaviro, Steven. "Kant, Deleuze and the Virtual." *Pinnochio Theory*. Blog Post. 9 May 2007. http://www.shaviro.com/Blog/?p=577

Shaviro, Steven. *Post-Cinematic Affect*. Winchester, UK: 0 [zero], 2010.

Shohat, Ella and Robert Stam. *Unthinking Eurocentrism: Multiculturalism and the Media*. London and New York: Routledge, 1994.

Silverman, Kaja. *The Subject of Semiotics*. New York: Oxford University Press, 1983.

Simondon, Gilbert. *L'individuation à la lumière des notions de forme et d'information*. Grenoble: Éditions Jérôme Millon, 2005.

Simondon, Gilbert. *L'individuation psychique et collective à la notion lumière des notions de Forme, Information, Potentiel et Métastabilité*. Paris: Éditions Aubier, 1989.

Simpson, Leanne. *Dancing On Our Turtle's Back: Stories of Nishnaabeg Re-Creation, Resurgence and a New Emergence*. Winnipeg: Arbeiter Ring Publishing, 2011.

Smith, Daniel W. "Introduction: 'A Life of Pure Immanence': Deleuze's 'Critique et Clinique' Project." *Essays Critical and Clinical*. Trans. Daniel W. Smith and Michael A. Greco. London and New York, 1998. xi-liii.

Solito, Auraeus. "Director's Statement". *Busong (Palawan Fate) Press Kit*. 2011.

Solomon, Andrew. *The Noonday Demon: An Atlas of Depression*. New York: Scribner, 2001.

Souriau, Étienne. *L'univers filmique*. Paris: Flammarion, 1953.

Stengers, Isabelle. "Beyond Conversation: The Risks of Peace". *Process and Difference: Between Cosmological and Poststructuralist Postmodernisms*. Ed. Catherine Keller and Anne Daniell. Albany: State University of New York Press, 2002. 235-255.

Thomas, M. Ladd. "Communist Insurgency in Thailand: Factors Contributing to Its Decline". *Asian Affairs* 13.1 (Spring, 1986): 17-26.

Thompson, Kristin and David Bordwell. *Film History: An Introduction*. Third Edition. New York: McGraw Hill, 2010.

Treichler, Paula A. *How to Have Theory in an Epidemic: Cultural Chronicles of AIDS*. Durham and London: Duke University Press, 1999.

UHM Center for Southeast Asian Studies Lecture Series Podcast. "Raymond Lee". *University of Hawaii*. Podcast.

Vinogradova, Maria. "The Berlin School as a Recent New Wave in German Cinema." *Acta Univ. Sapientiae, Film and Media Studies* 3 (2010): 157-168.

Watson, Janell. *Guattari's Diagrammatic Thought: Writing Between Lacan and Deleuze*. London and New York: Continuum, 2009.

Waziyatawin and Michael Yellow Bird, Eds. *For Indigenous Minds Only: A Decolonization Handbook*. Santa Fe: School for Advanced Research Press, 2013.

Weerasethakul, Apichatpong. "The Memory of Nabua: A Note on the Primitive Project". *Apichatpong Weerasethakul*. Ed. James Quandt. Vienna: Synema Publikationen, 2009a. 192-206.

Weerasethakul, Apichatpong. "The Folly and Future of Thai Cinema Under Military Dictatorship". *Apichatpong Weerasethakul*. Ed. James Quandt. Vienna: Synema Publikationen, 2009b. 178-181.

Whitaker, Robert. *Anatomy of an Epidemic: Magic Bullets, Psychiatric Drugs, and the Astonishing Rise of Mental Illness in America*. New York: Crown Publishers, 2010.

Whitehead, Alfred North. *Adventures of Ideas*. New York and London: The Free Press, 1967.

Whitehead, Alfred North. *Process and Reality: An Essay in Cosmology*. New York and London: The Free Press, 1978.

Williams, Blake. "Saying Something: The Films of Angela Schanelec." *Cinema Scope* 68 (Fall 2016): 12-15

World Health Organization. "Depression: Fact Sheet." *World Health Organization*. April 2016a. Online. www.who.int/mediacentre/factsheets/fs369/en

World Health Organization. "Investing in treatment for depression and anxiety leads to fourfold return. Depression and anxiety disorders cost the global economy US$1 trillion each year; countries and development partners to discuss way forward during World Bank-WHO events." Online. 13 April 2016b. http://www.who.int/mediacentre/news/releases/2016/depression-anxiety-treatment/en/

Worthmann, Merten. "Mit Vorsicht genießen." *Die Zeit* 27 (September 2001). Online. http://zeit.de

Zerehi, Sima Sahar. "Plight of Inuit healing centre in Ottawa highlights North's lack of mental health care." *CBC News*. 15 February 2016. Online. https://www.cbc.ca/news/canada/north/plight-of-inuit-healing-centre-in-ottawa-highlights-north-s-lack-of-mental-health-care-1.3448218

Zournazi, Mary. *Hope: New Philosophies for Change*. New York: Routledge, 2003.

Filmography

Oslo, August 31st. Dir. Joachim Trier. Don't Look Now, 2011.
Atanarjuat (*The Fast Runner*). Dir. Zacharias Kunuk. 2001.
Afternoon. Dir. Angela Schanelec. Nachmittagfilm. 2007.
Ballast. Dir. Lance Hamer. Prod. Alluvial Film Company. 2008.
Barbara. Dir. Christian Petzold. Schramm Film Kroener & Weber. 2012.
Barking Water. Dir. Serlin Harjo. 2009.
Boy. Taika Waititi. 2010.
BeDeviled. Dir. Tracey Moffatt. 1993.
Bicycle Thief, The. Dir. Vittorio De Sica. Produzioni De Sica. 1948.
Bungalow. Ulrich Köhler. Peter Stockhaus Filmproduktion. 2002.
Business of Fancydancing, The. Dir. Sherman Alexie. 2002.
Cabinet of Dr. Caligari, The. Dir. Robert Wiene. Decia-Bioscop. 1920.
Cemetery of Splendour. Dir. Apichatpong Weerasethaul. Kick the Machine, 2015.
Downfall. Dir. Oliver Hirschbiegel. Constantin Film Produktion. 2004.
The Dreamlike Path. Dir. Angela Schanelec. Dreamgalerie 451, 2016.
The Earth Trembles. Dir. Luchino Visconti. Universalia Film. 1948.
Forest for the Trees. Dir. Maren Ade. Komplizen Film, 2003.
Germany in Autumn. Dir. Alf Brustellin, Rainer Fassbinder, et al. Tango Film, 1978.
Germany Year Zero. Dir. Roberto Rossellini. Tevere Film, SAFDI, UCG. 1948.
Gold. Dir. Thomas Arslan. Schramm Film Koerner & Weber, Red Cedar Films. 2013.
Goodbye Lenin! Dir. Wolfgang Becker. X-FIlme Creative Pool, 2003.
History and Memory: For Akiko and Takashige. Dir. Rea Tajiri. 1992.
I Am Guilty. Dir. Christoph Hochhäusler. Filmsiftung Nordrhein-Westfalen, 2005.
In Vanda's Room. Dir. Pedro Costa. Contracosta Producoes, 2000.
Lives of Others, The. Dir. Florian Henckel von Donnersmarck. Wiedemann & Berg Filmproduktion. 2006.
Man Push Cart. Dir. Ramin Bahrani. Prod. Noruz Films. 2005.
Marseille. Dir. Angela Schanelec. Schramm Film Kroener & Weber. 2004.
Mauri. Dir. Merata Mita. 1988.
McFarland, USA. Dir. Niki Caro. 2015.
Meek's Cutoff. Dir. Kelly Reichardt. Perf. Michelle Williams. Prod. Evenstar Films. 2010.
Melancholia. Dir. Lars von Trier. Zentropa Studios, 2011.
Melancholia. Dir. Lav Diaz. Sine Olivia, 2008.
Ngati. Dir. Barry Barclay. 1985.
Night Moves. Dir. Kelly Reichardt. Perf. Jesse Eisenberg, Dakota Fanning. Prod. Maybach Film Productions. 2013.

Old Joy. Dir. Kelly Reichardt. Prod. Film Science. 2006.

Once Were Warriors. Dir. Lee Tamahori. 1994.

Orly. Dir. Angela Schanelec. Ringel Filmproduktion. 2010.

Palawan Fate (*Busong*). Dir. Auraeus Solito. 2011.

Pandora's Box. Dir. Georg Wilhelm Pabst. Nero Film. 1929.

Passing Summer. Dir. Angela Schanelec. Schramm Film. 2001.

The Pathfinder. Dir. Nils Gaup. 1987.

Phoenix. Dir. Christian Petzold. Schramm Film Koerner & Weber. 2014.

Places in Cities. Dir. Angela Schanelec. Schramm Film. 1998.

Playtime. Jacques Tati. Specta Films, 1967.

The Red Desert. Dir. Michelangelo Antonioni. Film Duemila, Federiz, Francoriz Production. 1964.

Samson & Delilah. Dir. Warwick Thornton. CAAMA Productions, 2009.

Shame. Dir. Steve McQueen. UK Film Council, 2011.

Silent Light. Dir. Carlos Reygadas. No Dream Cinema, 2007.

Sleeping Sickness. Ulrich Köhler. Komplizen Film, 2011.

Smoke Signals. Dir. Chris Eyre. 1998.

Sugar. Dir. Anna Boden and Ryan Fleck. HBO Films. 2008.

Te Rua. Dir. Barry Barclay. 1992.

Te Tangata Whai Rawa O Weneti (*The Maori Merchant of Venice*). Dir. Don Selwyn. 2004.

The Testament of Dr. Mabuse. Dir. Fritz Lang. Nero-Film AG, 1933.

This Very Moment. Dir. Christoph Hochhäusler. Cine Image, 2003.

Tropical Malady. Dir. Apichatpong Weerasethakul. Kick the Machine, 2004.

Umberto D. Dir. Vittorio De Sica. Rizzoli Film, 1952.

Uncle Boonmee Who Can Recall His Past Lives. Dir. Apichatpong Weerasethakul. Kick the Machine, 2010.

Voyage to Italy. Dir. Roberto Rossellini. Italia Film, Junior Film, Sveva Film. 1954.

Wendy and Lucy. Dir. Kelly Reichardt. Perf. Michelle Williams. Prod. Field Guide Films. 2008.

Windows on Monday. Dir. Ulrich Köhler. Ö-Filmproduktion. 2006.

Yella. Dir. Christian Petzold. Schramm Film Koerner & Weber, 2007.

You Are On Indian Land. Dir. Mort Ransen. 1969.

About the Author

Adam Szymanski is a Postdoctoral Fellow in the Department of Cinema and Media Studies at the University of Chicago.

Index

Abel, Marco 61
Abi-Rached, Joelle M. 14
Aboriginal Healing Foundation (AHF) 137–39
Aboriginalism 147n19
activism 88, 91, 153–54. *See also* Night Moves; therapeutic activism
actual occasions 122
Ade, Maren 60
aesthetics
- of *Afternoon* 74–77
- of the Berlin School 60
- expressionist 41
- free indirect 74–77, 107
- of imagist films 41
- melancholy 22–23, 31, 62, 107
- neorealist 40, 43–47
- of *Palawan Fate* 145
- of *The Red Desert* 54
- of *Uncle Boonmee* 114–17, 120n15, 125

Afternoon
- overview of 74
- characters, boundaries between 75–76
- contemporary film movements 23–24
- country and language 24–25
- framing 75
- free indirect aesthetics of 74–77
- images, plasticity of 75
- lighting 75–77
- melancholy in 74–78
- narrative of 74
- plastic depotentialization in 74, 76
- psychological suffering, conception of 63
- *versus The Red Desert* 63
- and transindividualism 75
- window motifs 75–76, 79

Alexie, Sherman 148
Alfred, Taiaiake 131, 135, 139n13, 140n14, 146, 147n19
alienation
- from common experience 19
- in melancholy 63–64
- in neorealism 45
- in *Night Moves* 96, 99–100
- in *The Red Desert* 27

alterity, encounters with 19, 113–16, 121, 126, 155
Antonioni, Michelangelo 48. *See also* The Red Desert
Apichatpong Weerasethakul. *See also* Uncle Boonmee Who Can Recall His Past Lives
- and the Berlin School 28–29
- *Cemetery of Splendor* 26–28
- censorship opposition 112n4
- and disappeared people 122–23
- films, socio-political contexts 111–12
- film watching as healing 111, 155
- Nabua disappearances 122n17
- *Primitive* project 122
- Thailand, relationship to 26–27
- and therapeutic activism 153

Aristarco, Guido 46n7
Arslan, Thomas 60, 62n5
art cinema. *See also* cinema of poetry
- contemporary 55
- criteria of 25n20
- global 25–29
- institution *versus* aesthetic debate 27n22
- and national cinemas 26–28

artists and medical classifications 18
assemblages
- and the free indirect 52
- machinic 16n8, 17, 19, 72
- in minor literature 30
- subject-world 95
- as symptomatology site 22

assemblages of enunciation
- overview of 16n8
- and the free indirect 51–52
- in minor literature 30
- ontological functors of 118–21

assemblage theory
- overview of 15–16
- beliefs in 95
- changes in 16n8
- cinematographic images 118–19
- contexts of creation 16
- events in 118

and symptoms, perception of 19
auteurism 51–52

Balintagos, Kanakan. *See also* Palawan Fate
- on films and healing 129, 141, 155
- films of 27–28
- Palawan heritage 141–43
- and Philippine film culture 28
- and therapeutic activism 153

Ballast 84–85
Barclay, Barry
- Fourth Cinema 129–33, 140, 143, 150
- *Te Rua* 148

Barking Water 148
Barnard, Timothy 115
Barnett, John 132
Barthes, Roland 104
Bazin, André
- découpage 115n8, 117
- image plasticity 73
- imagists *versus* realists 37–39

indexical readings of 104–6
neorealism 40–41, 43–47, 104
photography 105–6
readings of 44, 104–6
belief
and activism 88, 91
control, eluding 90
and creativity 90–91
Deleuze's conception of 88–91
filming 103–4
versus hope 87–91
and melancholy 95
in *Night Moves* 92, 96, 99–100, 102
non-terminal 93–94, 107
and pure experience 91–93
restoring the human-world link 89, 92
as subject-world assemblage 95
terminal 93–94
Benjamin, Walter 122
Bensmaïa, Réda 29
Berardi, Franco "Bifo," 23n19, 71
Bergson, Henri 146, 149–50
the Berlin School
overview of 59–60, 62n5
and cinema of poetry 59
criticisms of 60–61
filmmakers belonging to 60
free indirect perception use 60
as global art cinema 28–29
image plasticity 78
melancholy in 60–61
and national cinema 27
versus neo-neorealism 83
political aesthetics of 60
term origins 59–60
and transindividual psychology 60, 79
window tropes 78–79
Bertolucci, Bernardo 48
The Bicycle Thief 40
Bondanella, Peter 44
Bordwell, David 39n2
boundaries, exterior-interior 64, 75–76, 78–79
Boy 148
the brain. *See also* neuroplasticity
as boundary 64, 79
Deleuze's conception of 64, 66n8, 68, 95
screen metaphor for 64, 68
and subjectivity production 68–69
Brody, Richard 84n1
Brüggemann, Dietrich 61
Burton, Robert 20
The Business of Fancydancing 148–49
Busong. See Palawan Fate
Butler, Judith 63–65, 79

The Cabinet of Dr. Caligari 41
Canada 11n2, 134n6, 137–39
capitalist realism 69–70, 85
Caro, Niki 132
Cemetery of Splendor 26–28
cinema. *See also* art cinema; minor cinema
alterity encounters, foreclosures of 19
character psychology in 38
classical 89–90
critical perception of 30–31
and depression 19–20, 30–31, 156
experiences, representing 102–5
Guattari and 19
indexicality of 104–7
melancholy aesthetics 22–23, 31
modern 89–90, 92
and pure experience 107
and subjectivity 19
and subjectivity production 19, 147–48
symptomatology of 19–20
and time 89–90, 92
cinema of poetry. *See also* The Red Desert
overview of 29
arrival of 48
and art cinema, contemporary 55
and the Berlin School 59
character psychology in 38, 48
character subjectivity in 48
and faith in reality 55
and the free indirect 39, 48–49, 52, 62–63
images of 48–49, 55–56, 63
and the imagist-realist divide 38
and neorealism 43, 86
origins of 23
psychosociality of 53
realism of 53
techniques of 38–39
transindividual psychology of 54
Voyage to Italy 46
Clair, Jean 21
the clinical gaze
overview of 14
and assemblages 16
versus cinema's critical perception 30–31
and individuals 15, 17
and machinic assemblages 17, 19
and neoliberal subjects 30
and residual effects 103
clinical *versus* critical perception 19
Cloud, Dana L. 22n18
Cognitive Behaviour Therapy 11n3, 66
the collective unconscious 41–42
control and capitalist realism 69–70
control societies 69–71, 90
Coulthard, Glen 137–38, 140n14
creation stories 131
cultural appropriation 132–33

Dapice, Ann N. 134–35
decolonization and healing
overview of 133–34
Aboriginal Healing Foundation 137–39

contradictions in 134, 140
cooptation of 134, 137, 139–40
and cultural flourishing 134, 136, 141, 146–47, 150
and Fourth Cinema 140, 146, 149–50
government initiatives 137–40
Indigenous values 140, 155
political dimensions 135, 137
and reconciliation claims 138–39
techniques of 134–37
and war 146–47
découpage 115n7, 115n8, 117–18
Deleuze, Gilles. *See also* assemblage theory
Anti-Oedipus 54–55, 71–72
belief 87–90
the brain, conception of 64, 66n8, 68
cinema, classical *versus* modern 89–90
cinema of poetry and neorealism 86
commons of experience 94
communication excesses 71
control society theory 69
critical and clinical project 18–19
fabulation 147–48, 150
free indirect images 52
habit 92n8
minor literature 29–30
molecular fascism 72
movement-images 89–90
neorealism 40
on pure experience 93
time-images 89–90
Umberto D 45
depression
artists perceiving 18–19
and cinema 19–20, 30–31, 156
and the clinical gaze 14
desubjectification of 67–68
as economic issue 12–13
and hopelessness 88
versus melancholia 22
versus melancholy 21
political conditions causing 71
psychiatric positioning of 14
rates of, increasing 11
relapse prevalency 12
as subjectivity production 20
symptoms of 19–20
term connotations 20
treatment of 11–12, 66–67, 72–73
De Sica, Vittorio 40, 45
Designing Out Suicide zine 154
deterritorialization 16, 29, 31
Dewar, Jonathan 137
Doidge, Norman 66
Dudley, Andrew 26
Dürer, Albrecht 21

The Earth Trembles 40, 43–44
ecosophy 113–17, 120n15, 125
Eder, James 142
Eurocentrism 147
experiences. *See also* Night Moves
common 19, 94, 155
effects of 102–3
filming 103–4
pure 91–94, 103, 107
truth values of 102–3
expressionism 41–43, 46

fabulation 147–48, 150
fascism 41–42
feminism, liberal 133
filmmakers
Berlin School 60
imagist 37–38
realist 37
as therapeutic activists 23, 31, 108, 150, 155
Fisher, Mark 69–70
flexibility *versus* plasticity 70–71
Fluxes 118–20
Foucault, Michel 13–15, 23, 69, 71–72
Fourth Cinema. *See also* Palawan Fate
overview of 129–30
and fabulation 148
films of 129n2
geographic dispersal 141
and healing, decolonial 140, 146, 149–50
healing scenes, speechless 148–49
Indigenous values requirement 130–33, 140
interiority 130, 132, 143, 149–50
mystic intuition of 149–50
political import of 131
therapeutic potential of 133, 147
the Fourth World 141n15
the free indirect
aesthetics 74–77, 107
ambiguity of 39, 98
images 48–49, 51–53, 78, 95, 107
lighting and image composition 97–98, 100–1
obsessive framing 97–98
perception 60, 95, 101–2, 107, 108
point of view shots 39, 48–49, 52, 62–63
semi-subjective perspectives 97–98
Freud, Sigmund 21–22, 63

Galt, Rosalind 25–26
Gansera, Rainer 59n2
genocide 134
German national cinema 27, 61–62
Germany Year Zero 40, 44, 46
Godard, Jean-Luc 48
Granovetter, Mark 144n17
Guattari, Félix
alterity 113
Anti-Oedipus 54–55, 71–72
art 153

assemblages 15–16, 118–19
at La Borde 16–17
and cinema 19, 155
depression struggles 17–18
ecologies, the three 113
ecosophy 113
influences on 16
melancholy 65
mental illness 17
and minor cinema 29
minor literature 29–30
molecular fascism 72
schizoanalysis 17–18
subjectivity 15–17, 147, 156
Gunning, Tom 105–6

Harjo, Sterlin 148
healing. *See also* decolonization and healing
Apichatpong Weerasethakul on 111, 155
and Fourth Cinema 140, 146, 148–50
Kanakan Balintagos on 129, 141, 155
Palawan Fate as 144–46
HIV/AIDS activism 153–54
Hochhäusler, Christoph 28, 60, 79
Hollywood 85–86, 117
hope 85, 87–91
hopelessness 87–88, 96
Horton, Justin 46n6, 52
hypothetical sympathy 155

images
historical 122
psychosocial 51, 53, 55–56, 63, 78, 95
images, cinematographic. *See also* expressionism; free indirect images; neorealism
as assemblages of enunciation 118–19
cinema of poetry's 48–49, 55–56, 63
collective unconscious, expressing 41–42
dark 41
faith in 37–39, 41
free indirect 48–49, 51–53, 49, 78, 95, 107
healing 144–45
movement 89–90
plastic excess in 42, 46
plasticity of 73
subjective and objective poles of 45–47, 49, 52–53
time 89–90
truth-value of 104, 107
imagist film 37–39, 41. *See also* expressionism
indexes, semiotic 106–7
indexicality of cinema and film 104–7
Indigenous cultures and peoples. *See also* decolonization and healing
and Aboriginalism 147n19
in Canada 134n6, 137
contemporary problems 134
flourishing 134, 136, 141, 146–47, 150
and the Fourth World 141n15
health, conceptions of 134–35
historical violence against 134
Palawan 141–44
self-determination 140
Indigenous film 129n2, 130–31. *See also* Fourth Cinema
Indigenous values
decolonizing force of 131–32, 140, 155
erosion of 19
and Fourth Cinema 130–33, 140
and healing 140, 155
Palawan 143–45
stories transmitting 131
individuals
and the clinical gaze 15, 17
and illness 14
and medical institutions 14
mentally ill 30
as products of power 72–73
and pure experience 92–93
society, demarcations from 13–15
Irlbacher-Fox, Stephanie 139n12
Isaan province, Thailand 112–13, 114n7, 121–22, 126
Italian neorealism 39–40

James, William
analyses of psychological states 103n10
experience truth values 102
ideas 107
melancholy 102
pure experience 91–93
radical empiricism 93
streams of consciousness 93–94
thoughts 107
work of 92
Jeannerod, Marc 70–71

Kafka, Franz 29–30
Köhler, Ulrich 27–28, 60–62, 78
Kolker, Robert 43
Kracauer, Sigfriend 41–42

Lapoujade, David 91n7, 92
Lazzarato, Maurizio 56, 72

MacDonald, Charles 144
machinic assemblages 16n8, 17, 19, 72
Malabou, Catherine 65, 66n8, 70–71
Manning, Erin 90–91, 120, 154
Man Push Cart 84–85
Manuel, George 141n15
Maori cinema 130–32
Marazzi, Christian 67
Marquis de Sade 18
Massumi, Brian 13n5, 55n12, 87n2, 91, 120n15
material reductionism 64, 68
Meek's Cutoff 87
melancholia 21–22, 63

melancholy
  alienation, as causing 63–64
  ambiguity of 20
  and belief 95
  and the Berlin School 60–61
  cinema's critical perception of 31
  versus depression 21
  effects of 102–3
  event-based conceptions of 21
  and external-internal boundaries 65
  film indexing 104, 106–7
  free indirect images of 107
  historical development of 20–21
  images of 107–8
  and individuality 63, 79
  isolation, as causing 64–65
  versus melancholia 21
  and neoliberal power 65
  and Neo-Neorealism 83–84
  and non-terminal beliefs 94, 107–8
  relational fields of 31, 63, 154–56
  and subjectivity production 63–65
  symptoms 63–65
  term connotations 20
  and transindividuality 108
  truth of 102
  in the visual arts 21
Melancholy: Genius and Madness in the Occident 21
mental health 11–13, 17
mental illness 49, 64n7. *See also* depression
Mezernich, Michael 67–68
Million, Dian 134, 137–40
minor cinema 25, 29–31
minor literature 29–30
Mitchell, Mike 146n18
molecular fascism 72
Moore, Mary Elizabeth Mullino 113
Morgan, Daniel 106
movement-images 89–90
Munch, Edvard 21
mystic intuition 149–50

Nabua, Thailand 122
neoliberalism
  in control societies 69
  depression, as causing 71
  and expressivity 71
  flexibility, demand for 70
  and melancholy 65
  and neuroplasticity 65, 66n8, 67, 73
neoliberal subjects 30, 72–73
Neo-Neorealism, American 83–88. *See also* Night Moves; Reichardt, Kelly
neorealism
  alienation in 45
  Bazin on 40–41, 43–47, 104
  character psychology 40–49
  and cinema of poetry 43, 86
  The Earth Trembles 40, 43–44
  end of 45n5
  versus expressionism 42–43
  Germany Year Zero 40, 44, 46
  humanist spirit of 39–40
  images of 42–43, 47–48
  landscapes in 46–47
  as partial cinema 42
  poverty, images of 40
  poverty in 40, 43, 45
  reality, faith in 39, 47–48
  social realities in 43–44, 47–49
  sociological readings of 43
  socio-political reality emphasis 40–41
  techniques 44, 46
  Umberto D 45–46
  Voyage to Italy 45–47, 49, 53
  war in 40–43
neuroplasticity
  overview of 65–66
  and control society 69
  depotentialization of 19, 65
  and depression treatments 66–67, 72–73
  and material reductionism 68
  and neoliberal power 66n8, 67
  and subjectivity production theories 68
the neuroplastic paradox 66–67, 70–71, 73
neuroscience 67–68
Night Moves
  overviews of 84, 95–96
  alienation in 96, 99–100
  belief in 92, 96, 99–100, 102
  common worlds, undoing of 99–101
  common worlds in 94, 96–99
  contemporary film movements 23–24
  country and language 24–25
  free indirect perception in 95, 101–2, 108
  free indirect techniques used 96–101
  hopelessness in 87, 96
  individuals, isolation of 84
  melancholy in 84, 95–96, 99–102
  and pure experience 92
  versus Schanelec's work 84
  structure of 92, 99
  three-shots 97–98

objective shots 48
O'Hara, Lisa 154
Old Joy 86, 99
ontological functors 118–21
Orr, John 55n11
Orra, Josep Rafanelli i 23n19, 67

Palawan, Philippines 142
Palawan Fate
overview of 143–44
  aesthetics of 145
  and busong 143–45
  contemporary film movements 23–24

country and language 24–25
creation contexts 141–42
fabulatory subjectification 148
as Fourth Cinema 26, 141
as healing 144–46
Indigenous values in 143–45
and ingasiq 143–45
interiority of 143
narrative structure 143–44
and Palawan mythology 143
Palawan people 141–44
Pandora's Box 41
Panoho, Rangihiroa 130
Pasolini, Pier Paolo
as auteur 51
and cinema of poetry 38–39, 48, 56
free indirect schema 51–52
peace 113–14
Peirce, Charles Sanders 106
Petzold, Christian 60, 62n5
the Philippines 141–42
Phyla, machinic 118–20
Pignarre, Philippe 23
the plane of immanence 91–94, 107
plasticity 70–71, 73, 78. *See also* neuroplasticity
political resistance 69–70
Poslun, Michael 141n15
possibility *versus* potential 74n10
power
individuals as products of 72–73
neoliberal 65, 66n8, 67
and psychiatry 13–14
and subjectivity production 72, 108
and therapeutic activism 108
the present 122
the profilmic 106
profilmic reality 119n12
psychiatric perception 30
psychiatry 13–14, 17–18, 30
psychology 53, 55n12, 60, 79
psychosocial images 39, 51, 53, 55–56, 63, 78, 95
the “psy” to “neuro” turn 67–68
pure experience 91–94, 103, 107. *See also* the plane of immanence

Radden, Jennifer 21
radical empiricism 93, 103
realism 37–40. *See also* neorealism
realist *versus* imagist styles 37–39
reality, faith in 37–39, 47–48, 55
reality, psychosociality of 55
The Red Desert
overview of 23–25
aesthetics of 54
versus Afternoon 63
alienation theme 27
character psyche representation 49, 53–54
free indirect image use 49, 51, 54
neorealism, as shift from 48–49
stills from 50
style of 38
subjectivity-objectivity collapse 49, 51
techniques used 49
transindividuality of 53–54
versus Voyage to Italy 53
Reichardt, Kelly. *See also* Night Moves
and American cinema 27
as artist-physician 108
and the Berlin School 28
free indirect perception use 94–95
hope themes, use of 86
Meek's Cutoff 87
and Neo-Neorealism 83, 85–86
Old Joy 86, 99
shared belief, filming of 94
and therapeutic activism 153
Wendy and Lucy 84–87
relational fields 31, 63, 154–56
relational movement 120, 120n13
Rhodes, John David 55n11
Rivette, Jacques 46n7
Robbins, Julian 137
Roehler, Oskar 61
Rohmer, Eric 44
Rose, Nikolas 14
Rosen, Phil 104, 106n13
Rossellini, Roberto 44–45, 47, 49
Roy, Rajendra 28
Russell, Bertrand 155

Sacher-Masoch, Leopold von 18
Samson & Delilah 149
Sarris, Andrew 51
Schanelec, Angela. *See also* Afternoon
aesthetics, political 62
as artist-physician 108
and the Berlin School 60
The Dreamlike Path 28
individuals, view of 73
melancholy, uses of 62, 73–74
and therapeutic activism 153
window tropes, use of 79
schizoanalysis
overview of 17
art in 19
critical methods in 18–19
depression, approach to 17–18
and melancholy 21
and minor cinema 31
ontological functors 118–21
and therapeutic activism 155
and values 131
Schoonover, Karl 25–26
Schwartz, Jeffrey 65
Scott, A. O. 84–85
Seligman, Martin 12

Shaviro, Steven 74n10
Shohat, Ella 147
Simondon, Gilbert 53
Simpson, Leanne 136
Sleeping Sickness 28
social subjection 72
societies, control 69–71, 90
society and individuals 13–15
the socius 24, 37, 55, 63, 95, 111, 113, 155
Solito, Auraeus. *See* Balintagos, Kanakan
Souriau, Étienne 106n14, 119n12
Stam, Robert 147
Stengers, Isabelle 113
subjective shots 48
subjectivity 14–15, 17–18, 63. *See also* assemblage theory
subjectivity production
- the brain and 68–69
- capitalist 72
- and cinema 19, 147–48
- and control society 69
- depression as 20
- ecosophy and 113
- and machinic assemblages 72
- mental illness as problem of 17
- and the neoliberal individual 72
- neurological theories of 68
- and peace 114
- and power 72, 108

Sugar 84–85

terminal *versus* non-terminal beliefs 93–94
Territories, existential 118–20
Te Rua 148
The Testament of Dr. Mabuse 41
Thailand 111–13, 114n7, 121–23, 126
therapeutic activism
- approaches to 108
- cinema's relationship to 155
- definition of 23
- and film 153
- HIV/AIDS 153–54
- mental health 154–55
- platforms of relationality 155
- and power 108
- and schizoanalysis 155

therapeutic activists, filmmakers as 23, 31, 108, 150, 155
therapeutic capitalism 67
Thornton, Warwick 149
three-shots 97n9
time-images 89–90
transindividual creativity 90
transindividuality
- overview of 53
- and *Afternoon* 75
- and the Berlin School 60, 79
- the brain's 74–75
- of cinema of poetry 54, 56
- and desire and the social 55
- and melancholy 65, 102, 107–8
- and mental health platforms 155
- and psyche-socius links 55–56, 95
- psychosocial images of 55, 63, 94
- and pure experience 98
- of *The Red Desert* 53–54

Treichler, Paula A. 153

Umberto D 45–46
Uncle Boonmee Who Can Recall His Past Lives
- aesthetics, ecosophic 114–17, 120n15, 125
- alterity encounters 115–16, 121, 126
- background, absence of 118
- contemporary film movements 23–24
- country and language 24–25
- découpage of 115–18, 120
- depth of field in 117–18, 120
- and disappeared people 113, 122–23, 126
- futurity in 123–26
- group subjectivity 121
- historical and political contexts 112–13, 122–23, 126
- historical images in 122–23
- and Isaan communists, disappearance of 122–23
- and making peace 114, 121–22, 126
- ontological functors 120–21
- point-of-view shots, absence of 115–16
- spatiality in 116
- teen boys from Nabua 122
- and the three ecologies 113

Universes of value 118–20

values 131. *See also* Indigenous values
Visctoni, Luchino 43
visual arts 21, 153–54
Voyage to Italy 45–47, 49, 53

Waititi, Taiaka 148
war
- and colonization 146–47
- in expressionism 41–42
- in neorealism 40–43
- of subjectivity 147

Watson, Jannel 118
Waziyatawin 136
weak ties 144
Wendy and Lucy 84–87
Whale Rider 132–33
Whitehead, A. N. 113–14, 122, 123n19
Wickler, Henner 60
Windows on a Monday 78
window tropes 75–76, 78–79
Wollen, Peter 104–5, 106n13
Worthmann, Merten 59n2

Yellow Bird, Michael 136
Yong Kim, Jim 12–13

Made in the USA
Monee, IL
13 September 2026

62977124R10101